Elements of Literature®
Third Course

The Holt Reader, Adapted Version

INSTRUCTIONAL MAT. TECH. CNT.
COLLEGE OF EDUCATION
UNIVERSITY OF IDAHO

HOLT, RINEHART AND WINSTON

Copyright © by Holt, Rinehart and Winston

All rights reserved. No part of this publication may be reproduced or transmitted in any form or by any means, electronic or mechanical, including photocopy, recording, or any information storage and retrieval system, without permission in writing from the publisher.

Requests for permission to make copies of any part of the work should be mailed to the following address: Permissions Department, Holt, Rinehart and Winston, 10801 N. MoPac Expressway, Building 3, Austin, Texas 78759.

ELEMENTS OF LITERATURE, HOLT, HRW, and the **"Owl Design"** are trademarks licensed to Holt, Rinehart and Winston, registered in the United States of America and/or other jurisdictions.

Printed in the United States of America

If you have received these materials as examination copies free of charge, Holt, Rinehart and Winston retains title to the materials and they may not be resold. Resale of examination copies is strictly prohibited.

Possession of this publication in print format does not entitle users to convert this publication, or any portion of it, into electronic format.

ISBN 978-0-03-099642-9
ISBN 0-03-099642-2
2 3 4 5 6   179   11 10 09 08

Contents

To the Student xi

A Walk Through the Book xii

COLLECTION 1 Plot and Setting xiv

    Literary and Academic Vocabulary for Collection 1 1

        Preparing to Read: The Most Dangerous Game 2
        Literary Focus: Suspense and Foreshadowing 2
        Reading Focus: Making Predictions 2
        Vocabulary 2

        Interactive Selection: The Most Dangerous Game
        By Richard Connell 3
        Skills Practice: Use a Clues and Events Chart 32
        Applying Your Skills 33

        Preparing to Read: Liberty 34
        Literary Focus: Setting and Conflict 34
        Reading Focus: Analyzing Details 34
        Vocabulary 34

        Interactive Selection: Liberty
        Based on the story by Julia Alvarez 35
        Applying Your Skills 41

        Preparing to Read: The Great Escape 42
        Informational Text Focus: Main Idea 42
        Vocabulary 42

        Interactive Selection: The Great Escape
        ***Based on the article from* Boys' Life** 43
        Applying Your Skills 49

    Skills Review: Collection 1 50

COLLECTION 2 Character 52

    Literary and Academic Vocabulary for Collection 2 53

        Preparing to Read: Thank You M'am 54
        Literary Focus: Character and Dialogue 54

Reading Focus: Making Inferences 54

Vocabulary. 54

Interactive Selection: Thank You M'am
By Langston Hughes. 55

Skills Practice: Use an Inferences Table 62

Applying Your Skills 63

Preparing to Read: American History 64

Literary Focus: Round and Flat Characters 64

Reading Focus: Making Inferences About Characters 64

Vocabulary. 64

Interactive Selection: American History
Based on the story by Judith Ortiz Cofer 65

Skills Practice: Use a Comparison Table. 70

Applying Your Skills 71

Preparing to Read: An Interview with Dave Eggers 72

Informational Text Focus: Synthesizing Sources:
Main Idea, Audience, and Purpose 72

Vocabulary. 72

Interactive Selection: An Interview with Dave Eggers
from Writing Magazine 73

Skills Practice: Use a Concept Map 80

Applying Your Skills 81

Skills Review: Collection 2 82

COLLECTION 3 Narrator and Voice 84

Literary and Academic Vocabulary for Collection 3 85

Preparing to Read: The Interlopers 86

Literary Focus: Omniscient Narrator 86

Reading Focus: Drawing Conclusions 86

Vocabulary. 86

Interactive Selection: The Interlopers
Based on the story by Saki 87

Applying Your Skills 91

Preparing to Read: The Cask of Amontillado 92

Literary Focus: Unreliable Narrator 92

iv   Contents

Reading Focus: Drawing Conclusions 92
Vocabulary 92
Interactive Selection: The Cask of Amontillado
Based on the story by Edgar Allan Poe 93
Applying Your Skills 97

Preparing to Read: Three Readings About Poe's Death 98
Informational Text Focus: Synthesizing Sources:
Drawing Conclusions 98
Vocabulary 98
Interactive Selection: Poe's Final Days
By Kenneth Silverman 99
**Interactive Selection: Poe's Death Is Rewritten as
Case of Rabies, Not Telltale Alcohol**
Based on the article from the New York Times 104
**Interactive Selection: If Only Poe Had Succeeded
When He Said Nevermore to Drink**
Based on the article from the New York Times 105
Skills Practice: Use a Comparison Chart 106
Applying Your Skills 107

Skills Review: Collection 3 108

COLLECTION 4 **Symbolism and Irony** 110
Literary and Academic Vocabulary for Collection 4 111

Preparing to Read: The Scarlet Ibis 112
Literary Focus: Symbols and Theme 112
Reading Focus: Analyzing Details 112
Vocabulary 112
Interactive Selection: The Scarlet Ibis
By James Hurst 113
Applying Your Skills 131

Preparing to Read: The Gift of the Magi 132
Literary Focus: Situational Irony 132
Reading Focus: Analyzing Details 132
Vocabulary 132
Interactive Selection: The Gift of the Magi
Based on the story by O. Henry 133
Applying Your Skills 137

Contents v

Preparing to Read: Three Readings by Albert Einstein 138
  Informational Text Focus: Synthesizing Sources:
  Works by One Author 138
  Vocabulary 138
  Interactive Selection: Weapons of the Spirit
  Based on an interview from Einstein on Peace
  by Albert Einstein 139
  Interactive Selection: Letter to President Roosevelt
  Based on the letter by Albert Einstein 140
  Interactive Selection: On the Abolition of the Threat of War
  By Albert Einstein 141
  Applying Your Skills 143
Skills Review: Collection 4 144

COLLECTION 5 Form and Style 146

Literary and Academic Vocabulary for Collection 5 147

Preparing to Read: Cub Pilot on the Mississippi 148
  Literary Focus: Style and Tone 148
  Reading Focus: Reading Aloud and Paraphrasing 148
  Vocabulary 148
  Interactive Selection: Cub Pilot on the Mississippi
  Based on the autobiography by Mark Twain 149
  Applying Your Skills 153

Preparing to Read: The Grandfather 154
  Literary Focus: Style and Imagery 154
  Reading Focus: Making Generalizations 154
  Vocabulary 154
  Interactive Selection: The Grandfather
  Based on the personal essay by Gary Soto 155
  Applying Your Skills 157

Preparing to Read: About StoryCorps 158
  Informational Text Focus: Structure and Format
  of Functional Documents 158
  Vocabulary 158
  Interactive Selection: About StoryCorps
  Based on the document "About StoryCorps" 159
  Applying Your Skills 161
Skills Review: Collection 5 162

vi Contents

COLLECTION 6 **Persuasion** 164
  Literary and Academic Vocabulary for Collection 6 165

  Preparing to Read: Cinderella's Stepsisters 166
  Informational Text Focus: Argument: Intent and Tone 166
  Reading Focus: Questioning 166
  Vocabulary 166

  Interactive Selection: Cinderella's Stepsisters
  Based on the speech by Toni Morrison 167
  Applying Your Skills 169

  **Preparing to Read: Two Articles on
  Kaavya Viswanathan** 170
  Informational Text Focus: Evaluating Arguments 170
  Vocabulary 170

  **Interactive Selection: Kaavya Viswanathan: Unconscious
  Copycat or Plagiarist?**
  Based on the blog by Sandhya Nankani 171

  Interactive Selection: Kaavya Syndrome
  Based on the online article by Joshua Foer 174
  Applying Your Skills 177

  Skills Review: Collection 6 178

COLLECTION 7 **Poetry** 180
  Literary and Academic Vocabulary for Collection 7 181

  Preparing to Read: A Blessing 182
  Literary Focus: Imagery and Theme 182
  Reading Focus: Analyzing Details 182
  Vocabulary 182

  Interactive Selection: A Blessing
  By James Wright 183
  Applying Your Skills 185

  Preparing to Read: Women 186
  Literary Focus: Speaker and Tone 186
  Reading Focus: Analyzing Details 186
  Vocabulary 186

  Interactive Selection: Women
  By Alice Walker 187

Contents vii

Applying Your Skills 189

Preparing to Read: I Wandered Lonely as a Cloud 190
Literary Focus: Rhythm and Meter 190
Reading Focus: Reading Aloud 190
Vocabulary 190
Interactive Selection: I Wandered Lonely as a Cloud
By William Wordsworth 191
Applying Your Skills 193

Preparing to Read: Legal Alien/Extranjera Legal 194
Literary Focus: Speaker, Word Play, and Parallel Structures . . 194
Reading Focus: Analyzing Details 194
Vocabulary 194
Interactive Selection: Legal Alien/Extranjera Legal
By Pat Mora 195
Applying Your Skills 197

**Preparing to Read: The History Behind the Ballad,
Ballad of Birmingham, *and* 4 Little Girls** 198
Literary Focus: Historical Accounts Across Genres 198
Reading Focus: Comparing Messages in Different Forms 198
Vocabulary 198
Interactive Selection: The History Behind the Ballad
Based on the excerpt from Parting of the Waters
by Taylor Branch 199
Interactive Selection: Ballad of Birmingham
By Dudley Randall 200
Interactive Selection: 4 Little Girls
Based on the review by Roger Ebert 203
Skills Practice: Use a Comparison Chart 206
Applying Your Skills 207

**Preparing to Read: FBI Art Crime Team *and* Collection
Is Found to Contain Stolen Rockwell Art** 208
Informational Text Focus: Generating Research Questions . . . 208
Vocabulary 208
Interactive Selection: FBI Art Crime Team 209
Interactive Selection: Collection Is Found to Contain Stolen
Rockwell Art
Based on the article from The New York Times 211

Applying Your Skills 213

Skills Review: Collection 7 214

COLLECTION 8   Drama 216

Literary and Academic Vocabulary for Collection 8 217

Preparing to Read: *from* The Tragedy of Romeo and Juliet 218

Literary Focus: Tragedy 218

Reading Focus: Reading a Play 218

Vocabulary 218

Interactive Selection: *from* The Tragedy of Romeo and Juliet
By William Shakespeare 219

Applying Your Skills 233

Preparing to Read: "Dear Juliet": Seeking Succor From a Veteran of Love *and from* The Juliet Club 234

Informational Text Focus: Primary and Secondary Sources 234

Vocabulary 234

Interactive Selection: "Dear Juliet": Seeking Succor From a Veteran of Love
By Dinitia Smith 235

Interactive Selection: *from* The Juliet Club 241

Applying Your Skills 243

Skills Review: Collection 8 244

COLLECTION 9   Epic and Myth 246

Literary and Academic Vocabulary for Collection 9 247

Preparing to Read: *from the* Odyssey, Part One 248

Literary Focus: Epic Heroes and Conflict 248

Reading Focus: Reading an Epic 248

Vocabulary 248

Interactive Selection: *from the* Odyssey, Part One
By Homer, translated by Robert Fitzgerald 249

Applying Your Skills 265

Preparing to Read: *from* Shipwreck at the Bottom of the World *and* Tending Sir Ernest's Legacy 266

Contents   ix

Informational Text Focus: Synthesizing Sources: Making
Connections... 266
Vocabulary... 266

**Interactive Selection: *from* Shipwreck at the
Bottom of the World
By Jennifer Armstrong**............................... 267

**Interactive Selection: Tending Sir Ernest's Legacy
Based on the interview with Alexandra Shackleton
from NOVA Online**................................... 277

Applying Your Skills..................................... 281

Skills Review: Collection 9................................. 282

COLLECTION 10 Reading for Life................................. 284

Literary and Academic Vocabulary for Collection 10........... 285

Preparing to Read: Following Technical Directions......... 286
Informational Text Focus: Following Technical Directions..... 286
Reading Focus: Skimming and Scanning..................... 286
Vocabulary... 286

Interactive Selection: Following Technical Directions...... 287
Skills Practice: Use a Chain of Events Chart................ 290
Applying Your Skills..................................... 291

Preparing to Read: Functional Workplace Documents...... 292
Informational Text Focus: Analyzing Workplace Documents... 292
Reading Focus: Adjusting Reading Rate.................... 292
Vocabulary... 292

Interactive Selection: Functional Workplace Documents... 293
Skills Practice: Use a Concept Map........................ 298
Applying Your Skills..................................... 299

Skills Review: Collection 10................................ 300

Index of Authors and Titles................................ 302

To the Student

A Book for You

A book is like a garden carried in the pocket.
—Chinese Proverb

The more you put into reading, the more you get out of it. This book is designed to do just that—help you interact with the selections you read by marking them up, asking your own questions, taking notes, recording your own ideas, and responding to the questions of others.

A Book Designed for Your Success

The Holt Reader, *Adapted Version* goes hand in hand with *Elements of Literature*. It is designed to help you interact with the selections and master important language arts skills.

The Holt Reader, *Adapted Version* has three types of selections: literature, informational texts, and documents that you may encounter in your various activities. All the selections include the same basic preparation, support, and review materials. Vocabulary previews, skill descriptions, graphic organizers, review questions, and other tools help you understand and enjoy the selections. Moreover, tips and questions in the side margins ensure that you can apply and practice the skills you are learning as you read.

The selections in the book are all from your textbook, *Elements of Literature*. You will find that some of the selections are worded exactly as they were worded in *Elements of Literature*. In this book, those selections have been broken into section. Each section is followed by a short note titled "In Other Words." That note restates the previous text in different word. Other selections have been rewritten or retold slightly to make them easier to understand" these are called adapted selections. You can tell which ones are adapted because you will se the words "based on" in the Table of Contents or on the first page of the selection.

The original selections are exactly as they appear in the *Elements of Literature Student Edition*. The poems and play in this book are examples of original selections. In addition, some stories and articles are in their original form. These selections that are in their original form are broken into sections. Each section is followed by a short note titled "In Other Words" that paraphrases the preceding text. That is, the "In Other Words" notes restate the text in different words.

A Book for Your Own Thoughts and Feelings

Reading is about *you*. It is about connecting your thoughts and feelings to the thoughts and feelings of the writer. Make this book your own. The more you give of yourself to your reading, the more you will get out of it. We encourage you to write in this book. Jot down how you feel about the selection. Write down questions you have about the text. Note details you think need to be cleared up or topics that you would like to investigate further.

To the Student xi

A Walk Through the Book

The Holt Reader, Adapted Version is arranged in collections, just like *Elements of Literature*, the book on which this one is based. Each collection has a theme or basic idea. The stories, poems, articles, or documents within the collection follow that theme. Let's look at how the arrangement of *The Holt Reader, Adapted Version* helps you enjoy a collection as a whole and the individual selections within the collection.

Before Reading the Collection

Literary and Academic Vocabulary
Literary and academic vocabulary refers to the specialized language that is used to talk about books, tests, and formal writing. Each collection begins with the literary and academic terms that you need to know to master the skills for that collection.

Before Reading the Selection

Preparing to Read
From experience, you know that you understand something better if you have some idea of what's going to happen. So that you can get the most from the reading, this page previews the skills and vocabulary that you will see in the reading.

Literary Focus
For fiction selections—stories, poems, and plays—this feature introduces the literary skill that is the focus for the selection. Examples and graphic elements help explain the literary skill.

Reading Focus
Also in fiction selections, this feature highlights a reading skill you can apply to the story, poem, or play. The feature points out why this skill is important and how it can help you become a better reader.

Informational Text Focus
For informational, or nonfiction, selections, this feature introduces you to the format and characteristics of nonfiction texts. Those texts may be essays, newspaper articles, Web sites, employment regulations, application forms, or other similar documents.

Selection Vocabulary
This feature introduces you to selection vocabulary that may be unfamiliar. Each entry gives the pronunciation and definition of the word as well as a sentence in which the word is used correctly.

Into the Story
This feature provides an introduction about the selection related to the author, setting, historical events, or other topics that may be unfamiliar.

While Reading the Selection

Side-Column Notes
Each selection has notes in the side column that guide your reading. Many notes ask you to underline or circle in the text itself. Others provide lines on which you can write your responses to questions.

Quick Check These notes ask you to pause at certain points so that you can think about basic ideas before proceeding further. Your teacher may use these notes for class discussions.

A Walk Through the Book

Here's How This feature shows you how to apply a particular skill to what you are reading. It models how you might think through the text. Each Here's How note addresses the selection's Reading Focus, Literary Focus, Language Coach, or Vocabulary.

Your Turn In these notes, you have a chance to apply vocabulary skills and practice the same reading, literary, and language skills introduced and modeled earlier. You might be asked to underline or circle words in the text or to write responses in your own words.

Literary Analysis These notes take basic comprehension a step further and ask you to think more deeply about what you have just read.

After Reading the Selection

Skills Practice
For some selections, graphic organizers reinforce the skills you have practiced throughout the selection.

Applying Your Skills
This feature helps you review the selection. It provides additional practice with selection vocabulary and literary, reading, and informational text focus skills.

After Reading the Collection

Skills Review
On the first page of the Skills Review, you can practice using the collection's academic vocabulary and selection vocabulary.

Language Coach
The second Skills Review page draws on the Language Coach skills in the *Elements of Literature* Preparing to Read pages. This feature asks you to apply those skills to texts from throughout the collection.

Writing Activity
You may have found that you need more practice writing. These short writing activities challenge you to apply what you have learned to your own ideas and experiences.

Oral Language Activity
Writing Activities alternate with Oral Language Activities. These features are designed to help you express your thoughts clearly aloud. The features are particularly helpful if you are learning English or if you need practice with Standard English.

Collection 1

Plot and Setting

© Tom Collicott/Masterfile

Literary and Academic Vocabulary for Collection 1

LITERARY VOCABULARY

plot (PLAHT) *n.:* the series of events that make up a story.
   The most exciting part of the book's plot came right in the middle of the story.

flashback (FLASH BAK) *n.:* a scene that happens before the main time frame of the story.
   The story was about Sara's new job, and the information about her childhood was told in a flashback.

foreshadowing (FAWR SHA DOH ING) *n.:* the use of clues to hint at what is going to happen later in a story.
   The author's foreshadowing helped me realize that the detective was really the thief before I read the end of the story.

ACADEMIC VOCABULARY

convey (KUHN VAY) *v.:* to suggest or communicate.
   In this story, the author tries to convey an idea about war.

effect (UH FEHKT) *n.:* result.
   Describe one effect of the character's actions.

excerpt (EHK SURPT) *n.:* a part of a longer work.
   Choose an excerpt from the story that proves your point.

support (SUH PAWRT) *v.:* to back up; strengthen by giving evidence.
   It is a good idea to support your ideas by giving examples.

outcome (OWT KUHM) *n.:* result, ending.
   I was glad that the story had a happy ending, or outcome.

Preparing to Read

The Most Dangerous Game
By Richard Connell

LITERARY FOCUS: SUSPENSE AND FORESHADOWING

When you want to know what will happen next in a story, you are feeling **suspense**, an anxious or uncertain feeling. Perhaps you are worried about what will happen to a character. Will the main character survive? Will she defeat the bad guy? When you feel suspense, you might wonder about questions like these.

Writers try to build suspense into stories to make them exciting. One way writers build suspense is through **foreshadowing**. Foreshadowing is the use of clues early in the story to give you an idea of something that might happen later. For example, a writer might begin a story with the sentence, "A strange, icy wind blew into town." That clue might foreshadow disturbing things that happen later in the story. Foreshadowing can make you more interested in what happens next.

READING FOCUS: MAKING PREDICTIONS

A **prediction** is a guess based on evidence, or clues, in a story. For example, suppose you are reading the story of Cinderella. In the story, Cinderella and the prince meet and fall in love at the prince's ball. You might use this information to **predict** that Cinderella will marry the prince in the end. Clues in the story can help you make predictions. So can other things you know about how life or stories work.

VOCABULARY

receding (RIH SEED IHNG) *v.* used as *adj.:* moving into the distance.

disarming (DIHS AHRM IHNG) *adj.:* removing suspicion or fear; charming.

imprudent (IHM PROOD NT) *adj.:* unwise; foolish.

surmounted (SUHR MOWNT IHD) *v.:* overcame.

invariably (IHN VEHR EE UH BLEE) *adv.:* without changing.

INTO THE STORY

"The Most Dangerous Game" was written in 1924—more than 80 years ago. At that time, hunting large animals was a popular sport. Wealthy hunters in the early 1900s traveled all over the world to hunt wild and unusual animals.

SKILLS FOCUS

Literary Skills
Understand foreshadowing and suspense.

Reading Skills
Make predictions.

THE MOST DANGEROUS GAME

By Richard Connell

"Off there to the right—somewhere—is a large island," said Whitney. "It's rather a mystery—"

"What island is it?" Rainsford asked.

"The old charts call it Ship-Trap Island," Whitney replied. "A suggestive name, isn't it? Sailors have a curious dread of the place. I don't know why. Some superstition—" **A**

"Can't see it," remarked Rainsford, trying to peer through the dank tropical night that was palpable as it pressed its thick warm blackness in upon the yacht.

"You've good eyes," said Whitney, with a laugh, "and I've seen you pick off a moose moving in the brown fall bush at four hundred yards, but even you can't see four miles or so through a moonless Caribbean night."

"Nor four yards," admitted Rainsford. "Ugh! It's like moist black velvet."

"It will be light in Rio," promised Whitney. "We should make it in a few days. I hope the jaguar guns have come from Purdey's.[1] We should have some good hunting up the Amazon. Great sport, hunting." **B**

"The best sport in the world," agreed Rainsford.

"For the hunter," amended Whitney. "Not for the jaguar."

"Don't talk rot, Whitney," said Rainsford. "You're a big-game hunter, not a philosopher. Who cares how a jaguar feels?"

"Perhaps the jaguar does," observed Whitney.

"Bah! They've no understanding."

"Even so, I rather think they understand one thing—fear. The fear of pain and the fear of death."

"Nonsense," laughed Rainsford. "This hot weather is making you soft, Whitney. Be a realist. The world is made up of two

---

1. **Purdey's** was a British company that made hunting equipment.

"The Most Dangerous Game" by Richard Connell. Copyright © 1924 by Richard Connell; copyright renewed © 1952 by Louise Fox Connell. Reproduced by permission of **Brandt & Hochman Literary Agents, Inc.** Any electronic copying or distribution of this text is expressly forbidden. All rights reserved.

A HERE'S HOW

Literary Focus

In lines 3–6, Whitney is talking about Ship-Trap Island. Maybe the writer is using the name of the island to **foreshadow** something that will happen later in the story. Whitney also says sailors are afraid of the island. So maybe the ship will be trapped there and something frightening will happen.

B QUICK CHECK

What are Whitney and Rainsford planning to do when they reach their destination?

_____
_____
_____
_____

A HERE'S HOW

Reading Focus

I think Rainsford has an interesting point of view about the world. He says he sees it as divided into the hunters and the ones who are hunted. He tells Whitney that they are the hunters. I think Rainsford does not understand how it feels to be on the other side and to be hunted. I **predict** that, as the story goes along, he will somehow learn to understand this feeling.

B YOUR TURN

Literary Focus

In lines 41–47, Whitney is talking about Ship-Trap Island. Underline things Whitney says that build **suspense** about the island.

© Paul Sierra

30 classes—the hunters and the huntees. Luckily, you and I are the hunters. **A** Do you think we've passed that island yet?"

"I can't tell in the dark. I hope so."

"Why?" asked Rainsford.

"The place has a reputation—a bad one."

"Cannibals?" suggested Rainsford.

"Hardly. Even cannibals wouldn't live in such a Godforsaken place. But it's gotten into sailor lore, somehow. Didn't you notice that the crew's nerves seemed a bit jumpy today?"

"They were a bit strange, now you mention it. Even Captain
40 Nielsen—"

"Yes, even that tough-minded old Swede, who'd go up to the devil himself and ask him for a light. Those fishy blue eyes held a look I never saw there before. All I could get out of him was: 'This place has an evil name among seafaring men, sir.' Then he said to me, very gravely: 'Don't you feel anything?'—as if the air about us was actually poisonous. Now, you mustn't laugh when I tell you this—I did feel something like a sudden chill. **B**

"There was no breeze. The sea was as flat as a plate-glass window. We were drawing near the island then. What I felt was
50 a—a mental chill, a sort of sudden dread."

4   The Most Dangerous Game

"Pure imagination," said Rainsford. "One superstitious sailor can taint the whole ship's company with his fear."

"Maybe. But sometimes I think sailors have an extra sense that tells them when they are in danger. Sometimes I think evil is a tangible thing—with wavelengths, just as sound and light have. An evil place can, so to speak, broadcast vibrations of evil. Anyhow, I'm glad we're getting out of this zone. Well, I think I'll turn in now, Rainsford."

"I'm not sleepy," said Rainsford. "I'm going to smoke another pipe on the afterdeck."

"Good night, then, Rainsford. See you at breakfast."

"Right. Good night, Whitney."

IN OTHER WORDS Whitney and Rainsford are on a ship traveling to a hunting trip in South America. Whitney has heard from the sailors that the island they see in the distance is evil. He has a bad feeling about it. Rainsford insists that there is no reason to worry.

There was no sound in the night as Rainsford sat there but the muffled throb of the engine that drove the yacht swiftly through the darkness, and the swish and ripple of the wash of the propeller.

Rainsford, reclining in a steamer chair, indolently puffed on his favorite brier.[2] The sensuous drowsiness of the night was on him. "It's so dark," he thought, "that I could sleep without closing my eyes; the night would be my eyelids—"

An abrupt sound startled him. Off to the right he heard it, and his ears, expert in such matters, could not be mistaken. Again he heard the sound, and again. Somewhere, off in the blackness, someone had fired a gun three times.

Rainsford sprang up and moved quickly to the rail, mystified. He strained his eyes in the direction from which the reports had come, but it was like trying to see through a blanket. He leapt

C LITERARY ANALYSIS
Based on lines 67–77, how would you describe Rainsford's character?

_____
_____
_____

---

2. When Rainsford **puffed on his favorite brier**, he was smoking a tobacco pipe made from the root of a brier brush.

A HERE'S HOW

Vocabulary

Rainsford tried to reach the *receding* lights on the boat, but he could not. At first, I was not sure what *receding* meant. By the end of the paragraph, however, the lights are gone. So *receding* must mean "moving away."

B HERE'S HOW

Reading Focus

Rainsford hears an animal scream and a gunshot. Earlier, he and Whitney were talking about hunting. The scream and the gunshot probably have something to do with hunting. I **predict** that Rainsford will have to hunt later in the story.

---

upon the rail and balanced himself there, to get greater elevation; his pipe, striking a rope, was knocked from his mouth. He lunged for it; a short, hoarse cry came from his lips as he realized he had reached too far and had lost his balance. The cry was pinched off short as the blood-warm waters of the Caribbean Sea closed over his head.

IN OTHER WORDS Rainsford hears gunshots. He moves to the edge of the ship to see more. His pipe falls from his mouth. When he tries to catch it, he falls overboard.

He struggled up to the surface and tried to cry out, but the wash from the speeding yacht slapped him in the face and the salt water in his open mouth made him gag and strangle. Desperately he struck out with strong strokes after the receding lights of the yacht, but he stopped before he had swum fifty feet. A certain coolheadedness had come to him; it was not the first time he had been in a tight place. There was a chance that his cries could be heard by someone aboard the yacht, but that chance was slender and grew more slender as the yacht raced on. He wrestled himself out of his clothes and shouted with all his power. The lights of the yacht became faint and ever-vanishing fireflies; then they were blotted out entirely by the night. **A**

Rainsford remembered the shots. They had come from the right, and doggedly he swam in that direction, swimming with slow, deliberate strokes, conserving his strength. For a seemingly endless time he fought the sea. He began to count his strokes; he could do possibly a hundred more and then—

Rainsford heard a sound. It came out of the darkness, a high screaming sound, the sound of an animal in an extremity of anguish and terror.

He did not recognize the animal that made the sound; he did not try to; with fresh vitality he swam toward the sound. He heard it again; then it was cut short by another noise, crisp, staccato. "Pistol shot," muttered Rainsford, swimming on. **B**

Ten minutes of determined effort brought another sound to his ears—the most welcome he had ever heard—the muttering and growling of the sea breaking on a rocky shore. He was almost on the rocks before he saw them; on a night less calm he would have been shattered against them. With his remaining strength he dragged himself from the swirling waters. Jagged crags appeared to jut into the opaqueness.³ **C**

He forced himself upward, hand over hand. Gasping, his hands raw, he reached a flat place at the top. Dense jungle came down to the very edge of the cliffs. What perils that tangle of trees and underbrush might hold for him did not concern Rainsford just then. **D** All he knew was that he was safe from his enemy, the sea, and that utter weariness was on him. He flung himself down at the jungle edge and tumbled headlong into the deepest sleep of his life.

When he opened his eyes he knew from the position of the sun that it was late in the afternoon. Sleep had given him new vigor; a sharp hunger was picking at him. He looked about him, almost cheerfully.

"Where there are pistol shots, there are men. Where there are men, there is food," he thought. But what kind of men, he wondered, in so forbidding a place? An unbroken front of snarled and ragged jungle fringed the shore. **E**

He saw no sign of a trail through the closely knit web of weeds and trees; it was easier to go along the shore, and Rainsford floundered along by the water. Not far from where he had landed, he stopped.

Some wounded thing, by the evidence a large animal, had thrashed about in the underbrush; the jungle weeds were crushed down and the moss was lacerated; one patch of weeds was stained crimson. A small, glittering object not far away caught Rainsford's eye and he picked it up. It was an empty cartridge. "A twenty-two," he remarked. "That's odd. It must have been a fairly

---

3. Here, **opaqueness** (oh PAYK nehs) means darkness. Something opaque does not let light pass through.

C YOUR TURN

Vocabulary

Look up the word *jagged* in the dictionary. Then, in your own words, describe how the *"jagged* crags" would probably look.

D YOUR TURN

Vocabulary

Re-read lines 117–119. What do you think the word *perils* means? Write your definition on the lines, below. Then, use a dictionary to check if you are right.

E QUICK CHECK

Re-read lines 127–130. What clues does Rainsford use to figure out his surroundings?

The Most Dangerous Game 7

YOUR TURN

Reading Focus

In lines 128–130, Rainsford wonders what kind of men would be in the jungle. What clues in lines 146–148 might help you make a **prediction** about the kinds of people he will meet?

_____
_____
_____

large animal too. The hunter had his nerve with him to tackle it with a light gun. It's clear that the brute put up a fight. I suppose the first three shots I heard was when the hunter flushed his quarry[4] and wounded it. The last shot was when he trailed it here and finished it."

He examined the ground closely and found what he had hoped to find—the print of hunting boots. They pointed along the cliff in the direction he had been going. **A** Eagerly he hurried along, now slipping on a rotten log or a loose stone, but making headway; night was beginning to settle down on the island.

IN OTHER WORDS As Rainsford swims, he hears an animal scream and another gunshot. Finally, he reaches land. He discovers that it is a jungle and finds clues that the noises he heard were the end of a hunt. He also finds footprints and follows them along the island.

Bleak darkness was blacking out the sea and jungle when Rainsford sighted the lights. He came upon them as he turned a crook in the coastline, and his first thought was that he had come upon a village, for there were many lights. But as he forged along, he saw to his great astonishment that all the lights were in one enormous building—a lofty structure with pointed towers plunging upward into the gloom. His eyes made out the shadowy outlines of a palatial château; it was set on a high bluff, and on three sides of it cliffs dived down to where the sea licked greedy lips in the shadows.

"Mirage," thought Rainsford. But it was no mirage, he found, when he opened the tall spiked iron gate. The stone steps were real enough; the massive door with a leering gargoyle for a knocker was real enough; yet about it all hung an air of unreality.

He lifted the knocker, and it creaked up stiffly, as if it had never before been used. He let it fall, and it startled him with its

---

4. When the hunter **flushed his quarry**, he drove the animal he was hunting out of its hiding place.

8 The Most Dangerous Game

booming loudness. **B** He thought he heard steps within; the door remained closed. Again Rainsford lifted the heavy knocker and let it fall. The door opened then, opened as suddenly as if it were on a spring, and Rainsford stood blinking in the river of glaring gold light that poured out. The first thing Rainsford's eyes discerned was the largest man Rainsford had ever seen—a gigantic creature, solidly made and black-bearded to the waist. In his hand the man held a long-barreled revolver, and he was pointing it straight at Rainsford's heart.

Out of the snarl of beard two small eyes regarded Rainsford.

"Don't be alarmed," said Rainsford, with a smile which he hoped was disarming. **C** "I'm no robber. I fell off a yacht. My name is Sanger Rainsford of New York City."

The menacing look in the eyes did not change. The revolver pointed as rigidly as if the giant were a statue. He gave no sign that he understood Rainsford's words or that he had even heard them. He was dressed in uniform, a black uniform trimmed with gray astrakhan.[5]

"I'm Sanger Rainsford of New York," Rainsford began again. "I fell off a yacht. I am hungry."

The man's only answer was to raise with his thumb the hammer of his revolver. Then Rainsford saw the man's free hand go to his forehead in a military salute, and he saw him click his heels together and stand at attention. Another man was coming down the broad marble steps, an erect, slender man in evening clothes. He advanced to Rainsford and held out his hand.

In a cultivated voice marked by a slight accent that gave it added precision and deliberateness, he said: "It is a very great pleasure and honor to welcome Mr. Sanger Rainsford, the celebrated hunter, to my home."

Automatically Rainsford shook the man's hand.

"I've read your book about hunting snow leopards in Tibet, you see," explained the man. "I am General Zaroff." **D**

---

5. **Astrakhan** (AS truh kuhn) is the curly furlike wool of very young lambs.

B HERE'S HOW

Literary Focus
The description of the building sounds creepy. The descriptions of the spiked gate, the gargoyle knocker, and the knocker's loud sound make me worry about what is inside the building. I think the author is using these descriptions to build **suspense**.

C HERE'S HOW

Language Coach
A **prefix** is a word part that comes at the beginning of a word. A prefix can change a word's meaning. I can tell that the word *disarming* is made up of the word "arming" and the prefix *dis–*. To be armed means "to have weapons," and the prefix *dis–* means "not." So *disarming* could mean "taking away weapons." That does not make sense here, though. A smile cannot take away a gun. However, I think a smile might charm people. A smile could be *disarming* in the sense that it takes away the threat of violence and fear.

D QUICK CHECK

What new information about Rainsford does General Zaroff give in this paragraph?

_____
_____
_____
_____

The Most Dangerous Game 9

A YOUR TURN

Literary Focus

How does General Zaroff's description of Ivan and himself in lines 211–216 build **suspense**?

_____
_____
_____

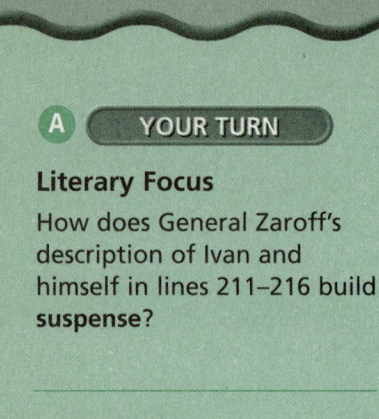

B YOUR TURN

Language Coach

Look at the word *reappeared*. The **prefix** *re–* means "again." What, then, does *reappeared* mean?

_____
_____

Rainsford's first impression was that the man was singularly handsome; his second was that there was an original, almost bizarre quality about the general's face. He was a tall man past middle age, for his hair was a vivid white; but his thick eyebrows and pointed military moustache were as black as the night from which Rainsford had come. His eyes, too, were black and very bright. He had high cheekbones, a sharp-cut nose, a spare, dark face, the face of a man used to giving orders, the face of an aristocrat. Turning to the giant in uniform, the general made a sign. The giant put away his pistol, saluted, withdrew.

"Ivan is an incredibly strong fellow," remarked the general, "but he has the misfortune to be deaf and dumb. A simple fellow, but, I'm afraid, like all his race, a bit of a savage."

"Is he Russian?"

"He is a Cossack,"[6] said the general, and his smile showed red lips and pointed teeth. "So am I. **A**

IN OTHER WORDS Rainsford reaches a large building. He knocks at the door and is met by a giant man with a gun. Before the giant can shoot, an elegant man stops him, introduces himself as General Zaroff, and welcomes Rainsford.

"Come," he said, "we shouldn't be chatting here. We can talk later. Now you want clothes, food, rest. You shall have them. This is a most restful spot."

Ivan had reappeared, and the general spoke to him with lips that moved but gave forth no sound. **B**

"Follow Ivan, if you please, Mr. Rainsford," said the general. "I was about to have my dinner when you came. I'll wait for you. You'll find that my clothes will fit you, I think."

It was to a huge, beam-ceilinged bedroom with a canopied bed big enough for six men that Rainsford followed the silent giant. Ivan laid out an evening suit, and Rainsford, as he put it

---

6. The **Cossacks** (KAHS AKZ) are a group from Ukraine. Many Cossacks served as horsemen to the Russian czars and were famous for their fierceness in battle.

10 The Most Dangerous Game

on, noticed that it came from a London tailor who ordinarily cut and sewed for none below the rank of duke.

230   The dining room to which Ivan conducted him was in many ways remarkable. There was a medieval magnificence about it; it suggested a baronial hall of feudal times, with its oaken panels, its high ceiling, its vast refectory table where two-score men could sit down to eat. About the hall were the mounted heads of many animals—lions, tigers, elephants, moose, bears; larger or more perfect specimens Rainsford had never seen. At the great table the general was sitting, alone. **C**

"You'll have a cocktail, Mr. Rainsford," he suggested. The cocktail was surpassingly good; and, Rainsford noted, the table
240   appointments were of the finest—the linen, the crystal, the silver, the china.

They were eating borscht, the rich red soup with sour cream so dear to Russian palates. Half apologetically General Zaroff said: "We do our best to preserve the amenities[7] of civilization here. Please forgive any lapses. We are well off the beaten track, you know. Do you think the champagne has suffered from its long ocean trip?"

"Not in the least," declared Rainsford. He was finding the general a most thoughtful and affable host, a true cosmopolite.[8]
250   But there was one small trait of the general's that made Rainsford uncomfortable. **D** Whenever he looked up from his plate he found the general studying him, appraising him narrowly.

"Perhaps," said General Zaroff, "you were surprised that I recognized your name. You see, I read all books on hunting published in English, French, and Russian. I have but one passion in my life, Mr. Rainsford, and it is the hunt."

"You have some wonderful heads here," said Rainsford as he ate a particularly well-cooked filet mignon. "That Cape buffalo is the largest I ever saw."

C LITERARY ANALYSIS
What is General Zaroff's home like? Why is this unusual or surprising?

D YOUR TURN
Language Coach
Un– is a **prefix** that means "not." What do you think the word *uncomfortable* means?

---

7. **Amenities** (UH MEHN UH TEEZ) are all kinds of comforts and conveniences.
8. A **cosmopolite** (KAH MAHP UH LYHT) is a knowledgeable citizen of the world or world traveler.

A YOUR TURN

Vocabulary

The word *game* refers to wild animals that can be hunted. The cape buffalo is one example of large *game*. What other kinds of large *game* can you think of?

_____
_____
_____

260 "Oh, that fellow. Yes, he was a monster."

"Did he charge you?"

"Hurled me against a tree," said the general. "Fractured my skull. But I got the brute."

"I've always thought," said Rainsford, "that the Cape buffalo is the most dangerous of all big game." **A**

For a moment the general did not reply; he was smiling his curious red-lipped smile. Then he said slowly: "No. You are wrong, sir. The Cape buffalo is not the most dangerous big game." He sipped his wine. "Here in my preserve on this island," 270 he said in the same slow tone, "I hunt more dangerous game."

Rainsford expressed his surprise. "Is there big game on this island?"

The general nodded. "The biggest."

"Really?"

"Oh, it isn't here naturally, of course. I have to stock the island."

"What have you imported, general?" Rainsford asked. "Tigers?"

The general smiled. "No," he said. "Hunting tigers ceased to 280 interest me some years ago. I exhausted their possibilities, you

12 The Most Dangerous Game

see. **B** No thrill left in tigers, no real danger. I live for danger, Mr. Rainsford."

The general took from his pocket a gold cigarette case and offered his guest a long black cigarette with a silver tip; it was perfumed and gave off a smell like incense.

"We will have some capital hunting, you and I," said the general. "I shall be most glad to have your society."

"But what game—" began Rainsford.

"I'll tell you," said the general. "You will be amused, I know. I think I may say, in all modesty, that I have done a rare thing. **C** I have invented a new sensation. May I pour you another glass of port, Mr. Rainsford?"

"Thank you, general."

The general filled both glasses and said: "God makes some men poets. Some He makes kings, some beggars. Me He made a hunter. My hand was made for the trigger, my father said. He was a very rich man, with a quarter of a million acres in the Crimea, and he was an ardent[9] sportsman. When I was only five years old, he gave me a little gun, specially made in Moscow for me, to shoot sparrows with. When I shot some of his prize turkeys with it, he did not punish me; he complimented me on marksmanship. I killed my first bear in the Caucasus when I was ten. My whole life has been one prolonged hunt. I went into the army—it was expected of noblemen's sons—and for a time commanded a division of Cossack cavalry, but my real interest was always the hunt. I have hunted every kind of game in every land. It would be impossible for me to tell you how many animals I have killed."

The general puffed at his cigarette.

"After the debacle[10] in Russia I left the country, for it was imprudent for an officer of the czar to stay there. **D** Many noble Russians lost everything. I, luckily, had invested heavily

---

9. Someone who is **ardent** (AHR DUHNT) about something is dedicated and enthusiastic.
10. A **debacle** (DIH BAH KUHL) is a disaster or sudden downfall. Zaroff is referring to the Russian Revolution of 1917, in which the czar and his government were overthrown.

B HERE'S HOW

Vocabulary

I am not sure what *exhausted* means. I think knowing that word is important to understanding General Zaroff. I checked my dictionary, and *exhausted* means "used something up completely." This tells me that the general has tried hunting tigers in every way in the past. Now he is looking for another animal to hunt.

C YOUR TURN

Vocabulary

Take a look at how the general uses the word *modesty*. This word can have more than one meaning. Circle the meaning that makes the most sense here: (a) not boastful (b) not large or extreme.

D HERE'S HOW

Language Coach

The word *imprudent* is made up of the word "prudent" plus the **prefix** *im–*, which means "not." I was not sure what "prudent" meant, so I looked it up in the dictionary. It means "sensible," or "wise." So if something is *imprudent*, it is not sensible.

The Most Dangerous Game 13

A QUICK CHECK

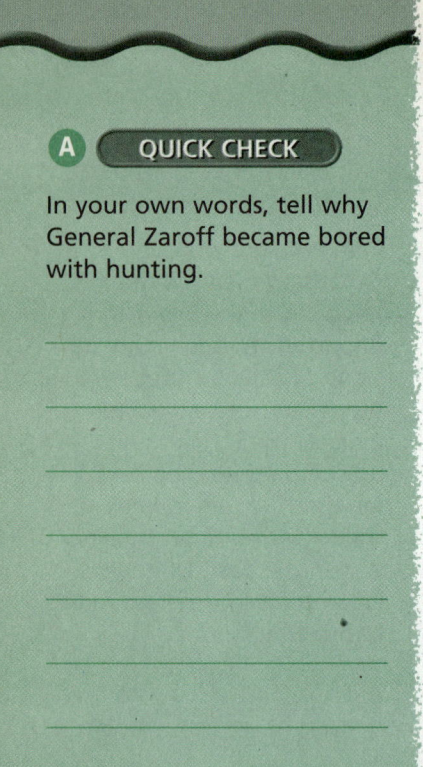

In your own words, tell why General Zaroff became bored with hunting.

___

in American securities, so I shall never have to open a tearoom in Monte Carlo or drive a taxi in Paris. Naturally, I continued to hunt—grizzlies in your Rockies, crocodiles in the Ganges, rhinoceroses in East Africa. It was in Africa that the Cape buffalo hit me and laid me up for six months. As soon as I recovered I started for the Amazon to hunt jaguars, for I had heard they were unusually cunning. They weren't." The Cossack sighed.

320 "They were no match at all for a hunter with his wits about him and a high-powered rifle. I was bitterly disappointed. I was lying in my tent with a splitting headache one night when a terrible thought pushed its way into my mind. Hunting was beginning to bore me! And hunting, remember, had been my life. I have heard that in America businessmen often go to pieces when they give up the business that has been their life."

"Yes, that's so," said Rainsford.

The general smiled. "I had no wish to go to pieces," he said. "I must do something. Now, mine is an analytical mind, Mr.
330 Rainsford. Doubtless that is why I enjoy the problems of the chase."

"No doubt, General Zaroff."

"So," continued the general, "I asked myself why the hunt no longer fascinated me. You are much younger than I am, Mr. Rainsford, and have not hunted as much, but you perhaps can guess the answer."

"What was it?"

"Simply this: Hunting had ceased to be what you call a sporting proposition. It had become too easy. I always got my quarry. Always. There is no greater bore than perfection." **A**

340 The general lit a fresh cigarette.

"No animal had a chance with me anymore. That is no boast; it is a mathematical certainty. The animal had nothing but his legs and his instinct. Instinct is no match for reason. When I thought of this, it was a tragic moment for me, I can tell you."

Rainsford leaned across the table, absorbed in what his host was saying.

14 The Most Dangerous Game

"It came to me as an inspiration what I must do," the general went on.

"And that was?"

350 The general smiled the quiet smile of one who has faced an obstacle and surmounted it with success. **B** "I had to invent a new animal to hunt," he said.

"A new animal? You're joking."

"Not at all," said the general. "I never joke about hunting. I needed a new animal. I found one. So I bought this island, built this house, and here I do my hunting. The island is perfect for my purposes—there are jungles with a maze of trails in them, hills, swamps—"

"But the animal, General Zaroff?"

360 "Oh," said the general, "it supplies me with the most exciting hunting in the world. No other hunting compares with it for an instant. Every day I hunt, and I never grow bored now, for I have a quarry with which I can match my wits."

Rainsford's bewilderment showed in his face. **C**

"I wanted the ideal animal to hunt," explained the general. "So I said: 'What are the attributes of an ideal quarry?' **D** And the answer was, of course: 'It must have courage, cunning, and, above all, it must be able to reason.'"

"But no animal can reason," objected Rainsford.

370 "My dear fellow," said the general, "there is one that can."

"But you can't mean—" gasped Rainsford.

"And why not?"

"I can't believe you are serious, General Zaroff. This is a grisly joke."

"Why should I not be serious? I am speaking of hunting."

"Hunting? Good God, General Zaroff, what you speak of is murder."

The general laughed with entire good nature. He regarded Rainsford quizzically. "I refuse to believe that so modern and 380 civilized a young man as you seem to be harbors romantic ideas

---

B HERE'S HOW

Vocabulary

I am not sure what the word *surmounted* means. I think I can figure it out. The sentence says that the general had successfully *surmounted* an obstacle. To have success getting around an obstacle is like overcoming a challenge. I think *surmounted* most likely means overcame or got through a difficulty or challenge.

C HERE'S HOW

Literary Focus

I can tell that the writer is building **suspense** in this conversation between General Zaroff and Rainsford. Rainsford wants to know what animal the general hunts. So do I! All I know so far is that the animal is very dangerous. Maybe if I keep reading, I will found out what this dangerous animal is.

D HERE'S HOW

Vocabulary

I am not sure what the word *quarry* means. I know General Zaroff is still talking about hunting. More specifically, I know that the general is talking about the ideal, or perfect, prey to hunt. Because of this, I think that *quarry* is another word for "prey." I checked my dictionary, and I was right.

A YOUR TURN

Reading Focus
Do you think Rainsford will agree to go hunting with the general? Explain the reasons for your **prediction**.

_____
_____
_____
_____
_____

about the value of human life. Surely your experiences in the war—"

"Did not make me condone coldblooded murder," finished Rainsford stiffly.

IN OTHER WORDS Over a fancy dinner, General Zaroff and Rainsford talk about hunting. The general tells about how he started hunting, the large animals he has hunted, and how he has become bored with the sport. Then he talks about the most challenging animal he has found to hunt: human beings. Rainsford is shocked by this.

Laughter shook the general. "How extraordinarily droll you are!" he said. "One does not expect nowadays to find a young man of the educated class, even in America, with such a naive, and, if I may say so, mid-Victorian point of view. It's like finding a snuffbox in a limousine. Ah, well, doubtless you had Puritan 390 ancestors. So many Americans appear to have had. I'll wager you'll forget your notions when you go hunting with me. **A** You've a genuine new thrill in store for you, Mr. Rainsford."

"Thank you, I'm a hunter, not a murderer."

"Dear me," said the general, quite unruffled, "again that unpleasant word. But I think I can show you that your scruples[11] are quite ill-founded."

"Yes?"

"Life is for the strong, to be lived by the strong, and if need be, taken by the strong. The weak of the world were put here 400 to give the strong pleasure. I am strong. Why should I not use my gift? If I wish to hunt, why should I not? I hunt the scum of the earth—sailors from tramp ships—lascars,[12] blacks, Chinese, whites, mongrels—a thoroughbred horse or hound is worth more than a score of them."

"But they are men," said Rainsford hotly.

---

11. **Scruples** (SKRRO PUHLZ) are feelings of doubt or guilt about a suggested action.
12. **Lascars** (LA SKURHZ) were sailors from the East Indies who worked on European ships.

16   The Most Dangerous Game

"Precisely," said the general. "That is why I use them. It gives me pleasure. They can reason, after a fashion. So they are dangerous."

"But where do you get them?"

The general's left eyelid fluttered down in a wink. "This island is called Ship-Trap," he answered. "Sometimes an angry god of the high seas sends them to me. Sometimes, when Providence is not so kind, I help Providence a bit. Come to the window with me."

Rainsford went to the window and looked out toward the sea.

"Watch! Out there!" exclaimed the general, pointing into the night. Rainsford's eyes saw only blackness, and then, as the general pressed a button, far out to sea Rainsford saw the flash of lights.

The general chuckled. "They indicate a channel," he said, "where there's none; giant rocks with razor edges crouch like a sea monster with wide-open jaws. They can crush a ship as easily as I crush this nut." He dropped a walnut on the hardwood floor and brought his heel grinding down on it. **B** "Oh, yes," he said, casually, as if in answer to a question, "I have electricity. We try to be civilized here."

"Civilized? And you shoot down men?"

A trace of anger was in the general's black eyes, but it was there for but a second, and he said, in his most pleasant manner: "Dear me, what a righteous young man you are! **C** I assure you I do not do the thing you suggest. That would be barbarous. I treat these visitors with every consideration. They get plenty of good food and exercise. They get into splendid physical condition. You shall see for yourself tomorrow."

"What do you mean?"

"We'll visit my training school," smiled the general. "It's in the cellar. I have about a dozen pupils down there now. They're from the Spanish bark *San Lucar* that had the bad luck to go on

B LITERARY ANALYSIS

General Zaroff explains why the island is called Ship-Trap. Compare what he says with what Whitney says about the island at the beginning of the story. How does this new information help explain Whitney's ideas and feelings about the island?

C YOUR TURN

Vocabulary

The general calls Rainsford *righteous*. From the surrounding sentences, what do you think *righteous* means? Write your definition on the lines, below. Use a dictionary to check your answer.

The Most Dangerous Game 17

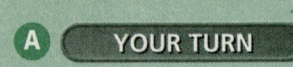

Vocabulary

Invariably means always or without changing. Why do General Zaroff's prisoners *invariably* choose to let him hunt them?

_____
_____
_____
_____
_____

440 the rocks out there. A very inferior lot, I regret to say. Poor specimens and more accustomed to the deck than to the jungle."

He raised his hand, and Ivan, who served as waiter, brought thick Turkish coffee. Rainsford, with an effort, held his tongue in check.

"It's a game, you see," pursued the general blandly. "I suggest to one of them that we go hunting. I give him a supply of food and an excellent hunting knife. I give him three hours' start. I am to follow, armed only with a pistol of the smallest caliber and range. If my quarry eludes me for three whole days, he wins the
450 game. If I find him"—the general smiled—"he loses."

"Suppose he refuses to be hunted?"

"Oh," said the general, "I give him his option, of course. He need not play that game if he doesn't wish to. If he does not wish to hunt, I turn him over to Ivan. Ivan once had the honor of serving as official knouter[13] to the Great White Czar, and he has his own ideas of sport. Invariably, Mr. Rainsford, invariably they choose the hunt." **A**

"And if they win?"

The smile on the general's face widened. "To date I have not
460 lost," he said.

IN OTHER WORDS The general explains how he captures ships, keeps the people onboard as prisoners, trains them, and hunts them. He sets it up like a game, with certain rules and supplies. Although it sounds as if the general gives his prisoners a fair chance, he always catches them in the end.

Then he added, hastily: "I don't wish you to think me a braggart, Mr. Rainsford. Many of them afford only the most elementary sort of problem. Occasionally I strike a tartar.[14] One almost did win. I eventually had to use the dogs."

"The dogs?"

---

13. A **knouter** (NOWT uhr) was a person who beat criminals with a knout, a kind of leather whip.
14. To **strike a tartar** means to take on someone stronger than you. A tartar is a violent, unmanageable person.

18 The Most Dangerous Game

"This way, please. I'll show you."

The general steered Rainsford to a window. The lights from the windows sent a flickering illumination that made grotesque patterns on the courtyard below, and Rainsford could see moving about there a dozen or so huge black shapes; as they turned toward him, their eyes glittered greenly. **B**

"A rather good lot, I think," observed the general. "They are let out at seven every night. If anyone should try to get into my house—or out of it—something extremely regrettable would occur to him." He hummed a snatch of song from the Folies-Bergère.

"And now," said the general, "I want to show you my new collection of heads. Will you come with me to the library?"

"I hope," said Rainsford, "that you will excuse me tonight, General Zaroff. I'm really not feeling at all well."

"Ah, indeed?" the general inquired solicitously.[15] "Well, I suppose that's only natural, after your long swim. You need a good, restful night's sleep. Tomorrow you'll feel like a new man, I'll wager. Then we'll hunt, eh? I've one rather promising prospect—"

Rainsford was hurrying from the room.

"Sorry you can't go with me tonight," called the general. "I expect rather fair sport—a big, strong black. He looks resourceful— Well, good night, Mr. Rainsford; I hope you have a good night's rest."

The bed was good and the pajamas of the softest silk, and he was tired in every fiber of his being, but nevertheless Rainsford could not quiet his brain with the opiate[16] of sleep. He lay, eyes wide open. **C** Once he thought he heard stealthy steps in the corridor outside his room. He sought to throw open the door; it would not open. He went to the window and looked out. His room was high up in one of the towers. The lights of the château were out now, and it was dark and silent, but there was a frag-

---

15. To inquire or ask of **solicitously** (SUH LIH SIH THUS LEE) means to speak in a concerned manner.
16. An **opiate** (OH PEE IHT) is anything that tends to soothe or calm someone. An opiate may also be a medicine containing opium or a related drug used to relieve pain.

B HERE'S HOW

Literary Focus
General Zaroff shows Rainsford his dogs. Maybe the writer is **foreshadowing** that the general will be using the dogs when he and Rainsford go hunting.

C LITERARY ANALYSIS

Why do you think Rainsford is having trouble sleeping here?

_____
_____
_____
_____
_____

A HERE'S HOW

Vocabulary

I have never seen the words *sallow* or *wan* before. In this sentence, the author uses the words to describe the moon and the light that is given off by the moon. I checked my dictionary, and *sallow* means "of a grayish, greenish, yellow color." This makes sense when describing the color of the moon. The word *wan* means "washed-out," or "pale." This means that there was not much light coming from the moon, but there was a little. There was just enough light for Rainsford to see the shapes moving.

B QUICK CHECK

Why is General Zaroff unhappy with the last night's hunt?

_____
_____
_____
_____
_____

---

ment of sallow moon, and by its wan light he could see, dimly, the courtyard; there, weaving in and out in the pattern of shadow, were black, noiseless forms; the hounds heard him at the window and looked up, expectantly, with their green eyes. **A** Rainsford went back to the bed and lay down. By many methods he tried to put himself to sleep. He had achieved a doze when, just as morning began to come, he heard, far off in the jungle, the faint report of a pistol.

IN OTHER WORDS The general shows off his fierce, or mean, hunting dogs. He talks about hunting a man, and about his collection of human heads. That night, Rainsford cannot sleep. He realizes that he is a prisoner in this beautiful room. He hears someone leave in the evening. Then, in the morning, he hears a gunshot.

General Zaroff did not appear until luncheon. He was dressed faultlessly in the tweeds of a country squire. He was solicitous about the state of Rainsford's health.

"As for me," sighed the general, "I do not feel so well. I am worried, Mr. Rainsford. Last night I detected traces of my old complaint."

To Rainsford's questioning glance the general said: "Ennui. Boredom."

Then, taking a second helping of crêpes suzette, the general explained: "The hunting was not good last night. The fellow lost his head. He made a straight trail that offered no problems at all. That's the trouble with these sailors; they have dull brains to begin with, and they do not know how to get about in the woods. They do excessively stupid and obvious things. It's most annoying. **B** Will you have another glass of Chablis, Mr. Rainsford?"

"General," said Rainsford firmly, "I wish to leave this island at once."

The general raised his thickets of eyebrows; he seemed hurt. "But, my dear fellow," the general protested, "you've only just come. You've had no hunting—"

"I wish to go today," said Rainsford. He saw the dead black eyes of the general on him, studying him. General Zaroff's face suddenly brightened.

He filled Rainsford's glass with venerable Chablis from a dusty bottle.

"Tonight," said the general, "we will hunt—you and I."

Rainsford shook his head. "No, general," he said. "I will not hunt."

The general shrugged his shoulders and delicately ate a hothouse grape. "As you wish, my friend," he said. "The choice rests entirely with you. But may I not venture to suggest that you will find my idea of sport more diverting[17] than Ivan's?"

He nodded toward the corner where the giant stood, scowling, his thick arms crossed on his hogshead of chest.

"You don't mean—" cried Rainsford.

"My dear fellow," said the general, "have I not told you I always mean what I say about hunting? This is really an inspiration. I drink to a foeman worthy of my steel—at last."

The general raised his glass, but Rainsford sat staring at him.

"You'll find this game worth playing," the general said enthusiastically. **C** "Your brain against mine. Your woodcraft against mine. Your strength and stamina against mine. Outdoor chess! And the stake is not without value; eh?" **D**

"And if I win—" began Rainsford huskily.

"I'll cheerfully acknowledge myself defeated if I do not find you by midnight of the third day," said General Zaroff. "My sloop will place you on the mainland near a town."

The general read what Rainsford was thinking.

"Oh, you can trust me," said the Cossack. "I will give you my word as a gentleman and a sportsman. Of course you, in turn, must agree to say nothing of your visit here."

"I'll agree to nothing of the kind," said Rainsford.

---

17. Something **diverting** (DUH VUR THING) is amusing or entertaining.

YOUR TURN

Vocabulary

Knowing what you do about how the general feels about this new game, what do you think *enthusiastically* means? Write a definition, below.

_____

_____

YOUR TURN

Reading Focus

Think about what you already know about both Rainsford and General Zaroff. Then make a **prediction** about who will win the hunting game. Explain your answer.

_____

_____

_____

_____

_____

_____

A HERE'S HOW

Literary Skills

The things Ivan brings Rainsford here sound familiar to me. I think maybe this moment was **foreshadowed** earlier in the story. I looked back, and I was right! In lines 445–449, General Zaroff talked about the equipment he gives his prisoners before the hunt.

B HERE'S HOW

Vocabulary

Rainsford tells himself he must keep his *nerve*. I looked up *nerve* in the dictionary. One definition I found was "a fiber that sends messages from the brain so the entire body can move and feel." That does not seem to be what Rainsford is talking about. Another definition was "courage." That makes more sense. Rainsford needs to keep up his courage to escape General Zaroff.

---

560 "Oh," said the general, "in that case— But why discuss that now? Three days hence we can discuss it over a bottle of Veuve Clicquot, unless—"

The general sipped his wine.

Then a businesslike air animated him. "Ivan," he said to Rainsford, "will supply you with hunting clothes, food, a knife. I suggest you wear moccasins; they leave a poorer trail. I suggest too that you avoid the big swamp in the southeast corner of the island. We call it Death Swamp. There's quicksand there. One foolish fellow tried it. The deplorable part of it was that Lazarus
570 followed him. You can imagine my feelings, Mr. Rainsford. I loved Lazarus; he was the finest hound in my pack. Well, I must beg you to excuse me now. I always take a siesta after lunch. You'll hardly have time for a nap, I fear. You'll want to start, no doubt. I shall not follow till dusk. Hunting at night is so much more exciting than by day, don't you think? Au revoir,[18] Mr. Rainsford, au revoir."

General Zaroff, with a deep, courtly bow, strolled from the room.

From another door came Ivan. Under one arm he carried
580 khaki hunting clothes, a haversack of food, a leather sheath containing a long-bladed hunting knife; his right hand rested on a cocked revolver thrust in the crimson sash about his waist.... **A**

IN OTHER WORDS At lunch, Rainsford asks to leave the island, but the general insists that Rainsford go hunting with him. Zaroff explains the rules. If Rainsford escapes for three days, he may leave. The general also warns Rainsford about a dangerous swamp on the island and has Ivan give him food, clothes, and a knife. Rainsford can start right away, and Zaroff will follow him in the evening.

Rainsford had fought his way through the bush for two hours. "I must keep my nerve. **B** I must keep my nerve," he said through tight teeth.

---

18. **Au revoir** (OH RUH VWAHR) is French for "goodbye."

22 The Most Dangerous Game

He had not been entirely clearheaded when the château gates snapped shut behind him. His whole idea at first was to put distance between himself and General Zaroff, and, to this end, he had plunged along, spurred on by the sharp rowels of something very like panic. Now he had got a grip on himself, had stopped, and was taking stock of himself and the situation.

He saw that straight flight was futile; inevitably it would bring him face to face with the sea. He was in a picture with a frame of water, and his operations, clearly, must take place within that frame.

"I'll give him a trail to follow," muttered Rainsford, and he struck off from the rude paths he had been following into the trackless wilderness. He executed a series of intricate loops; he doubled on his trail again and again, recalling all the lore of the fox hunt and all the dodges of the fox. **C** Night found him leg-weary, with hands and face lashed by the branches, on a thickly wooded ridge. He knew it would be insane to blunder on through the dark, even if he had the strength. His need for rest was imperative and he thought: "I have played the fox; now I must play the cat of the fable." A big tree with a thick trunk and outspread branches was nearby, and taking care to leave not the slightest mark, he climbed up into the crotch and stretching out on one of the broad limbs, after a fashion, rested. Rest brought him new confidence and almost a feeling of security. Even so zealous a hunter as General Zaroff could not trace him there, he told himself; only the devil himself could follow that complicated trail through the jungle after dark. But, perhaps, the general was a devil—

An apprehensive night crawled slowly by like a wounded snake, and sleep did not visit Rainsford, although the silence of a dead world was on the jungle. **D** Toward morning, when a dingy gray was varnishing the sky, the cry of some startled bird focused Rainsford's attention in that direction. Something was coming through the bush, coming slowly, carefully, coming by the same winding way Rainsford had come. He flattened himself down

---

C QUICK CHECK

Why is Rainsford making a complex trail like a fox?

_____
_____
_____
_____

D LITERARY ANALYSIS

The author compares the night Rainsford is having to a wounded snake. In what way or ways are these two things similar?

_____
_____
_____
_____

YOUR TURN

Literary Focus

Reread lines 633–641. How does the writer build **suspense** about what will happen next in the story?

_____
_____
_____
_____
_____

on the limb, and through a screen of leaves almost as thick as tapestry, he watched. The thing that was approaching was a man.

It was General Zaroff. He made his way along with his eyes fixed in utmost concentration on the ground before him. He paused, almost beneath the tree, dropped to his knees and studied the ground. Rainsford's impulse was to hurl himself down like a panther, but he saw the general's right hand held something metallic—a small automatic pistol.

The hunter shook his head several times, as if he were puzzled. Then he straightened up and took from his case one of his black cigarettes; its pungent incenselike smoke floated up to Rainsford's nostrils.

Rainsford held his breath. The general's eyes had left the ground and were traveling inch by inch up the tree. Rainsford froze there, every muscle tensed for a spring. But the sharp eyes of the hunter stopped before they reached the limb where Rainsford lay; a smile spread over his brown face. Very deliberately he blew a smoke ring into the air; then he turned his back on the tree and walked carelessly away, back along the trail he had come. The swish of the underbrush against his hunting boots grew fainter and fainter. **A**

Then pent-up air burst hotly from Rainsford's lungs. His first thought made him feel sick and numb. The general could follow a trail through the woods at night; he could follow an extremely difficult trail; he must have uncanny powers; only by the merest chance had the Cossack failed to see his quarry.

Rainsford's second thought was even more terrible. It sent a shudder of cold horror through his whole being. Why had the general smiled? Why had he turned back?

Rainsford did not want to believe what his reason told him was true, but the truth was as evident as the sun that had by now pushed through the morning mists. The general was playing with him! The general was saving him for another day's sport! The Cossack was the cat; he was the mouse. Then it was that Rainsford knew the full meaning of terror.

24   The Most Dangerous Game

IN OTHER WORDS Rainsford starts running, but then he stops to think. He creates a complicated trail that will be difficult to follow. At night, he climbs a tree. Just before dawn, General Zaroff reaches the tree. The general stops for long enough to show that he has found his prey but leaves without harming his prisoner. Rainsford, frightened, understands that this is because Zaroff wants to keep playing the game.

"I will not lose my nerve. I will not."

He slid down from the tree and struck off again into the woods. His face was set and he forced the machinery of his mind to function. Three hundred yards from his hiding place he stopped where a huge dead tree leaned precariously on a smaller living one. Throwing off his sack of food, Rainsford took his knife from its sheath and began to work with all his energy.

The job was finished at last, and he threw himself down behind a fallen log a hundred feet away. He did not have to wait long. The cat was coming again to play with the mouse.

Following the trail with the sureness of a bloodhound came General Zaroff. Nothing escaped those searching black eyes, no crushed blade of grass, no bent twig, no mark, no matter how faint, in the moss. So intent was the Cossack on his stalking that he was upon the thing Rainsford had made before he saw it. His foot touched the protruding bough that was the trigger. Even as he touched it, the general sensed his danger and leapt back with the agility of an ape. But he was not quite quick enough; the dead tree, delicately adjusted to rest on the cut living one, crashed down and struck the general a glancing blow on the shoulder as it fell; but for his alertness, he must have been smashed beneath it. He staggered, but he did not fall; nor did he drop his revolver.

B He stood there, rubbing his injured shoulder, and Rainsford, with fear again gripping his heart, heard the general's mocking laugh ring through the jungle. **C**

"Rainsford," called the general, "if you are within the sound of my voice, as I suppose you are, let me congratulate you. Not many men know how to make a Malay man-catcher. Luckily for

---

B HERE'S HOW

Vocabulary

General Zaroff *staggered* but did not fall when the dead tree hit his shoulder. That sounds like he almost fell down. I looked the word up in the dictionary, and I was right! When a person *staggers*, he or she has trouble walking or standing steady.

C YOUR TURN

Vocabulary

Think about how General Zaroff feels during this "game." He seems to enjoy the game, and the situation he has put Rainsford in, very much. Knowing this, what do you think a *mocking* laugh is?

_____
_____
_____

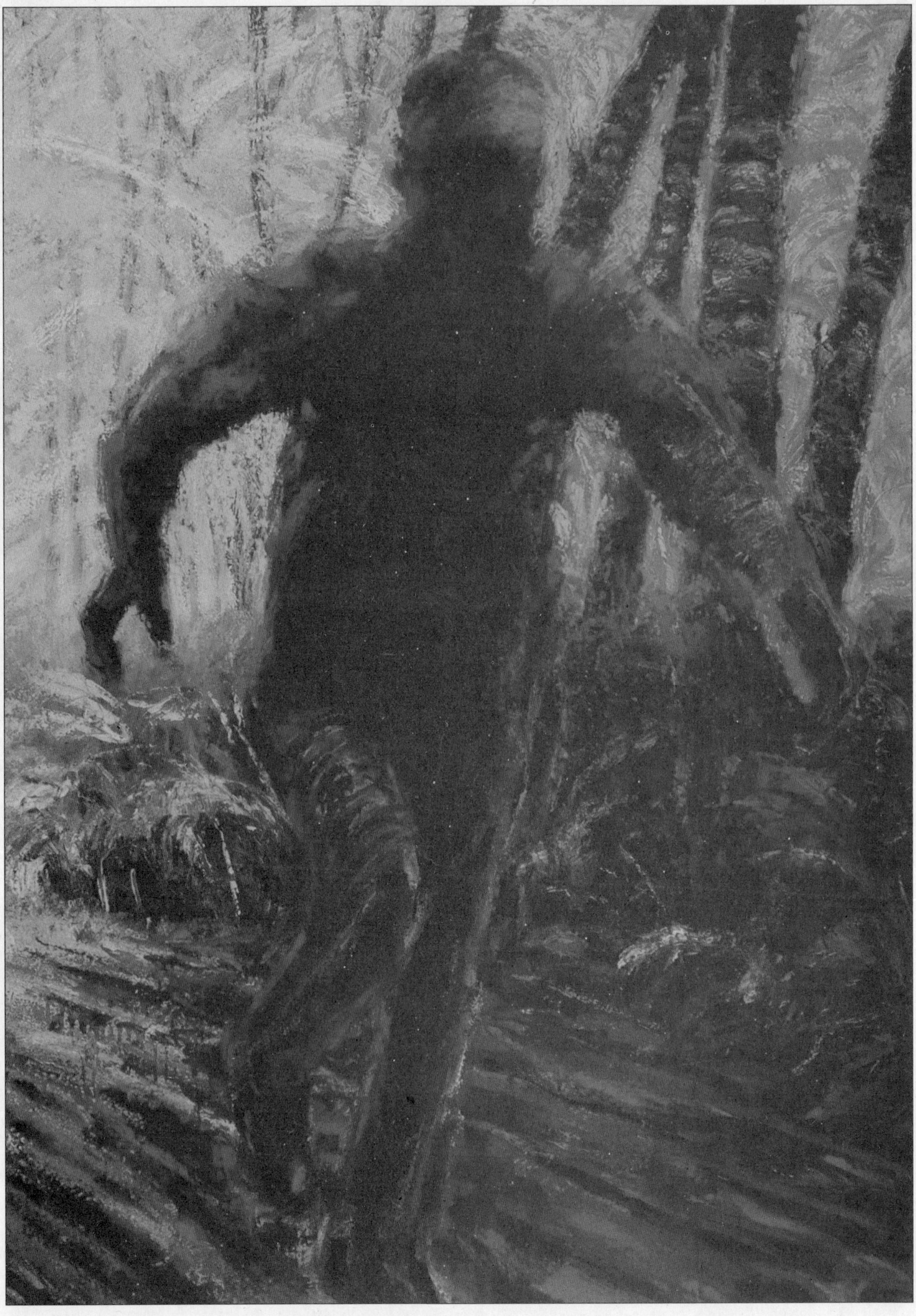

me, I too have hunted in Malacca. You are proving interesting, Mr. Rainsford. I am going now to have my wound dressed; it's only a slight one. But I shall be back. I shall be back."

IN OTHER WORDS Rainsford sets up a trap with a dead tree. General Zaroff walks into it but pulls back just in time. He escapes with only a small injury and promises to return.

When the general, nursing his bruised shoulder, had gone, Rainsford took up his flight again. It was flight now, a desperate, hopeless flight, that carried him on for some hours. Dusk came, then darkness, and still he pressed on. The ground grew softer under his moccasins; the vegetation grew ranker, denser; insects bit him savagely. Then, as he stepped forward, his foot sank into the ooze. He tried to wrench it back, but the muck sucked viciously at his foot as if it were a giant leech. With a violent effort, he tore loose. He knew where he was now. Death Swamp and its quicksand. **A**

His hands were tight closed as if his nerve were something tangible that someone in the darkness was trying to tear from his grip. The softness of the earth had given him an idea. He stepped back from the quicksand a dozen feet or so, and, like some huge prehistoric beaver, he began to dig.

Rainsford had dug himself in in France, when a second's delay meant death. That had been a placid pastime compared to his digging now. The pit grew deeper; when it was above his shoulders, he climbed out and from some hard saplings cut stakes and sharpened them to a fine point. These stakes he planted in the bottom of the pit with the points sticking up. With flying fingers he wove a rough carpet of weeds and branches and with it he covered the mouth of the pit. Then, wet with sweat and aching with tiredness, he crouched behind the stump of a lightning-charred tree. **B**

He knew his pursuer was coming; he heard the padding sound of feet on the soft earth, and the night breeze brought him the perfume of the general's cigarette. It seemed to Rainsford that

---

A YOUR TURN

Literary Focus

Look back through the story. Find the place where the author **foreshadows** Rainsford's arrival in the swamp.

B HERE'S HOW

Reading Focus

It looks like Rainsford has made a trap. He already tried a similar idea to stop the general. It did not work, but it did hurt him. I **predict** that this trap will not stop the general either, but it might slow him down.

A **HERE'S HOW**

Vocabulary

I am not sure what *swiftness* means, but I think I can make a guess based on the way it is used here. The general was coming with *swiftness*. He was not feeling his way along and moving slowly. I think *swiftness* is another word for "quickness."

B **YOUR TURN**

Reading Focus

What do you think Rainsford's new idea to stop the general will be? Use information from the story to make a **prediction**.

_____
_____
_____
_____
_____

C **YOUR TURN**

Vocabulary

What does the word *straining* mean? What was Rainsford doing *straining* his eyes to see?

_____
_____

---

the general was coming with unusual swiftness; he was not feeling his way along, foot by foot. **A** Rainsford, crouching there, could not see the general, nor could he see the pit. He lived a year in a minute. Then he felt an impulse to cry aloud with joy, for he heard the sharp crackle of the breaking branches as the cover of the pit gave way; he heard the sharp scream of pain as the pointed stakes found their mark. He leapt up from his place of concealment. Then he cowered back. Three feet from the pit a man was standing, with an electric torch in his hand.

"You've done well, Rainsford," the voice of the general called. "Your Burmese tiger pit has claimed one of my best dogs. Again you score. I think, Mr. Rainsford, I'll see what you can do against my whole pack. I'm going home for a rest now. Thank you for a most amusing evening."

IN OTHER WORDS Near the swamp, Rainsford makes a trap with a hidden pit. Something falls into it, but it is not the general. It is one of his dogs. The general is pleased with the game, and the "player" that Rainsford is turning out to be. The general says he will come back with all the dogs.

At daybreak Rainsford, lying near the swamp, was awakened by the sound that made him know that he had new things to learn about fear. It was a distant sound, faint and wavering, but he knew it. It was the baying of a pack of hounds.

Rainsford knew he could do one of two things. He could stay where he was and wait. That was suicide. He could flee. That was postponing the inevitable. For a moment he stood there, thinking. An idea that held a wild chance came to him, and, tightening his belt, he headed away from the swamp. **B**

The baying of the hounds drew nearer, then still nearer, nearer, ever nearer. On a ridge Rainsford climbed a tree. Down a watercourse, not a quarter of a mile away, he could see the bush moving. Straining his eyes, he saw the lean figure of General Zaroff; just ahead of him Rainsford made out another figure whose wide shoulders surged through the tall jungle weeds. **C** It was the giant Ivan, and he seemed pulled forward by some unseen force. Rainsford knew that Ivan must be holding the pack in leash.

They would be on him any minute now. His mind worked frantically. He thought of a native trick he had learned in Uganda. He slid down the tree. He caught hold of a springy young sapling and to it he fastened his hunting knife, with the blade pointing down the trail; with a bit of wild grapevine he tied back the sapling. Then he ran for his life. The hounds raised their voices as they hit the fresh scent. Rainsford knew now how an animal at bay feels. **D**

He had to stop to get his breath. The baying of the hounds stopped abruptly, and Rainsford's heart stopped too. They must have reached the knife.

He shinnied excitedly up a tree and looked back. His pursuers had stopped. But the hope that was in Rainsford's brain when he climbed died, for he saw in the shallow valley that General Zaroff was still on his feet. But Ivan was not. The knife, driven by the recoil of the springing tree, had not wholly failed.

"Nerve, nerve, nerve!" he panted, as he dashed along. A blue gap showed between the trees dead ahead. Ever nearer drew the hounds. Rainsford forced himself on toward that gap. He reached it. It was the shore of the sea. Across a cove he could see the gloomy gray stone of the château. Twenty feet below him the sea

D YOUR TURN

Literary Focus
Underline the words and phrases in lines 747–754 that help build **suspense**.

A HERE'S HOW

Language Coach
General Zaroff thinks it will be hard to *replace* Ivan. That makes sense. I know that the **prefix** *re–* means "again." The word *replace* probably means "to get something again," or "to get something similar to a thing that has been lost."

rumbled and hissed. Rainsford hesitated. He heard the hounds. Then he leapt far out into the sea. . . .

770 When the general and his pack reached the place by the sea, the Cossack stopped. For some minutes he stood regarding the blue-green expanse of water. He shrugged his shoulders. Then he sat down, took a drink of brandy from a silver flask, lit a perfumed cigarette, and hummed a bit from *Madama Butterfly*.

IN OTHER WORDS As the general and his dogs get closer, Rainsford sets up one more trap with his knife. He misses the general but kills Ivan, who is holding the dogs. As Zaroff and the dogs continue the chase, Rainsford makes a final run and dives into the sea.

General Zaroff had an exceedingly good dinner in his great paneled dining hall that evening. With it he had a bottle of Pol Roger and half a bottle of Chambertin. Two slight annoyances kept him from perfect enjoyment. One was the thought that it would be difficult to replace Ivan; the other was that his 780 quarry had escaped him; of course the American hadn't played the game—so thought the general as he tasted his after-dinner liqueur. **A** In his library he read, to soothe himself, from the works of Marcus Aurelius. At ten he went up to his bedroom. He was deliciously tired, he said to himself as he locked himself in. There was a little moonlight, so before turning on his light, he went to the window and looked down at the courtyard. He could see the great hounds, and he called: "Better luck another time," to them. Then he switched on the light.

A man, who had been hiding in the curtains of the bed, was 790 standing there.

"Rainsford!" screamed the general. "How in God's name did you get here?"

"Swam," said Rainsford. "I found it quicker than walking through the jungle."

The general sucked in his breath and smiled. "I congratulate you," he said. "You have won the game."

30 The Most Dangerous Game

Rainsford did not smile. "I am still a beast at bay," he said, in a low, hoarse voice. "Get ready, General Zaroff."

The general made one of his deepest bows. "I see," he said. "Splendid! One of us is to furnish a repast[19] for the hounds. The other will sleep in this very excellent bed. On guard, Rainsford...."

IN OTHER WORDS When General Zaroff goes to bed, Rainsford is waiting for him. The general admits that Rainsford has won, but Rainsford is still "playing" the game. The two fight. That night, the winner will sleep in Zaroff's bed. The loser will not survive.

He had never slept in a better bed, Rainsford decided. **B**

IN OTHER WORDS Rainsford thought he slept very well that night.

---

19. A **repast** (RIH PAST) is a meal.

B QUICK CHECK

Who won the game?

Skills Practice

The Most Dangerous Game

USE A CLUES AND EVENTS CHART

Sometimes authors provide clues that **foreshadow** future events in a story. You can record how clues relate to events in a story by using a chart like the one below.

DIRECTIONS: Complete the chart below. Find clues in "The Most Dangerous Game" that **foreshadow** the events listed below. Also, write about the events from the story that are **foreshadowed** by the clues listed.

Clues	Event
Rainsford and Whitney talk about hunting and how a jaguar feels.	
The island is called "Ship-Trap Island."	
	General Zaroff hunts people, including Rainsford.
	Rainsford wins the hunting game.

Applying Your Skills

The Most Dangerous Game

LITERARY FOCUS: SUSPENSE AND FORESHADOWING

DIRECTIONS: Read the short story below. Underline the sentences that you think are examples of **foreshadowing**.

The sky in the little town turned as black as ink. The wind howled. James and Michael had to stay at school late to finish a science project. "It's six o'clock," Michael said to James. "We should really get going." As the students began packing up their supplies, a loud rumble of thunder startled them. Looking out the window, James saw that the rain was getting heavier. The two started to rush now. They quickly threw their books in their bags and headed for the classroom door.

The late bus was long gone, so the two boys walked through the dark and empty hallways out to the front of the building. Michael's mom was supposed to pick them up, but she was nowhere in sight. James and Michael decided that all they could do now was go back inside and wait.

READING FOCUS: MAKING PREDICTIONS

DIRECTIONS: Answer the following questions in complete sentences.

1. What do you think will happen to Rainsford after the story is over?
   _____

2. What evidence, or clues, in the story supports your **prediction**?
   _____
   _____
   _____

VOCABULARY REVIEW

DIRECTIONS: Fill in each blank space with the correct vocabulary word from the Word Box.

Word Box
- receding
- imprudent
- surmounted
- invariably

1. That young woman _____ many obstacles to become a famous athlete.
2. It would be _____ to spend all your money on that prom dress.
3. I am _____ late for work on rainy mornings.
4. I waved goodbye while the bus was _____ into the distance.

The Most Dangerous Game   33

Preparing to Read

Liberty

Based on the story by Julia Alvarez

LITERARY FOCUS: SETTING AND CONFLICT

When you think about **setting**, think about what surrounds a character:

- Where does the character live?
- What is the time period?
- What is life like for people in that place and time?

The setting of a story can sometimes lead to **conflict**, or a problem or argument. Look at these examples.

Setting	Conflict
1930s Kansas, there is no rain and so no food is growing on the farms	Families must struggle to survive.
World War II, prison camp	Prisoners must decide if and how to escape.

As you will see in "Liberty," conflicts can also take place between characters.

READING FOCUS: ANALYZING DETAILS

Details are small pieces of information. For example, the writer of "Liberty" tells us that the dog in the story is black and white, a special type of dog, a puppy, and full of energy. Details can tell you about the story's setting, conflict, and characters.

VOCABULARY

Work with a friend to practice using these words in complete sentences.

embassy (EHM BUH SEE) *n.*: a government office in a foreign country.

expedition (EHKS PUH DIH SHUHN) *n.*: a journey or a trip.

hesitated (HEHZ IH TAY TEHD) *v.*: paused or stopped, often out of nervousness.

SKILLS FOCUS

Literary Skills Understand setting; understand conflict.

Reading Skills Analyze story details.

LIBERTY

Based on the Story by Julia Alvarez

INTO THE STORY

In "Liberty," a family is preparing to move to the United States. The writer never tells us exactly where they live. We do know that Julia Alvarez, the story's writer, is from the Dominican Republic in Central America. It is likely that the characters in the story also live in the Dominican Republic. In the 1950s, the government of this small country did not allow many rights for its citizens. Those who disagreed with the government were often attacked by secret police. Julia Alvarez's family had to leave their country because her father disagreed with the government. "Liberty" tells the story of a family in a similar situation. For this family, going to the United States is not just a move, it is a move toward a life of new freedoms.

Papi came home with a dog. We had never seen one like it before. The black-and-white puppy was a special breed and full of energy. "It looks like a mess!" said Mami. "Take it back."

"Mami, it is a gift from Mister Victor!" Papi said. Returning the puppy would insult Mister Victor, who worked for the American embassy. We had helped him learn to live in our country, and now he wanted to thank us.

"If he wanted to thank us, he'd give us our visas,"[1] Mami said. My parents had been talking about going to the United States for a while. **A**

"Those visas[1] will come soon," Papi promised. But Mami kept shaking her head. She had enough to do with four daughters. Papi explained that the dog would not be allowed in the house. He would not poop in Mami's garden or bark late at night. "He will be a well-behaved dog," Papi said. "An American dog."

---

1. **Visas** (VEE SUHZ) are certificates granting official approval to enter a country.

"Liberty" by Julia Alvarez. Copyright © 1996 by Julia Alvarez. First published in *Writer's Harvest 2*, edited by Ethan Canin, published by Harcourt Brace and Company, 1996. All rights reserved. Reproduced by permission of **Susan Bergholz Literary Services, New York.**

A HERE'S HOW

Vocabulary
I am not sure if I have ever seen the word *embassy*. I can use context clues to figure out what it means, though. This man is an American. I see from lines 8–10 that he is trying to help the family get permission to move to the United States. An *embassy* must be a government office in a foreign country.

A HERE'S HOW

Literary Focus

I can see that this story starts with a **conflict**. Papi wants to keep the dog but Mami does not. I will read closely to see how the conflict ends.

B HERE'S HOW

Reading Focus

By **analyzing details** on this page, I learn a lot about the characters. I notice in lines 31–32 Papi suggests that Mami should speak English to the dog. Maybe this detail is the author's way of showing how much Papi wants to move to the United States. But the detail about Mami's facial expression in lines 33–34 tells me that Mami is not so happy about this change.

"What shall we call you?" Papi asked the puppy.

"Trouble," Mami suggested. The puppy was slobbering on her leg. She kicked him away.

20 "We will call him Liberty, like in the U.S.A. Constitution. Life, liberty, and the pursuit of happiness," Papi said. "Liberty, you are a lucky sign!"

Liberty barked. All us kids laughed. "Trouble," Mami said as she walked away. Liberty ran behind her. He seemed to agree that "Trouble" would be a better name for him. **A**

Mami was right—Liberty was trouble. He ate all of Mami's orchids, knocked things off the coffee table, and left footprints on the flowered couch. He tore up Mami's garden looking for buried treasure. Mami screamed at Liberty and stamped her foot. "Perro 30 sin vergüenza!"[2] But Liberty just barked back at her.

"He doesn't understand Spanish," Papi said. "Maybe if you correct him in English, he'll behave better!"

Mami turned to Papi. Her face looked as if she'd attack him after she was done with Liberty. "Let him go be a pet in his own country if he wants instructions in English!" Mami had changed her mind about going to the United States. She wanted to stay in her own country. **B**

"All liberty involves sacrifice," Papi said in a careful voice. Liberty barked as if he agreed.

40 Mami glared at Papi. "I told you I don't want trouble—" She was going to say more, but her eye fell on me. She stopped herself. "Why aren't you with the others?" she scolded.

The truth was that after Liberty arrived, I never played with the others. I had always been a tomboy and a troublemaker. While my sisters played nicely inside, I was out roaming the world looking for trouble. And now I had found someone to share my adventures.

"I'll take Liberty back to his pen," I offered. Unlike the dog, I knew when to get out of Mami's way.

---

2. The Spanish phrase **"Perro sin vergüenza!"** means "shameless dog."

36 Liberty

Mami didn't answer. She seemed to have something else on her mind. As I led Liberty away by his collar, I could see her talking to Papi. Suddenly she started to cry, and Papi held her.

"It's okay," I told Liberty. "Mami doesn't mean it. She really does love you. She's just nervous." It was what my father always said when Mami yelled at me.

At the back of the property stood Liberty's pen—a chain-link fence around a dirt square. Papi had built Liberty a cute little house inside, but then he painted it an unpleasant shade of green. It was always a job to get Liberty into that pen.

Sure enough, as soon as he saw where we were headed, he ran to our favorite spot in the front yard. Whenever I did something wrong, I hid out on a grassy mound surrounded by tall bushes. Liberty headed there, and I was right behind him.

Inside the clearing I stopped short. Two strange men in dark glasses were crouched behind the bushes. The fat one grabbed Liberty's collar. He pulled on it until poor Liberty was almost standing on his hind legs. Liberty began to bark. The man yanked his collar so hard that I felt sick to my stomach. I began to back away, but the other man grabbed my arm. "Not so fast," he said. I saw my scared face reflected in his glasses.

"I came for my dog," I said. I was about to cry.

"Good thing you found him," the man said. "Give her the dog," he ordered his friend. Then he turned to me. "You haven't seen us, you understand?"

I nodded—glad to escape—but I didn't understand.

"It's okay, Liberty." I hugged him when I put him back in his pen. We were both shaken. The fat man had almost broken Liberty's neck. The other one had hurt my arm. After I locked up the pen, Liberty wandered back to his house and actually went inside. He usually avoided that ugly doghouse. I walked back to my own house to tell my parents what had happened. After that, Mister Victor practically moved in. When he had to leave, someone from the embassy stayed "to keep an eye on things." Now, when Papi and Mister Victor talked or when

---

HERE'S HOW

Language Coach

Some words have **multiple**, or more than one, **meanings**. I know that a *pen* can be something to write with. But lines 56–57 describe Liberty's *pen* as "a chain-link fence around a dirt square." So, here, *pen* must mean "a closed area where animals are kept."

YOUR TURN

Literary Focus

The **setting** in this story is a country that limits people's rights. This setting may offer clues about the two men in the glasses who appear in lines 64–74. Who do you think they are?

_____
_____
_____
_____
_____

YOUR TURN

Language Coach

The word *practically* can have **multiple meanings**. It can mean "sensibly" or "almost." In line 82, which meaning makes more sense?

_____

Liberty 37

A HERE'S HOW

Reading Focus

By **analyzing details**, I can figure out why Mami says it is no longer safe to talk in the house. Lines 86–87 say that Mami found wires in the study. I think that these wires have something to do with the strange men in dark glasses. Because the family is afraid to talk in the house, I think the wires were put in to record what the family says.

B HERE'S HOW

Vocabulary

Papi and his friends are talking about a hunting *expedition*. From reading this sentence, I think an *expedition* must be a trip. Just to be sure, I checked the dictionary, and I was right!

C YOUR TURN

Reading Focus

There are many **details** in this paragraph, including where the character is sitting, what language is being spoken, and what is being said. Which details suggest that the adults are making secret plans?

_____
_____
_____
_____
_____

the *tíos*[3] came over, they all went to the back of the property near Liberty's pen to talk. Mami had found some wires in the study. The wires ran behind a screen and then out a window, where there was a little box with lots of other wires coming from different parts of the house.

Mami explained that it was no longer safe to talk in the house about certain things. **A** But the only way you knew what not to say was when Mami stared at you, demanding silence. She did this every time I asked her what was going on.

"Nothing," she said, and then she urged me to go outside and play. Mami forgot about enforcing rules. She seemed tense and always in tears. Papi was right—she was too nervous.

One day my *tíos* came to talk with Mister Victor and Papi. I wandered into the pen and sat beside Liberty with my back to the house and listened. The men were speaking in English, but I could understand most of what they said. They were planning some hunting expedition for a goat with guns to be delivered by Mister Charlie. **B** Papi was going to leave the goat to the others because his tennis shoes were missing. I thought I understood the words, but nothing made sense. My father did not own a pair of tennis shoes, we didn't know a Mister Charlie, and who ever heard of hunting a goat? **C**

---

3. *Tíos* is the Spanish word for "uncles."

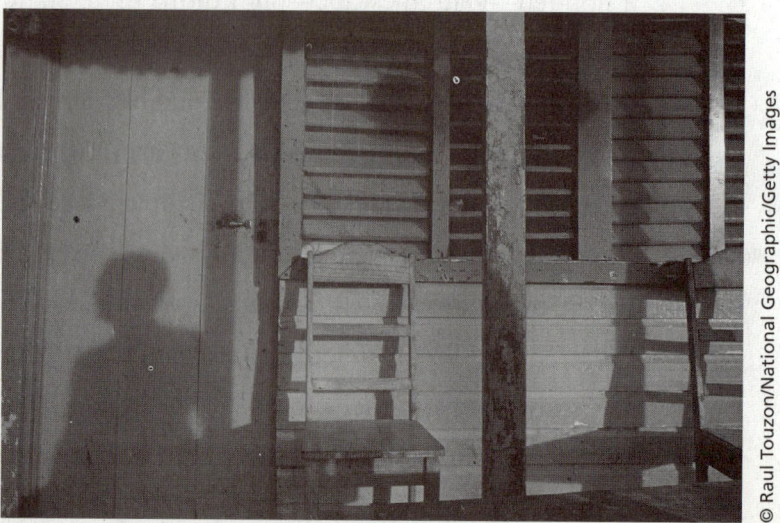

38 Liberty

Liberty and I sat there with the sun baking the tops of our heads. I had a sense that the world as I knew it was about to end. The image of the two men in glasses flashed through my head. To stop thinking, I put my arm around Liberty and buried my face in his neck.

Late one morning Mami told my sisters and me the news. Our visa had come. Mister Victor had arranged everything. That very night we were going to the United States of America! Wasn't that wonderful! She flashed us a bright smile, as if someone were taking her picture.

She smiled, but at the same time she looked like she wanted to cry. All morning aunts had been stopping by, kissing us and asking us to promise we would be very good. Until now, we hadn't a clue why they were so upset. **D**

Mami kept smiling her company smile. She had a job for each of us. There would not be room in our bags for everything. We had to pick just one toy to take with us to the United States.

I didn't even have to think twice about my choice. "I want to take Liberty."

Mami started shaking her head no. We could not take a dog into the United States of America. That was not allowed.

I burst into tears. I was not going to the United States unless I could take Liberty! Mami shook me and whispered that we had to go to the United States or else. But a world without Liberty would break my heart. Mami began to cry. *Tía*[4] Mimi took me aside. She had gone to school in the States and loved reading. I loved her because she always had smart things to say. "I'm going to tell you a little secret," she offered now. "You're going to find liberty when you get to the United States."

"Really?" I asked.

She hesitated a minute, and then she gave me a quick nod. **E** "You'll see what I mean," she said. And then, giving me a pat, she added, "Come on, let's go pack."

---

4. *Tía* is the Spanish word for "aunt."

D LITERARY ANALYSIS

Pause at line 120. Why do you think Mami looks like she wants to cry? Why are the narrator's aunts "so upset"?

_____
_____
_____
_____

E YOUR TURN

Vocabulary

Based in *Tía* Mimi's response, write a definition for the word *hesitated*.

_____
_____
_____
_____

Liberty 39

A YOUR TURN

Literary Focus

This scene is the first time in the story that the narrator has said or done anything unkind to her dog. What problem or **conflict** causes her to kick Liberty?

_____
_____
_____
_____
_____

B YOUR TURN

Language Coach

In this story, the word *liberty* often means "freedom." In other places, Liberty is the name of a dog. In the last sentence of this story, which **meaning** does liberty have—or does it have both meanings?

_____
_____
_____
_____

Late in the night someone comes in and shakes us awake. "It's time!" Half asleep, we put on our clothes.

"Go sit by the door," we are ordered. We file out of the bedroom and go sit on a bench. There is much rushing around. Mister Victor comes by and pats us on the head like dogs. "We'll have to wait a few more minutes," he says.

© Bo Zaunders/Corbis

In that wait, one sister has to go to the bathroom. Another wants a drink of water. My baby sister is dozing with her head on my shoulder. I lay her down on the bench and sneak outside.

I go through the dark patio down the path to the back of the yard. I have said good-bye to Liberty a dozen times already, but there is something else I have to do. I am afraid those two men in glasses may come back to the house and hurt Liberty.

I run quickly, because I hear my family calling. I open the pen, and Liberty jumps all over me, wagging his tail.

"Get away!" I order sharply. He is not used to hearing this tone of voice from me. I begin walking back to the house. I do not look around so as not to encourage him. I want him to run away before the bad men come.

He doesn't understand and keeps following me. Finally I have to treat him like Mami does. I kick him, softly at first. When he keeps tagging behind me, I kick him hard. **A** He whimpers and dashes away toward the front yard. He keeps on going down the drive, through the big gates, to the world out there. I tell myself that he will beat me to the United States. I will find Liberty there, like Tía Mimi says. But I know that my aunt meant a different kind of liberty. All I can do is hope that when we come back—as Mami has promised we will—my Liberty will be waiting for me here. **B**

40 Liberty

Applying Your Skills

Liberty

LITERARY FOCUS: SETTING AND CONFLICT

DIRECTIONS: When a **conflict** is worked out, it is called a *resolution*. What is the resolution for each of the following conflicts? Complete the chart below with information from the story. The first one has been done as an example.

Conflict	Resolution
Mami and Papi disagree about the dog.	The family keeps the dog.
The girl must decide whether to tell her parents about the mysterious men.	
The family must decide whether or not to go to the United States.	
Mami and the girl argue over leaving the dog behind.	

READING FOCUS: ANALYZING DETAILS

DIRECTIONS: Match each set of **details** from "Liberty" with the character they describe.

_____ 1. American, works at the embassy   **a.** Narrator

_____ 2. Nervous, grows orchids, has a bright "company smile"   **b.** Mister Victor

_____ 3. Tomboy, doesn't like school, loves her dog   **c.** *Tía* Mimi

_____ 4. Went to school in the United States, loves to read   **d.** Mami

VOCABULARY REVIEW

DIRECTIONS: Write "yes" after each sentence if the vocabulary word is being used correctly. Write "no" if it is not being used correctly.

1. Steve felt **embassy** when he answered the question incorrectly. _____

2. The **expedition** up the mountain was very hard on the climbers. _____

Preparing to Read

The Great Escape
Based on the article by Thomas Fleming

INFORMATIONAL TEXT FOCUS: MAIN IDEA

When you read for information, you should ask yourself: "What is the writer trying to say?" The most important point in an informational piece of writing is called the **main idea**. How can you find the main idea? Try these tips:

- Read the article's title. Does it tell you what the article will be about?
- Read the first sentence or paragraph. Does anything there sound like it could be the writer's most important point?
- Look for headings to give you an idea of the article's important points.
- Read the last sentence or paragraph. Does the writer focus on one big idea?

Use the chart below to help you organize information in "The Great Escape" that may help you find the main idea.

Main Idea Chart	
Title	The Great Escape
Headings	
Important words in first sentence or paragraph	
Important words in last sentence or paragraph	

VOCABULARY

Using index cards, make a flashcard for each of the words below. Write the word on the front and the definition on the back. Then, with a partner, practice using the flashcards to learn the meanings of each word.

forgery (FOHR JUHR EE) *n.*: something created to fool people.

civilian (SUH VIL YUHN) *n.*: anyone not in the armed forces or police.

violation (VY UH LAY SHUHN) *n.*: breaking of a law or rule.

fugitives (FYOO JIH TIHVZ) *n.*: people who run from danger or from the law.

SKILLS FOCUS

Informational Text Skills
Identify the main idea of an article.

42 The Great Escape

THE GREAT ESCAPE

Based on the article by Thomas Fleming

> **INTO THE ARTICLE**
>
> In World War II, the Allied Powers, or Allies, fought the Axis Powers. The major Allies included the United States, Great Britain, Russia, France, and China. The largest Axis Powers were Germany, Japan, and Italy. The war lasted from 1939 until 1945. During this time, Germany was ruled by the Nazi Party, led by Adolf Hitler. This article tells the story of prisoners of war, or POWs, in a German prison camp.

© Australian War Memorial Negative Number ART34781.021

The seven hundred fliers in the prisoner of war camp called Stalag Luft III came from many different countries. They had two things in common. All had been shot down fighting Germany during World War II in the early 1940s. And all wanted to escape. **A**

They had tried to escape from many other camps and had been caught. That was why they were in this camp. It was supposed to be escape-proof.

"The Great Escape" by Thomas Fleming adapted from *Boys' Life*, March 1997. Copyright © 1997 by **Thomas Fleming**. Retold by Holt, Rinehart and Winston. Reproduced by permission of the author.

A HERE'S HOW

Reading Focus

I know I should look for the **main idea** in the first paragraph. The first paragraph tells me what I think will be the main idea of this article. In my own words, the main idea is: "The Great Escape is the name for a famous escape in World War II when lots of POWs wanted to escape from a Nazi prison camp." Now I should check the rest of the article to make sure this is really the main idea.

A — HERE'S HOW

Reading Focus

Roger Bushell is mentioned by name, so he must be important. The author calls him a genius and the other prisoners seem to look up to him.

B — QUICK CHECK

What are "Tom, Dick, and Harry"?

_____

C — HERE'S HOW

Vocabulary

Civilian must mean the oposite of *uniform*. So civilian clothes are worn by people not in the military.

D — YOUR TURN

Reading Focus

Underline the headings on this page. On the lines below, write how they relate to the **main idea** of this article.

_____
_____
_____
_____

Two tall barbed wire fences with big towers, searchlights, and machine guns surrounded the camp. The prisoners called the towers "goon boxes," and they called the German guards inside the camp "ferrets."

Anyone the ferrets caught planning an escape was sent to "the cooler"—a cell where the prisoner was kept all alone and lived on nothing but bread and water.

The Escape Genius

The Germans seemed to have thought of everything. But Roger Bushell from South Africa was an escape genius. He was called Big X by the rest of the prisoners. He announced to his fellow prisoners that they were going to make the greatest escape in history. **A**

Big X's plan called for the prisoners to start three tunnels—called Tom, Dick and Harry. **B** The men cut trapdoors through the stone floors of three huts and inserted removable slabs made from stolen concrete. "Tunnel rats" dropped through the trapdoors and began digging.

Big X wanted deep tunnels. If they were too shallow, the Germans would be able to hear the men working in them. There was danger of the tunnels collapsing and burying them alive, but the tunnel rats went down thirty feet before they started for the fences.

The Escape Factory

The tunnels were only the beginning. "I want each escaping man to be equipped with a set of forged documents that will fool the German police," Big X said. "I want them to be wearing civilian clothes or fake German uniforms. **C** I want them to have compasses and maps that will help them reach the borders of neutral countries." **D**

The prisoners bribed some guards with chocolate from their Red Cross aid packages. Soon they had ink and pens, a camera, and a set of official documents. A forgery factory ran day and night. **E**

In other huts prisoners created civilian clothes by cutting and reshaping prisoners' uniforms, the linings of winter coats and other pieces of cloth. An Australian officer ran a factory that made two hundred compasses out of melted phonograph records and razor blades.

An engineering factory built air pumps so the tunnel rats could breathe. The engineers also made small flatbed trolleys from wooden bed boards. They even stole light bulbs and wiring for the tunnels.

The diggers lay on their stomachs in the two-foot-wide tunnels and filled boxes on the trolleys with sand. Other prisoners poured the sand into bags made from towels—bags that could be inserted under a man's pants.

Fifty Americans worked as sand carriers. They were called "penguins" because they had to spend most of their time outside, walking up and down, waiting for the right moment to pull a string on the bags and let the sand run out.

All around the camp were dozens of "stooges" who signaled when a ferret approached. This gave the forgers, tailors, penguins, and the others time to hide their work or take cover. Thirty feet underground, the tunnel rats kept digging. **F G**

E HERE'S HOW

Vocabulary

I'm not sure what *forgery* is, but if the prisoners want *forged* documents to fool the German police, it must mean "something made to fool others."

F YOUR TURN

Language Coach

Some words (called compounds) are made up of two other words. Recognizing and correctly pronouncing such words can improve your **oral fluency.** For example, the word *underground* in line 60 is made up of *under* and *ground*. Underline three other compound words in the next two paragraphs.

G HERE'S HOW

Reading Focus

I still think the **main idea** of this article is, "The Great Escape is the name for a famous event in World War II when lots of people wanted to escape from a prison camp." The details in lines 40–60 support this idea. These details show how determined prisoners were to escape and also to hide their plans from the Germans.

A QUICK CHECK

Reading Focus
What happens that might stop the escape?

_____
_____
_____

B HERE'S HOW

Vocabulary
Fugitives, in line 94, is an unfamiliar word. But in the next sentence, it is clear that *fugitives* and *escaped prisoners* mean the same thing, "people running away."

Pretending Defeat

Then disaster struck. The Germans discovered the trapdoor for Tom, the longest tunnel. The diggers had gotten past the wire fence and were only one hundred feet from the woods around the camp. Big X ordered a halt to all digging for more than a month. He wanted the Germans to think they had given up.

Then Big X ordered more digging in Harry. Soon they were under the wire and—they thought—into the woods. It was time for "the great escape." Big X was hoping to spring no fewer that 250 men. Not even a six-inch snowfall was going to stop them.

At 9 P.M. on March 24, 1944, the breakout began. Men wearing German uniforms, business suits and tattered workers' outfits crowded into the hut containing Harry's trapdoor. At the other end, the tunnel rats finished the thirty-foot shaft to the surface.

They finally broke through and stared around in horror. They were ten feet short of the trees! **A**

After a frantic conference, Big X decided they had to keep going. All their forged documents were dated. If they dug another ten feet and waited a month for the next moonless night, the forgery factory would have to do its work all over again.

They stretched a rope from the hole to the trees. The first man out lay in the trees and pulled the rope to signal when the guard was not looking. Over the next seven hours, seventy-six men ran through the woods towards freedom.

It was almost dawn when a German guard outside the fence discovered the hole. The guard raised his rifle to shoot the man crawling out. The rope controller leaped from the woods crying: "*Nicht schiessen*!" ("Don't shoot!"). The surprised guard's shot went wild.

By this time Big X and his friends were far away from Stalag Luft III.

The German dictator, Adolf Hitler, was furious. He ordered one of the biggest manhunts in history. More than 70,000 policemen and soldiers chased the fugitives. **B** Big X's plan to humiliate

46 The Great Escape

Map of Germany, Austria and Czechoslovakia during WWII

the Germans and make them worry about escaped prisoners—and not the war front—was successful.

But only three men made it to freedom. Fifty of the captured men, including Big X, were shot by the German secret police, the Gestapo, at Hitler's order. This was a terrible violation of the rules of war. **C** The bodies were cremated to hide the murders.

The rest of the escapers were returned to Stalag Luft III and other camps for long stays in the cooler. A year later, Allied armies freed the survivors as Germany surrendered.

C YOUR TURN

Vocabulary
The word *violation* is made up of a shorter word, *violate*. To *violate* means "to break a law or rule." Based on this, what do you think *violation* means?

_____
_____
_____
_____

A LITERARY ANALYSIS

Many men tried to escape, even though it was both difficult and dangerous to do so. How does the fact that so many tried to escape in the face of great danger connect to the first paragraph of the selection?

_____
_____
_____
_____
_____

B HERE'S HOW

Reading Focus

I should check the end of the selection to see if the author gives more details to support the **main idea**. *Escape* is still the most important idea of this article along with the importance of working with others to achieve a goal.

After the war, the British sent a team of investigators to Germany. They tracked down those who had carried out Hitler's order. Twenty-one were hanged for murder; seventeen received prison terms.

What had the great escape accomplished? **A** One writer summed it up this way: It proved that "there is nothing that can stop a group of men, regardless of race, creed, color or nationality, from achieving a goal once they agree to what that goal is." **B**

48   The Great Escape

Applying Your Skills

The Great Escape

INFORMATIONAL TEXT FOCUS: MAIN IDEA

DIRECTIONS: In the graphic organizer below, write the **main idea** of "The Great Escape" in the center bubble. Then, fill in details in the connecting bubbles. Each detail should support the main idea.

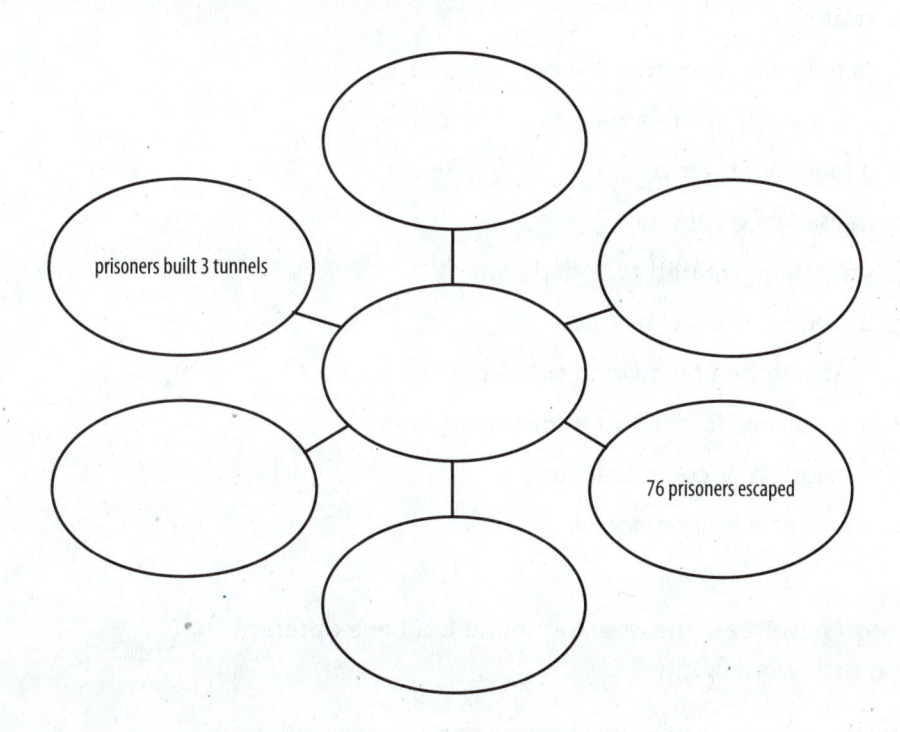

- prisoners built 3 tunnels
- 76 prisoners escaped

VOCABULARY REVIEW

DIRECTIONS: Fill in the blanks below with the correct words from the Word Box. Not every word will be used.

Word Box
- forgery
- civilian
- violation
- fugitives

1. Prisoners were punished for _____ of the rule against planning an escape.

2. German soldiers and police hunted the _____ who had escaped.

3. An important part of the escape plan was the _____ of documents to fool the German police.

The Great Escape   49

Skills Review

Collection 1

VOCABULARY REVIEW

DIRECTIONS: Match each vocabulary word in the left column with its correct meaning in the right column. Write the letters indicating your answers on the blanks.

1. convey _____
2. effect _____
3. excerpt _____
4. support _____
5. forgery _____
6. embassy _____
7. civilian _____
8. expedition _____
9. violation _____
10. hesitated _____
11. fugitives _____

a. result
b. people who run from danger or the law
c. anyone not in the armed forces or police
d. a journey or a trip
e. paused or stopped
f. something created to fool people
g. breaking of a law or rule
h. to strengthen by giving evidence
i. a government office in a foreign country
j. to suggest or communicate
k. a part of a longer story

DIRECTIONS: *Expedition* and *excerpt* have the same opening sound but have different meanings. Write a sentence using each word below.

_____
_____
_____
_____

50 Plot and Setting

Skills Review

Collection 1

LANGUAGE COACH: MULTIPLE MEANINGS

Many words have **multiple**, or more than one, **meanings**. In each sentence below, the bold word has multiple meanings. Some of the sentences come from the selections you have just read. Others do not. Circle the meaning beneath the sentence that makes the most sense in the sentence.

1. Two strange men in dark **glasses** were crouched behind the bushes.
    a. cups to drink from   b. things you wear to see better
2. The kitten's fur was black, shiny, and **soft**.
    a. kind   b. smooth to the touch   c. quiet
3. When the teacher called my name, I answered "**present**."
    a. here   b. gift
4. Jimmy James helped with this **part** of the job.
    a. divide   b. portion   c. an actor's lines in a play
5. Guards destroyed the tunnel **just** a week before it was ready to be used.
    a. fair   b. only

ORAL LANGUAGE ACTIVITY

All of the selections you have just read deal with the theme, or idea, of people adjusting to an unfamiliar place. With a partner, discuss how this theme is presented in each story or article. What unfamiliar place did the characters have to go to? How well did they deal with the situation?

Collection 2

Character

© Hyacinth Manning/Super Stock

Literary and Academic Vocabulary for Collection 2

LITERARY VOCABULARY

characters (KAR IHK TUHRZ) *n.:* the people you meet in a story, poem, or play.
   Mrs. Jones and Roger are the two main characters in Thank You, M'am.

characterization (KAR IHK TUHR UH ZAY SHUHN) *n.:* the way in which a writer reveals a character's personality.
   The author's characterization of the woman told me that she was kind and generous.

inferences (IHN FRUHN SUHZ) *n.:* educated guesses.
   You can make inferences about characters based on how they act.

ACADEMIC VOCABULARY

observation (AWB ZUHR VAY SHUHN) *n.:* statement based on what you see.
   My observations about the new baseball stadium were that it was smaller and much less crowded than the old one.

incident (IHN SIH DUHNT) *n.:* an event; something that took place.
   I read in the newspaper this morning about the incident downtown.

complex (KAHM PLEHKS) *adj.:* having more than one part; complicated.
   Although the old man's words are simple, the feelings behind what he says are complex.

significant (SIHG NIHF UH KUHNT) *adj.:* important.
   The girl does not say much, but what little she says is significant.

Preparing to Read

Thank You, M'am

By Langston Hughes

LITERARY FOCUS: CHARACTER AND DIALOGUE

Writers sometimes use conversation, or **dialogue**, between **characters** to tell us more about them. As a reader, you listen in on those conversations. You form opinions about the characters based on what they say and how they say it. For example, the woman in "Thank You, M'am" asks the boy, "Ain't you got nobody home to tell you to wash your face?" This leads her to believe that the boy has nobody to look after him. This shows that she seems to care about the boy.

As you read, keep notes in a chart, like the one below, to help you better understand the characters through their dialogue.

Lines of dialogue	What does this tell me about the characters?
"Ain't you got nobody home to tell you to wash your face?" "No'm," said the boy.	The woman notices that the boy's face is dirty. She seems to care about him.

READING FOCUS: MAKING INFERENCES

Writers do not always tell you what their characters are like. Instead, they allow you to make **inferences**, or form your own ideas about the characters based on what they say and do. When you make an inference, you use information from the story or your own experience to make an educated guess. For example, in the conversation above, you learn the detail that the boy lives alone or does not see his parents much. Based on this information, you can infer that he is probably lonely.

VOCABULARY

Work with a friend to practice using these words in complete sentences.

permit (PUHR MIHT) *v.*: allow.

frail (FRAYL) *adj.*: thin and weak.

barren (BAR UHN) *adj.*: empty.

SKILLS FOCUS

Literary Skills Understand characterization, understand dialogue.

Reading Skills Make inferences about characters.

Thank You, M'am

Thank You, M'am

By Langston Hughes

> **INTO THE STORY**
> Langston Hughes is best known for the stories and poems he wrote while living in Harlem, an African American neighborhood in New York City. When Hughes lived there in the 1920s, he saw his neighbors struggling against poverty, crime, and overcrowding. That setting influenced the action in this story.

She was a large woman with a large purse that had everything in it but a hammer and nails. It had a long strap, and she carried it slung across her shoulder. It was about eleven o'clock at night, dark, and she was walking alone, when a boy ran up behind her and tried to snatch her purse. The strap broke with the sudden single tug the boy gave it from behind. But the boy's weight and the weight of the purse combined caused him to lose his balance. **A** Instead of taking off full blast as he had hoped, the boy fell on his back on the sidewalk and his legs flew up. The large woman simply turned around and kicked him right square in his blue-jeaned sitter. Then she reached down, picked the boy up by his shirt front, and shook him until his teeth rattled.

After that the woman said, "Pick up my pocketbook, boy, and give it here."

She still held him tightly. But she bent down enough to permit him to stoop and pick up her purse. Then she said, "Now ain't you ashamed of yourself?" **B**

Firmly gripped by his shirt front, the boy said, "Yes'm."

The woman said, "What did you want to do it for?"

The boy said, "I didn't aim to."

She said, "You a lie!"

"Thank You, M'am" from *Short Stories* by Langston Hughes. Copyright © 1996 by Ramona Bass and Arnold Rampersad. All rights reserved. Reproduced by permission of **Hill and Wang, a division of Farrar, Straus and Giroux, LLC.**

A — HERE'S HOW

Vocabulary

I am not sure what *combined* means. When I read the sentence, I can tell that the boy's weight and the weight of the purse are the two things that *combined* to knock him over. I think *combined* means "put together." I checked my dictionary, and I was right.

B — HERE'S HOW

Literary Focus

The **dialogue** in lines 13–17 tells me about the characters. It sounds like the woman is not afraid of the boy who tried to rob her. In fact, she tells him he should be ashamed! She uses slang words, like *ain't*. I think the author wants me to understand that this woman does not speak formally, but she is very smart and strong.

A   YOUR TURN

Literary Focus
Once again, the boy answers "Yes'm," which is short for "Yes, m'am," which shows respect. What does the boy's answer tell you about his **character**?

_____
_____
_____
_____
_____
_____

© Underwood & Underwood/Corbis.

IN OTHER WORDS It is late at night, and a woman is walking home by herself. On her way, a young boy tries to steal her purse. The boy tries, but cannot grab the purse. Instead, as he reaches for the purse, the straps break and the boy trips and falls. While he is on the ground, the woman kicks him and starts to yell at him. The woman grabs the boy's shirt and holds onto him tightly so he cannot run away.

By that time two or three people passed, stopped, turned to look, and some stood watching.

"If I turn you loose, will you run?" asked the woman.

"Yes'm," said the boy. **A**

56   Thank You, M'am

"Then I won't turn you loose," said the woman. She did not release him.

"Lady, I'm sorry," whispered the boy.

"Um-hum! Your face is dirty. I got a great mind to wash your face for you. Ain't you got nobody home to tell you to wash your face?"

"No'm," said the boy.

"Then it will get washed this evening," said the large woman starting up the street, dragging the frightened boy behind her. **B**

He looked as if he were fourteen or fifteen, frail and willow-wild, in tennis shoes and blue jeans. **C**

The woman said, "You ought to be my son. I would teach you right from wrong. Least I can do right now is to wash your face. Are you hungry?"

"No'm," said the being-dragged boy. "I just want you to turn me loose."

"Was I bothering *you* when I turned that corner?" asked the woman.

"No'm."

"But you put yourself in contact with *me*," said the woman. "If you think that that contact is not going to last awhile, you got another thought coming. When I get through with you, sir, you are going to remember Mrs. Luella Bates Washington Jones."

Sweat popped out on the boy's face and he began to struggle. Mrs. Jones stopped, jerked him around in front of her, put a half nelson about his neck, and continued to drag him up the street. When she got to her door, she dragged the boy inside, down a hall, and into a large kitchenette-furnished room at the rear of the house. **D E** She switched on the light and left the door open. The boy could hear other roomers laughing and talking in the large house. Some of their doors were open, too, so he knew he and the woman were not alone. The woman still had him by the neck in the middle of her room.

IN OTHER WORDS The woman asks the boy if he will run away when she lets go of him. The boy says yes, so the

---

B QUICK CHECK

What does the woman want to do with the boy now that she has caught him trying to steal from her?

C HERE'S HOW

Vocabulary

I am not sure what *frail* means. But I think it is an important word that can help me understand what the boy looks like. I checked my dictionary, and *frail* means "thin and weak."

D YOUR TURN

Vocabulary

Mrs. Jones *dragged* the boy up the street and into her home. After reading lines 52–54, what do you think *dragged* means?

E HERE'S HOW

Vocabulary

I think the word *furnished* sounds like "furniture." I think a *furnished* room is one that already has furniture in it.

Thank You, M'am 57

A YOUR TURN

Language Coach
Some words have **multiple**, or more than one, **meanings** as verbs and nouns. As a verb, *sink* means to go down to the bottom. As a noun, *sink* means a basin with a drain where you wash. Underline the meaning above that makes the most sense in line 61.

B HERE'S HOW

Reading Focus
I am thinking about Roger's character and what kind of **inference** I can make about him from his actions in lines 62–64. He looks at the door, so I guess he thinks about running. But then he looks at Mrs. Jones and follows her instructions. My **inference** is that he has decided to trust her.

C YOUR TURN

Literary Focus
What does the **dialogue** in lines 77–79 tell you about Mrs. Jones?

_____
_____
_____

---

woman keeps holding onto him. She then tells the boy that his face is dirty and asks him if he has someone at home to take care of him. When the boy says no, the woman tells him she will take him to her house and wash his face. The boy says he just wants to be let go, and the woman says no. She says her name is Mrs. Luella Bates Washington Jones, and she is going to teach the boy a lesson. She takes him to her home.

She said, "What is your name?"

60 "Roger," answered the boy.

"Then, Roger, you go to that sink and wash your face," said the woman, whereupon she turned him loose—at last. **A** Roger looked at the door—looked at the woman—looked at the door—*and went to the sink.* **B**

"Let the water run until it gets warm," she said. "Here's a clean towel."

"You gonna take me to jail?" asked the boy, bending over the sink.

"Not with that face, I would not take you nowhere," said the 70 woman. "Here I am trying to get home to cook me a bite to eat, and you snatch my pocketbook! Maybe you ain't been to your supper either, late as it be. Have you?"

"There's nobody home at my house," said the boy.

"Then we'll eat," said the woman. "I believe you're hungry—or been hungry—to try to snatch my pocketbook."

"I want a pair of blue suede shoes," said the boy.

"Well, you didn't have to snatch *my* pocketbook to get some suede shoes," said Mrs. Luella Bates Washington Jones. "You could've asked me." **C**

80 "M'am?"

The water dripping from his face, the boy looked at her. There was a long pause. A very long pause. After he had dried his face and not knowing what else to do, dried it again, the boy turned around, wondering what next. The door was open. He could make a dash for it down the hall. He could run, run, run, *run!*

58 Thank You, M'am

Harlem Street Scene, 1942. Gouache on paper, 21 x 20 ¾". © 2007 The Jacob and Gwendolyn Lawrence Foundation, Seattle/Artists Rights Society (ARS), New York

The woman was sitting on the daybed[1]. After a while she said, "I were young once and I wanted things I could not get." There was another long pause. The boy's mouth opened. Then
90 he frowned, not knowing he frowned. **D**

The woman said, "Um-hum! You thought I was going to say but, didn't you? You thought I was going to say, *but I didn't snatch people's pocketbooks*. Well, I wasn't going to say that." Pause. Silence. "I have done things, too, which I would not tell you,

---

1. A **daybed** is a couch that can be turned into a bed.

D QUICK CHECK

Why does Roger frown as Mrs. Jones begins speaking?

_____
_____
_____

Thank You, M'am 59

A YOUR TURN

Reading Focus

What **inferences** can you make about Mrs. Jones from what you learn about her past in lines 91–96?

_____
_____
_____
_____

B YOUR TURN

Vocabulary

Look at the word *mistrusted*. Circle the prefix *mis–*. This prefix means "not." Now write a definition for *mistrusted*.

_____
_____
_____

C LITERARY ANALYSIS

Pause at line 117. Think about what you know about Roger from earlier in the story. Why does Mrs. Jones think that talking about Roger's home or family might embarrass him?

_____
_____
_____

---

son—neither tell God, if He didn't already know. Everybody's got something in common. **A** So you set down while I fix us something to eat. You might run that comb through your hair so you will look presentable."

IN OTHER WORDS The boy tells Mrs. Jones that his name is Roger. Mrs. Jones tells Roger to wash his face in the sink. Roger thinks about running away, but decides not to. Mrs. Jones asks Roger if he has eaten supper. Again, Roger says there is no one at home for him. Mrs. Jones says she thinks Roger is hungry, and that is why he tried to take her purse. Roger says he wanted the purse and the money in it to buy shoes. Mrs. Jones tells him that when she was his age, she did some things that she is not proud of to buy things that she could not afford.

100   In another corner of the room behind a screen was a gas plate and an icebox. Mrs. Jones got up and went behind the screen. The woman did not watch the boy to see if he was going to run now, nor did she watch her purse, which she left behind her on the daybed. But the boy took care to sit on the far side of the room, away from the purse, where he thought she could easily see him out of the corner of her eye if she wanted to. He did not trust the woman *not* to trust him. And he did not want to be mistrusted now. **B**

"Do you need somebody to go the store," asked the boy, "maybe to get some milk or something?"

110   "Don't believe I do," said the woman, "unless you just want sweet milk yourself. I was going to make cocoa out of this canned milk I got here."

"That will be fine," said the boy.

She heated some lima beans and ham she had in the icebox, made the cocoa, and set the table. The woman did not ask the boy anything about where he lived, or his folks, or anything else that would embarrass him. **C** Instead, as they ate, she told him about her job in a hotel beauty shop that stayed open late, what the work was like, and how all kinds of women came in and out, blondes, redheads, and Spanish. Then she cut him a half of her ten-cent cake.

"Eat some more, son," she said.

When they were finished eating, she got up and said,

"Now here, take this ten dollars and buy yourself some blue suede shoes. And next time, do not make the mistake of latching onto *my* pocketbook *nor nobody else's*—because shoes got by devilish ways will burn your feet. **D** I got to get my rest now. But from here on in, son, I hope you will behave yourself."

She led him down the hall to the front door and opened it. "Good night! Behave yourself, boy!" she said, looking out into the street as he went down the steps.

The boy wanted to say something other than "Thank you, m'am" to Mrs. Luella Bates Washington Jones, but although his lips moved, he couldn't even say that as he turned at the foot of the barren stoop and looked up at the large woman in the door. Then she shut the door. **E**

IN OTHER WORDS Mrs. Jones starts cooking supper, and she turns her back to Roger. She leaves her purse out on the couch, and Roger can easily take the money inside it. Roger wants Mrs. Jones to trust him, so he sits down far away from the purse. Mrs. Jones puts supper on the table, and they eat together. Mrs. Jones makes sure that she does not bring up Roger's family, because she does not want to embarrass him. When they are done eating, Mrs. Jones gives Roger ten dollars so he can buy those shoes that he wants. She leads him to the door and tells him to be good and not to steal anymore. Before Mrs. Jones shuts the door, all Roger can say is "Thank you, m'am," even though he wants to say much more.

D HERE'S HOW

Vocabulary

Latching is an unfamiliar word to me. Here, the phrase, "*latching* onto my pocketbook," makes me think the word probably means "holding" or "grabbing."

E YOUR TURN

Literary Focus

Sometimes thinking about what the characters do not say is an important part of understanding **dialogue**. What do you think Roger wished he could say to Mrs. Jones other than "Thank you, m'am"?

_____

_____

_____

_____

Thank You, M'am

Skills Practice

Thank You, M'am

USE AN INFERENCES TABLE

When you **make inferences**, you form your own ideas about characters in a story. What inferences can you make about Roger based on the three details from the story? Fill in the right side of the table with your inferences about Roger's character.

Details about Roger	Inferences about Roger
1. Tries to snatch purse.	
2. Has dirty face.	
3. Listens to Mrs. Jones.	

Applying Your Skills

Thank You, M'am

LITERARY FOCUS: CHARACTER AND DIALOGUE

DIRECTIONS: For each line of **dialogue** below from "Thank You, M'am," write the name of the character who says it and what you learned about each character from the dialogue.

1. "If you think that that contact is not going to last awhile, you got another thought coming." _____
_____

2. "I want a pair of blue suede shoes." _____
_____

3. "Everybody's got something in common." _____
_____

READING FOCUS: MAKING INFERENCES

DIRECTIONS: Based on the details in the story, circle the sentence that gives the best **inference** about each character.

1. Roger
    a. is a scared and lonely boy who has a hard life.
    b. is a rich kid who steals purses for fun.
    c. is going to try to rob Mrs. Jones again tomorrow.

2. Mrs. Jones
    a. is scared of all the people she meets on the street.
    b. hates Roger and plans to call the police in the morning.
    c. is a hardworking woman who wants to help young people in trouble.

Word Box

permit
frail
barren

VOCABULARY REVIEW

1. Write a sentence about Roger using the word **frail**. _____
_____

2. Fill in the blank with the correct word from the Word Box:

   Only when you raise your hand will your teacher _____ you to speak.

Thank You, M'am   63

Preparing to Read

American History
Based on the story by Judith Ortiz Cofer

LITERARY FOCUS: ROUND AND FLAT CHARACTERS

The main characters in a story are called **round characters.** They are called round because the reader sees many sides of their personalities as the story goes along. On the other hand, characters that the reader does not learn as much about are called **flat characters.** Flat characters are not necessarily bad; they are less detailed, **minor** characters. For example, "American History" is narrated by a round character, Elena. We learn a lot about Elena throughout the story. There are also numerous flat characters, like Gail, in the story. We learn Gail's name, but not much else about her personality.

READING FOCUS: MAKING INFERENCES ABOUT CHARACTERS

You can often learn a lot about characters just from what the narrator tells you. Sometimes, though, you need to figure out a character's personality by **making inferences,** or educated guesses. You can do this by looking at a character's words, thoughts, and actions. For example, a writer might tell you that his main character likes to play baseball, football, and basketball. From that, you can make the **inference** that this character is an athletic person. As you read, keep track of what the characters do, and decide what that tells you about their personalities.

VOCABULARY

Look for these words and their context as you read the selection.

humiliating (HYOO MILH EE AYT HING) *v.:* embarrassing; causing a loss of pride.

disciplinarian (DIHS UH PLUH NEHR EE UHN) *n.:* someone who enforces the rules.

INTO THE STORY

President John F. Kennedy was killed on November 22, 1963, in Dallas, Texas. Just about any American living then can tell you where he or she was that day. The date is a part of our national memory, much like September 11, 2001, when the World Trade Center buildings were destroyed. These tragic days have left an impact on our memories and have affected how we think of ourselves as a nation.

SKILLS FOCUS

Literary Skills Understand flat and round characters.

Reading Skills Make inferences about characters.

64 American History

American History

Based on the Story by Judith Ortiz Cofer

It was a cold gray day in Paterson, and I was miserable. "Hey, Skinny Bones, pump it, girl," Gail yelled. "Didn't you eat your rice and beans and pork chops for breakfast today?"

I could not manage to coordinate the jump rope with Gail. The chill was entering my bones, making me cry, humiliating me. **A B** I hated the city, especially in winter. I hated Public School 13, and I hated my skinny, flat-chested body. **C**

Seeing Eugene was the one source of beauty and light that school year. In August, Eugene and his family had moved into the only house on the block that had a yard. I could see his kitchen and backyard from my window in El Building. Eugene was tall and blond, and he wore glasses. I liked him right away because he sat at the kitchen table and read books for hours.

Once school started, I looked for him in all my classes, but PS 13 was a huge crowded place. It took me days to discover that Eugene was in honors classes. These classes were not open to me because English was not my first language, though I was a straight-A student. After much skillful planning I managed to "run into him" in the hallway. One day I blurted out, "You're Eugene. Right?" I was ready for rejection, but he smiled and nodded. In the following weeks, we walked home together.

My father had a good job at the bluejeans factory in Passaic and soon, he kept assuring us, we would be moving to a house there. Every Sunday we drove out to the suburbs where children made snowmen from pure white snow, not like the gray slush of Paterson, which seemed to fall from the sky in that color. I listened to my parents' dreams, spoken in Spanish, like their stories about life in Puerto Rico before I was born. My dreams were about going to college and becoming a teacher.

Slight adaptation of "American History" from *The Latin Deli: Prose and Poetry* by Judith Ortiz Cofer. Copyright © 1993 by Judith Ortiz Cofer. Retold by Holt, Rinehart and Winston. Reproduced by permission of **The University of Georgia Press**.

A HERE'S HOW

Vocabulary

I am not sure what the word *humiliating* means. Because the narrator cannot jump rope and is crying, I am guessing that it means "embarrassing" or "causing a loss of pride."

B YOUR TURN

Language Coach

The word *humiliate* comes from the Latin verb *humiliare*, meaning "to humble." How does this **word origin** relate to your understanding of the word *humiliating*?

_____
_____
_____

C HERE'S HOW

Literary Focus

In the first seven lines the narrator does not tell me much about Gail's personality. So far, I think that Gail is a **flat character**. On the other hand, I learn more about the narrator. I think that she is a **round character**.

American History 65

A YOUR TURN

Vocabulary

Discipline is a way to enforce rules. What do you think the word *disciplinarian* means? Write your definition, below. Use a dictionary to check your answer.

_____

_____

_____

B HERE'S HOW

Reading Focus

By **making inferences,** I can find out about a character's personality. Based on what he says in lines 39–44, I can tell that Mr. DePalma is a tough teacher. I can make the inference that he most likely yells at his students. But, because he is so upset here, I think there may be more to Mr. DePalma than he lets on.

---

30   Eugene's family had come from Georgia. The kids at school called him "the Hick" and made fun of the way he talked. "Skinny Bones and the Hick" was what they called us at school when we were seen together.

On the day that President Kennedy was shot, Mr. DePalma asked us to line up in front of him. A short, muscular man with slicked-down black hair, Mr. DePalma was the science teacher, PE coach, and disciplinarian at PS 13. **A** We were shocked to see he was crying. Someone giggled behind me.

"Listen," Mr. DePalma said. His voice broke, and he covered
40   his face with his hands. "Listen," he repeated, "something awful has happened." There was a lot of laughter. Mr. DePalma shrieked, "The president is dead, you idiots. I should have known that wouldn't mean anything to a bunch of losers like you kids. Go home." **B** No one moved for a minute; then we all scrambled madly to get out of there.

As I headed home there was an eerie feeling on the streets. There were no horns blasting that day. There was a profound[1] silence in El Building, with no music spilling out from open doors. I found my mother sitting in front of our television set.
50   She looked at me with a tear-streaked face. I went into my room.

Though I wanted to feel the right thing about President Kennedy's death, I could not fight the elation[2] that stirred in my chest. Today I was to visit Eugene in his house. He had asked me to study for an American history test with him.

I got my books together. When I went in to tell my mother that I was going to a friend's house to study, I did not expect her reaction.

"You are going out *today*? The president has been killed. We must show respect. He was a great man. Come to church with me
60   tonight." My first impulse was to comfort her because she seemed so bewildered, but I had to meet Eugene.

"I have a test to study for, Mama. I will be home by eight," I said.

---

1. **profound** (PROH FOWND): deeply felt.
2. **elation** (EE LAY SHUHN): a feeling of great happiness.

"You are forgetting who you are," Mama said. "I have seen you staring down at that boy's house. You are heading for humiliation and pain." She spoke in Spanish in a resigned tone that surprised me, as if she did not intend to stop me from "heading for humiliation and pain." **C**

70 I walked around the chain-link fence that separated El Building from Eugene's house. His door was painted deep green, *verde*—the color of hope. Moments after my knock, the door

> **C** YOUR TURN
>
> **Reading Focus**
> Read lines 58–68. What **inferences** can you make about the narrator's mother?
> _____
> _____
> _____

American History **67**

A LITERARY ANALYSIS

The narrator says that Eugene's house is separated from hers by a fence. She also describes Eugene's door as being "the color of hope." How does this connect to the narrator's dreams about leaving El Building?

_____
_____
_____
_____
_____

opened a crack and the red, swollen face of a woman appeared. She had a halo of red hair floating over a delicate white face. **A**

"What do you want?" Her voice sounded sweet, as if drenched with honey, but her tone was not friendly.

"I'm Eugene's friend. He asked me over. To study." I said.

"You live there?" She pointed up to El Building, which looked like a gray prison.

"Yes. I do."

80   She looked intently at me for a couple of heartbeats, then said, as if to herself, "I don't know how you people do it." Then directly to me, she said, "Listen. Honey. Eugene doesn't want to study with you. He is a smart boy. Doesn't need help. You understand me. I am truly sorry if he said you could come over. He cannot study with you. It's nothing personal. You understand? We won't be in this place much longer, no need for him to get close to people. It'll just make it harder for him later. Run back home now."

© Time Life Pictures *and* © 2007 Corbis/Jupiter Images

68   American History

I stood there in shock.

"Didn't you hear what I said?" She seemed very angry, and I finally snapped out of my trance. As I turned away from the green door I heard her close it gently.

That night I lay in my bed trying to feel the right thing for our dead president, but my tears were strictly for me. Sometime during the night, I went to my window and pressed my face to the glass. Looking up at the streetlight, I could see the white snow falling like a lace veil over its face. I did not look down to see it turning gray as it touched the ground below. **B**

B YOUR TURN

Literary Focus
What have you learned about the narrator's personality in this story? Underline portions of the final paragraph that support, or back or up, the argument that she is a **round character**.

American History **69**

Skills Practice

American History

USE A COMPARISON TABLE

Stories can have both **round** and **flat characters**. You can compare characters in a story by using a comparison table.

DIRECTIONS: Make a list of every character in the story. Determine whether each character is a round character or a flat character. Write each character's name in the correct column in the chart below.

American History	
Round Character	Flat Characters

Applying Your Skills

American History

LITERARY FOCUS: ROUND AND FLAT CHARACTERS

DIRECTIONS: Review the story and determine which characters are **round** and which are **flat**. Write whether each character below is round or flat. Then explain why you labeled each as such.

The narrator's mother _____

Mr. DePalma _____

The narrator _____

Eugene _____

READING FOCUS: MAKING INFERENCES ABOUT CHARACTERS

DIRECTIONS: Use the **inferences** you made while reading the story to complete the activity below. Circle the letter that best describes each character.

1. Mr. DePalma is
   A. kind and understanding.
   B. the school's disciplinarian.
2. The narrator is
   A. mature and curious.
   B. athletic and humiliating.
3. Eugene is
   A. intelligent and shy.
   B. mean and pushy.

VOCABULARY REVIEW

DIRECTIONS: Write 1–2 sentences describing either a *disciplinarian* you know or a time when someone or something was *humiliating* you.

_____
_____
_____

Preparing to Read

An Interview with Dave Eggers
from Writing Magazine

INFORMATIONAL TEXT FOCUS: SYNTHESIZING SOURCES: MAIN IDEA, AUDIENCE, AND PURPOSE

A **primary source** is a document in which events are described by a person who experienced them. For example, a diary is a primary source because the person writing the diary had a part in all of the experiences described. An interview, like the one you are about to read, is also a primary source, because the person being interviewed can give you personal knowledge of the subjects being discussed.

To get the most out of a primary source, ask yourself these questions:

Audience: Who is this written for?

Purpose: Why does the author want me to know this?

Main Idea: What point is the author trying to tell me?

VOCABULARY

Make flashcards for each of the words below with a word on one side and its definition on the other.

unconventional (UHN KUHN VEHN SHUH NUHL) *adj.:* not conforming to accepted practices.

memoir (MEHM WAHR) *n.:* a piece of writing in which the author describes his or her personal experiences or memories.

enabled (EHN AY BUHLD) *v.:* made possible or allowed.

aspect (A SPEHKT) *n.:* a way in which something can be looked at.

aspiring (UH SPY RIHNG) *adj.:* hoping to accomplish a goal.

INTO THE INTERVIEW

Dave Eggers is an award-winning author who tries to share his love of writing and reading with others, especially young people. He has created a number of tutoring centers around the country, including one in San Francisco called 826 Valencia. These centers are meant to help students become more comfortable with writing and, if they want, to learn to become professional writers as adults. In this interview from *Writing* magazine, Eggers talks about his love of writing, what he thinks about fame, and why 826 Valencia is important to him. After the introduction to the article, the interview follows a question-and-answer format. A person from *Writing* (**Writing:**) magazine asks the questions and Dave Eggers (**Eggers:**) answers them.

SKILLS FOCUS

Informational Text Skills Understand main idea, audience, and purpose; synthesize sources.

An Interview with Dave Eggers

from Writing Magazine

A "Staggering Genius" Talks About Writing, Fame, and... Trout.

When Dave Eggers was 21, he lost his parents to cancer. Each died within five weeks of the other, leaving Eggers to raise his 7-year-old brother, Christopher, or "Toph," on his own. A few years later, Eggers published his story in a highly unconventional, funny and sad memoir called *A Heartbreaking Work of Staggering Genius* (2000). **A** The title hints at the self-mocking[1] tone of the book, but it's not kidding—at least not totally. Critics called Eggers "refreshingly honest," "an original new voice," and oh, yes, "a staggering genius."

IN OTHER WORDS Dave Eggers is a writer who became very successful at a young age. He was only 21 when both of his parents died of cancer. Eggers had to take care of his younger brother. Then a few years later he published a book about his own life. He gave it a title that was meant to make fun of himself. People who read the book had very good things to say about it.

The success of his first book, which he refers to as *AHWOSG*, enabled Eggers to pursue a number of writing projects, including the creation of the superhip[2] online literary journal *McSweeney's* (www.mcsweeneys.net). **B** He has written several novels; edits an annual anthology of nonfiction, *The Best American*

---

1. **Self-mocking** (SEHLF MAHK ihng) means making fun of yourself. In a self-mocking book, the author does not take himself or herself too seriously.
2. The adjective **superhip** (SOO pur hihp) is slang for very involved in the newest styles or trends.

A HERE'S HOW

Vocabulary
Memoir looks like the word *memories*. I think that a *memoir* is someone's story of his or her own experiences or memories.

B YOUR TURN

Vocabulary
What word is at the center of *enabled* in line 13?

After studying this word, what do you think *enabled* means in this sentence?

_____

_____

_____

From "A 'Staggering Genius' Talks about Writing, Fame, and ...Trout. An Interview With Dave Eggers" from *Writing Magazine*, vol. 27, no. 4, January 2005. Copyright © 2005 by Weekly Reader Corporation. All rights reserved. Reproduced by permission of **Weekly Reader**.

> **A** **HERE'S HOW**
>
> **Reading Focus**
>
> I think the **main idea** of this paragraph is: Eggers is involved in a number of writing projects.

> **B** **QUICK CHECK**
>
> What subjects did Eggers like most in school?
>
> _____
> _____

> **C** **HERE'S HOW**
>
> **Reading Focus**
>
> As I read Eggers's answer here, I want to look for the **purpose**—why the author wants me to know this information. Eggers is trying to say that you do not have to know what you want to do as an adult right away. It took Eggers until his last year of college to realize he wanted to be a writer.

Nonrequired Reading; and recently published a book of short stories, *How We Are Hungry.* He also founded 826 Valencia, a writing center for kids in San Francisco. Recently, *Writing* caught up with Eggers and tossed him a few questions. **A**

IN OTHER WORDS Eggers has continued to build his career as a writer. He runs an Internet magazine called McSweeney's. He has written several more books and edits a collection of informational pieces that comes out once every year. He also started a center in San Francisco to help kids with their writing skills. It is called 826 Valencia. The interviewer from Writing magazine asked him about all of these things, and their conversation is below.

Writing: First, let's talk a little about you. What kind of student were you in school?

Dave Eggers: I guess I always liked school. I wasn't all about school—I didn't go running to the bus stop every day—but I did well in school, and I had a string of great teachers and enjoyed my time there. English and art were my favorite subjects, and I would take after-school art classes to learn more. I wanted to be a cartoonist. **B**

Writing: When and why did you start writing?

Eggers: At various points—fifth grade, seventh grade, eighth grade—we were asked to create books, where we would write and illustrate them and spend a lot of time making them look official and spiffy,[3] and I remember those books sparking an interest in writing. I still wanted, first and foremost,[4] to be a comic-book artist, but I was doing well in English classes and started thinking I could combine my interest in art and in writing. It wasn't until college, though—not until my junior year—that I really thought about writing for a living. I studied painting for three years in college and switched to the journalism program my last year. **C**

---

3. The description **spiffy** (SPIH FEE) means attractive or smart-looking.
4. **Foremost** (FAWR MOHST) means most important.

IN OTHER WORDS Eggers always enjoyed school, especially English and art. He remembers school projects in which he created books. He thinks these projects helped him to later become a writer. He didn't really think seriously about becoming a writer, though, until his last year in college.

Writing: So many people today seem to think fame is the ultimate goal of life. What's the deal with fame anyway?
Eggers: The aspect of being well known that's important is that sometimes you can use your fame to help people or to change those things that need changing. **D** Because people read my books, I can sometimes raise money for good causes easier than I could when I was younger and not known. I can write about an issue—like the need to pay teachers better—and people will listen to me in a way they wouldn't have before I had some success. I'm really happy that I can help that way. That's the main upshot[5] of any measure of fame.

Writing: A little about the writing process: How do you write? Do you, like some writers, sit down and write for a set amount of time every day? Or do you write only when inspiration hits?
Eggers: I write most days. Sometimes I write for about 10 hours a day, sometimes only a few hours. Sometimes I sit at the computer and stall forever; sometimes the words shoot onto the page at lightning speed. But I do write pretty much every day, even weekends. And I usually write late at night, from about 10 P.M. to 3 A.M. **E**

IN OTHER WORDS Eggers feels that the important part about being famous is the chance it gives him to help other people. When he writes about things in the world that need to be changed, others listen. Eggers tries to write every day, usually late at night, no matter how easy or difficult it is to write that day.

---

5. The word **upshot** (UHP SHAHT) is used to mean what happens, or the outcome or result.

D HERE'S HOW

Vocabulary
When I look in my dictionary for the word *aspect*, there are many meanings listed. I think the meaning that makes the most sense here is "a way in which something can be looked at." I think Eggers means that he looks at being well-known as a way to help other people.

E YOUR TURN

Reading Focus
Here, do you think Eggers is talking about how most people write, how his teacher writes, or how he writes? How does Eggers's answer show that this is a **primary source**?

_____
_____
_____
_____
_____

An Interview with Dave Eggers 75

A HERE'S HOW

Reading Focus

I should be thinking about the **audience** for this interview as I read. Since this was published in a magazine called *Writing*, I think the audience is supposed to be people who are already interested in writing.

B HERE'S HOW

Vocabulary

Since the word *aspiring* in line 74 is used before "writers," I think it is an adjective describing the writers. These are students who want to be writers someday. So I think *aspiring* must mean "wanting to reach a goal."

C LITERARY ANALYSIS

How can meeting professional writers help students who hope to be writers someday?

_____
_____
_____
_____
_____

Writing: Tell us about your work with 826 Valencia.

Eggers: 826 Valencia is a drop-in tutoring, writing, and publishing center in San Francisco. We help local students with writing-related homework, and we teach classes in tons of different fields: journalism, radio, film, poetry, and bookmaking—you name it. **A** We also publish student work in various collections that are then sold in bookstores all over the city and on Amazon.[6]

Writing: Why did you want to help young people learn to write?

Eggers: Over the years, I'd worked with the YMCA and other groups, teaching middle school and high school students about cartooning, writing, and publishing, and we always had a great time. I learned a lot of what I know about writing and design while I was in high school, so I think if we at 826 Valencia can help aspiring writers when they're very young and if we can introduce them to actual writers who have been successful, then those students can get a clear idea of a writer's life, and how to get from *A* to *Z*. **B C** I meet hundreds of students every year who could be successful writers—as novelists, journalists, poets. Our goal at 826 Valencia is to make sure these aspirants[7] know that they can actually do it and to give them as many tools as possible. On the other hand, we also help tons of students who need assistance with the basics—lots of students new to this country who are just learning English. So it varies, from the basics to the most advanced. That's what makes 826 Valencia a good place to be.

IN OTHER WORDS Students come to 826 Valencia for help with writing. They can take classes in how to write for newspapers, poetry, how to make books, and other areas. The center publishes and sells books of student writing. Students who want to be writers someday meet successful writers and learn what that life is like. Other students may not want to

---

6. **Amazon** (A MUH ZAHN) is the name of an Internet bookstore.
7. The word **aspirants** is related to *aspiring*. Aspirants are people who hope to do something successfully.

be writers but use the center to get help with homework, to learn English, or for other reasons.

Writing: A lot of people complain that kids today don't read. Some blame TV, computers, fast food. (Just kidding, but who knows?) What are your thoughts about it?

Eggers: I watched a whole lot of TV when I was growing up. I lived in a house where the TV was on most of the day and night, but I still found a lot of time to read, and I spent most of my time outside, running around in the woods. I think there's a balance—you have to get out there and see the world, learn from books, and also know what's happening via the TV, the Web, and other media. **D** Any young person who's interested in writing should be reading (outside of school) about 10 books a year. That's only one a month—you could definitely read more—but 10 a year is a guideline. **E** I still keep track of my reading, making sure I'm reading a book every week or two. Again, it's part of the balance, because I still love TV.

Writing: What books would you recommend to young people?

Eggers: I recommend any book that grabs you, any book you can't put down. There are millions of books in the world, so I don't feel like we should spend too much time slogging[8] our way through books we feel no connection to. I don't like Jane Austen[9] very much. After reading a few of her books and feeling no particular connection to that world, I've decided I probably won't read any more. If you don't consider yourself a big reader, start by reading books about things you're interested in, like fishing. **F** Maybe you're like LeBron James and you love trout, but you don't like reading so much, because you think books are always about people in the 19th century eating cucumber sandwiches. **G** So go find some books about trout and trout fishing, trout preparation, trout eating. The point is to begin to love books. I guarantee there are at least 100 books out there for

---

8. If you are **slogging** (SLAHG IHNG) through something, you are working very hard and slowly to get through it.
9. **Jane Austen** (1775–1817) was an English author who wrote novels about romance and society.

D YOUR TURN

Reading Focus
What do you think is the **purpose** of Eggers' comments in lines 89–95?

_____
_____
_____
_____
_____

E QUICK CHECK

How many books a year does Eggers suggest a young person interested in writing should read?

_____
_____

F YOUR TURN

Reading Focus
When Eggers says "you", who do you think his **audience** is?

_____
_____
_____

G HERE'S HOW

Language Coach
I do not know very much about the word *trout*. I looked it up in my dictionary. I learned it comes from the Greek word *troktes*, which means "gnawer," a fish with sharp teeth. By finding **word origins** like this, I can get a better idea of a word's meaning.

An Interview with Dave Eggers

A HERE'S HOW

Reading Focus

I can use the headings in an article to help me find out more about the **audience**. Because this heading is "Dave's Advice for Young Writers," I know that the audience for this section is young people, or students like me.

B YOUR TURN

Reading Focus

What is the **main idea** of the section called "Dave's Advice for Young Writers"?

_____
_____
_____
_____
_____

---

everyone—100 books that will knock you over and change your life—so get started looking for those. (That doesn't mean you shouldn't finish the books you're reading in class. Your teachers know why they're asking you to read a certain book. You have to trust them.) Sometimes a book will bore the life out of you for 50 pages, then get really interesting. You have to have patience, but if you're reading a book for fun and you're not having fun, maybe it's time to try something else.

IN OTHER WORDS Eggers thinks it is important to balance TV, reading, and being outside. He recommends that any student who is interested in writing should read at least 10 books a year outside of school. It's important to find books that are fun to read. He suggests looking for books about something you are already interested in, such as a hobby.

Dave's Advice for Young Writers A

Wear a helmet. Write every day. Keep a journal—buy one small enough to keep in your pocket. Listen to people, to the way they talk. Get lost in the woods or in new neighborhoods, explore. Swim a lot. Come up with new and better names for llamas. Listen to a lot of music, loud. Read as much as you can. Watch *Time Bandits* and *Napoleon Dynamite*. Don't let any one person discourage you. Don't count on your friends' liking your work. Maybe you like to write about zombies, and none of your friends are zombies—this doesn't mean there aren't thousands of people all over the world who are just dying (excuse the pun) to read your work about zombies. And when you write about zombies or anything else, try to describe them in ways never before done by humankind. A writer's job is to make the world new, to charge it full of new life, so you have to start over, from scratch; you can't rehash stories that have been told a hundred times. You have to give readers something brand-spanking new. Especially if it involves trout. B

---

78   An Interview with Dave Eggers

IN OTHER WORDS Dave's advice for young writers is to do a little of everything—read, write, listen, explore outside, watch movies. Write about what you like to write about no matter what anyone else says. Look for something new and different to say, especially about things that interest you.

© AP Images/Susan Ragan

Skills Practice

An Interview with Dave Eggers

USE A CONCEPT MAP

In this interview, the **main idea** that Dave Eggers is trying to relate is that students should read, write about, and do what most interests them. You can record details about an interview by using a concept map. Concept maps have an idea in the center circle. The outer circles have details to support that idea. In the outer circles below, record details from the interview that support Eggers's main idea.

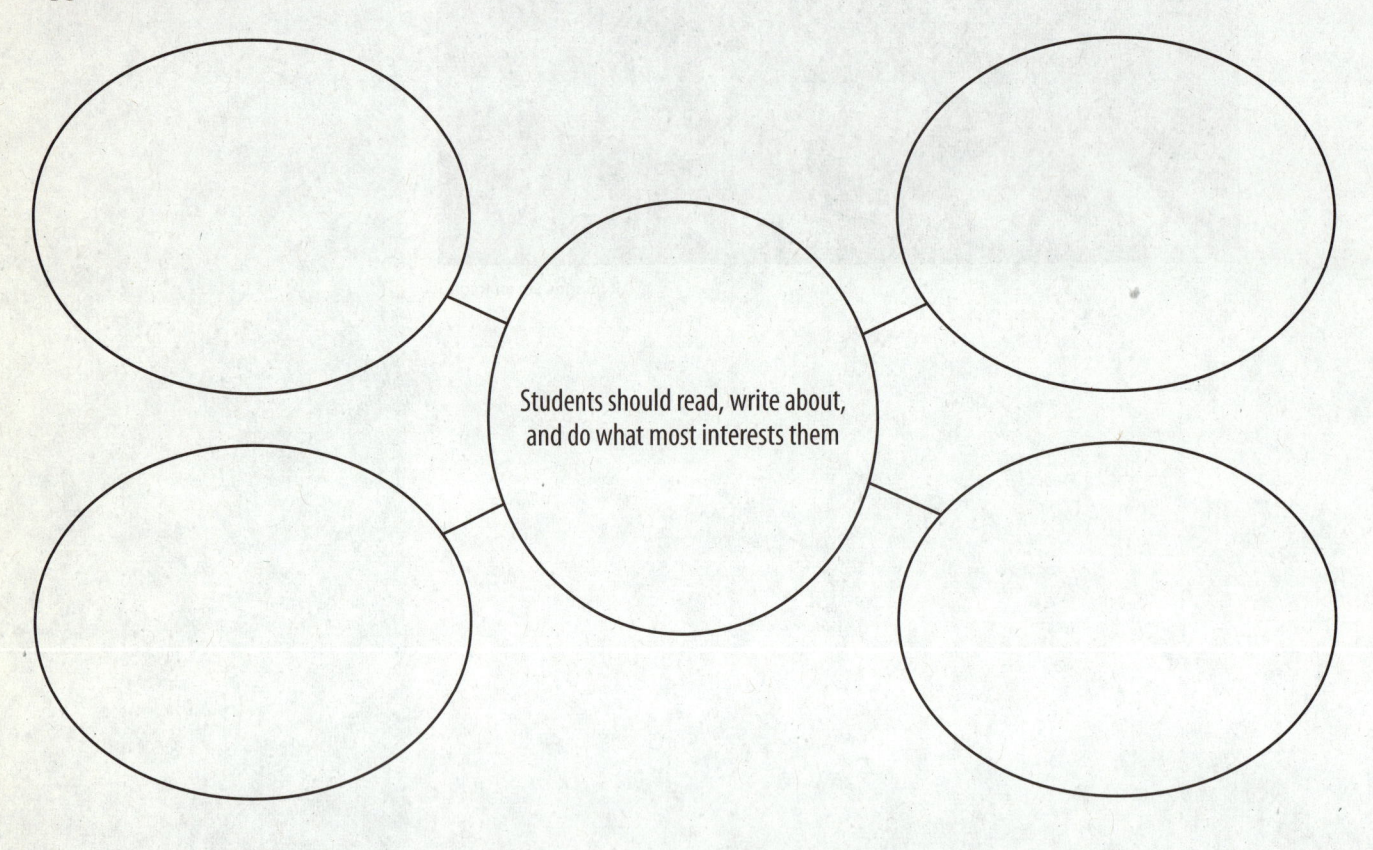

(Center circle: Students should read, write about, and do what most interests them)

80 An Interview with Dave Eggers

Applying Your Skills

An Interview with Dave Eggers

INFORMATIONAL TEXT FOCUS: SYNTHESIZING SOURCES: MAIN IDEA, AUDIENCE, AND PURPOSE

DIRECTIONS: Use what you have learned about analyzing **primary sources** to choose the best answer for each question below.

1. Who is the **audience** for the interview with Dave Eggers?
    A. only people who teach writing
    B. aspiring writers and people interested in reading
    C. students in the third and fourth grades

2. What is the **purpose** of the part of the interview about fame?
    A. Eggers wants everyone to know how great his memoir is.
    B. Eggers believes people should use their fame to help other people.
    C. Eggers wants to make the students at 826 Valencia famous.

3. Which of the following sentences supports the statement, "The interview with Dave Eggers is an example of a **primary source**"?
    A. The interviewer explains Eggers's life without ever letting Eggers talk.
    B. Eggers describes events he had never seen or experienced.
    C. Eggers describes his life and work, in his own words and from his own point of view.

VOCABULARY REVIEW

DIRECTIONS: Complete the following sentences with words from the Word Box. Not every word will be used.

Word Box

- unconventional
- memoir
- enabled
- aspect
- aspiring

1. Dave Eggers's fame has _____ him to help others.
2. Eggers's book, *A Heartbreaking Work of Staggering Genius*, is an example of a _____.

An Interview with Dave Eggers 81

Skills Review

Collection 2

VOCABULARY REVIEW

DIRECTIONS: Choose the word from the Word Box that best completes each sentence. Some of the words will not be used.

Word Box

memoir
aspect
aspiring
complex
furnished
incident
mistrusted
observation
significant
latching
enabled

1. My knowledge about engines _____ me to help fix my uncle's car.

2. I wanted to believe her, but because she had lied to me before, I _____ her.

3. I watched the dogs in the park for an hour, and my _____ was that they all got along very well.

4. Marie hoped to rent a _____ apartment because she did not want to have to buy a new sofa when she moved.

5. Susan decided to write a _____ because she wanted to write about her own life and experiences growing up.

6. The first part of the article was unimportant. However, the second part was _____ to me because it explained what the mayor thought about giving more money to the library.

7. Not all of the students who take drama are _____ Hollywood actors.

8. The little girl was so nervous about her first day at kindergarten that I saw her _____ onto her mother's hand.

Skills Review

Collection 2

LANGUAGE COACH: MULTIPLE MEANINGS

Some words can be both nouns and verbs. These words may also have **multiple meanings**. The part of speech being used changes the meaning.

DIRECTIONS: For each sentence below, decide whether the underlined word is used as a noun or as a verb. Then, circle the correct meaning of the word.

1. Mark had to shift the order of batters in the baseball game because John could not play on Saturday.

    A. *noun:* time to work   **B.** *verb:* change or move

2. Next year, my little sister will begin the fifth grade.

    A. *noun:* a class arranged according to year   **B.** *verb:* to rate or score

3. I hope my parents will permit me to go to the party on Saturday.

    A. *noun:* license   **B.** *verb:* allow

4. Please make sure that you take out the trash before you leave.

    A. *noun:* garbage   **B.** *verb:* destroy

5. Thelma looked at the schedule board in the airport to see if Jeremy's plane would land on time.

    A. *noun:* ground or property   **B.** *verb:* to set down or come to rest

WRITING ACTIVITY

You have been learning about **dialogue** and what it reveals about characters. Think about Mrs. Jones and Roger in "Thank You, M'am." Imagine that they meet again one month later. Write a short conversation between them. Your dialogue should reflect what you know about the characters.

_____
_____
_____
_____
_____
_____

Collection

3

Narrator and Voice

© Noma/Images.com

Literary and Academic Vocabulary for Collection 3

LITERARY VOCABULARY

narrator (NAR AY TUHR) *n.:* the person who tells the story.
The story's narrator is a young boy with four brothers.

first-person narrator (FUHRST PUHR SUHN NAR AY TUHR) *n.:* a character in the story who tells the story from his or her point of view.
In my favorite book, the first-person narrator begins by saying "I was only 15 when it happened."

omniscient narrator (AHM NIHSH UHNT NAR AY TUHR) *adj.:* all-knowing character; able to tell readers what each character thinks and feels.
An omniscient narrator tells the readers what the characters think and feel in The Interlopers.

ACADEMIC VOCABULARY

distinct (DIHS TIHNGKT) *adj.:* different; unique.
The narrator's description of Clara reveals a distinct personality.

impression (IHM PREHSH UHN) *n.:* strong effect; feeling.
The story's events leave readers with the impression that life in the main character's house is unusual.

insight (IHN SEYT) *n.:* clear understanding.
A history book can provide insight to a different time period.

portray (PAWR TRAY) *v.:* describe; show.
A younger narrator might portray the events in the story differently than an older narrator.

Preparing to Read

The Interlopers
Based on the story by Saki

LITERARY FOCUS: OMNISCIENT NARRATOR

An **omniscient narrator** knows everything about every character in the story. He or she knows what everyone in the story is thinking and doing. An omniscient narrator tells readers everything they know about people, places, and other things in the story. As you will see, "The Interlopers" has an omniscient narrator. Be careful, though, because an omniscient narrator can also hide information from the reader to create a surprise ending to the story.

READING FOCUS: DRAWING CONCLUSIONS

Writers do not always directly tell readers everything about characters in stories. Instead, writers plant clues to help readers **draw conclusions** about the characters and their actions. For example, in "The Interlopers," you can draw conclusions about human nature based on how the characters act. While you read, look for places where you can draw conclusions about the characters and their actions in different situations.

VOCABULARY

Look for these words and their context as you read the selection.

interlopers (IHN TUHR LOH PURS) *n.*: people who enter a place when they are not wanted.

game (GAYM) *n.*: wild animals that are hunted for food, sport, or profit.

snarled (SNAR ALD) *v.*: spoke angrily; growled.

condolences (KUHN DOHL UHNS UHZ) *n.*: messages of sorrow.

INTO THE STORY

This story is set in a thick forest on the slopes of the Carpathian (KAHR PAY THEE UHN) Mountains. These mountains stretch through Poland, Slovakia, Romania, and Ukraine. The story is set around the end of the 1800s. At this time, wealthy, noble families owned much of the land—almost entire countries. Poachers would sometimes try to enter these lands. A poacher is someone who goes onto private property to hunt or fish illegally. Someone who was caught poaching in Europe at this time could be put to death.

SKILLS FOCUS

Literary Skills Understand omniscient narrator.

Reading Skills Draw conclusions.

THE INTERLOPERS

Based on the story by Saki

A man stood watching and listening one winter night in a dark forest on the eastern side of the Carpathian Mountains. He acted as if he were hunting game. But this man was hunting a different sort of animal. Ulrich von Gradwitz[1] was searching for a human enemy.

His family's large forestland was full of game; however, few animals could be found where Ulrich waited. **A** Still, Ulrich guarded this land jealously. In a famous lawsuit during the days of his grandfather, his family had won back the land from a neighboring family. The losing family had no legal claim to the land, but still they had never accepted the court's ruling. For three generations now, the two families had been enemies. **B**

Now that Ulrich was the head of his family, the fighting had become personal. Ulrich detested Georg Znaeym,[2] his warring neighbor. **C** Georg went on killing game in Ulrich's forest. The feud continued because the two men hated each other so much.

On this windy winter night, Ulrich had ordered his servants to watch for thieves in the forest.

---

1. **Ulrich von Gradwitz** (UHL RIHK FAHN GRAHT VIHTS).
2. **Georg Znaeym** (JAWRJ ZNY UHM).

A HERE'S HOW

Vocabulary

The word *game* usually means an activity. That is not the case here. The word "animal" in line 4 hints at the meaning of *game* here.

B HERE'S HOW

Reading Focus

I can re-read the first two paragraphs to **draw conclusions**. I learn that the conflict between these two families has been going on for a long time and is serious.

C HERE'S HOW

Language Coach

The adjective *warring* (WAWR ING) means "fighting" or "engaged in a fight." To improve my **oral fluency**, I will practice pronouncing this word aloud.

> **A** HERE'S HOW
>
> **Vocabulary**
>
> I see that Ulrich is searching for *poachers*. I remember reading that *poachers* are people who hunt or fish without permission on someone else's land. I checked my dictionary, and I was right.

> **B** HERE'S HOW
>
> **Vocabulary**
>
> I am not sure what the word *condolences* means. I think it means "messages of sorrow" because it is followed by the words "how sorry I am."

All the animals in the forest usually hid in safe places in bad weather, but tonight they were restless. Something was upsetting the forest and the animals that night. Ulrich could guess what it was.

He had his watchers hiding on the hilltop. Then he wandered alone listening through the wild, whistling wind for poachers. **A** His greatest wish was to come face to face with Georg Znaeym, to meet him alone. As he stepped around a huge tree trunk, he met Georg.

The two enemies glared at each other for a long moment. Each held a rifle, and each had hate in his heart and murder on his mind. Finally, they had the chance of a lifetime, but neither could just shoot a man in cold blood without a word spoken.

Before either could act, a fierce wind blew against the massive tree over their heads. With a splitting crash, the tree thundered down upon them. Ulrich found himself on the ground with one arm numb beneath him, the other arm caught in the branches, and both legs pinned beneath the trunk. Twigs had slashed his face, causing him to blink blood from his eyelashes in order to see. Georg lay close by his side. He was alive and struggling, pinned down like Ulrich.

Ulrich was glad to be alive, but he was angry at being trapped. He mumbled a strange mixture of thanks and sharp curses.

"So you're not dead, but you're caught anyway," Georg cried. "What a joke! Ulrich von Gradwitz caught in his stolen forest!"

"I'm caught in my own forest," Ulrich replied. "My men will free me soon. Then you'll wish you hadn't been caught stealing game."

Georg was silent a moment, then answered quietly: "Are you sure your men will find much to release? I have men, too. They're in the forest tonight, close behind me. *They* will be here first. When they drag me out from under these branches, it won't take much clumsiness on their part to roll this trunk on top of you. Your men will find you dead under a fallen tree. I'll send condolences to let your family know how sorry I am." **B**

"That's a useful plan," said Ulrich fiercely. "My men had orders to follow in ten minutes, and seven minutes must have passed already. When they get me out, I'll remember that plan. But since you will have met your death while poaching on my land, I don't think I can decently send any condolences to your family."

"Good," snarled Georg. "You and I and our men will fight this to the death, with no interfering outsiders here." **C**

60 Both men knew that they might be defeated or found too late. Which team would get there first was a matter of chance.

Both stopped struggling to get free. Ulrich managed to get his wine flask[3] from his pocket. Though it was a mild winter and Ulrich felt the cold less than he might have, the drink warmed and revived the wounded man. He looked over at Georg with a throb of pity.

"Could you reach this flask if I tossed it to you?" asked Ulrich suddenly. "There is good wine in it. We may as well be as comfortable as we can."

"No. I can't see to catch it," said Georg. "Anyway, I don't
70 drink with an enemy."

Ulrich was silent for a few minutes. An idea was slowly forming in him, an idea that gained strength every time he looked at Georg. In his pain and weariness, the old hatred seemed to be dying. **D**

"Neighbor," he said, "do what you like if your men come first. But, I've changed my mind. If my men come first, they will help you first. We have fought like devils over this stupid forest. I see we've been fools. If you'll help me end this fight, we can be friends."

80 After a silence, Georg finally spoke. "Think how people would stare if we rode into the market square together! No one living can remember our families being friendly. And if we choose to make peace, there is none other to interfere, no interlopers from outside. **E** I never thought of anything but hating you. But I think I've changed my mind, too. Ulrich von Gradwitz, I will be your friend."

For a time, both men thought about the wonderful changes peace would bring. In the cold, gloomy forest on that windy night,

---

3. **flask**: a flat container that fits in a pocket. A flask usually holds alcohol.

C HERE'S HOW

Vocabulary

I have heard the word *snarl* before, usually used with angry animals. When Georg *snarls*, I think it means that he speaks angrily.

D YOUR TURN

Literary Focus

Underline two sentences on this page that show that this story has an **omniscient narrator**.

E YOUR TURN

Vocabulary

The word *interlopers* is important because it is in the title of the story. Underline the clues that help you figure out the meaning of *interloper*. Write your definition on the lines below.

_____
_____
_____

A **YOUR TURN**

Reading Focus

After three generations of family conflict, Ulrich and Georg have become friends. Based on the two men's words and actions, what **conclusions** can you draw about what the author is saying about family conflicts?

_____
_____
_____
_____
_____

B **LITERARY ANALYSIS**

How does this surprise ending connect to the events of this story and the feelings that Ulrich and Georg have about each other?

_____
_____
_____
_____
_____
_____

Rampaging Wolves Attacking, illustration from 'The Hobbit,' by J.R.R. Tolkien (1892-1973), edition published 1976 (engraving), Belomlinsky, Mikhail (Contemporary Artist)/Private Collection/Bridgeman Art Library

they lay and waited for help. Each prayed that his men would arrive first. Then, he might be the first to help his new friend. **A**

Soon, the wind died down. Ulrich said, "Let's shout for help."

"Our voices won't carry far," said Georg, "but we can try. Together, then."

The two men cried out.

"Together again," said Ulrich after waiting a few minutes. Then he said, "I heard something that time, I think."

"I heard nothing but the cursed wind," said Georg.

After a few minutes of silence, Ulrich gave a joyful cry.

"I can see figures coming through the wood."

Both men shouted as loudly as they could.

"They hear us! They're running down the hill toward us," cried Ulrich.

"How many of them are there?" asked Georg.

"I can't see clearly. Nine or ten," said Ulrich.

"Then they are yours," said Georg. "I had only seven men."

"They are hurrying as fast as they can," said Ulrich gladly.

"Are they your men?" asked Georg. "Are they your men?" he repeated impatiently, as Ulrich did not answer.

"No," said Ulrich with a strange laugh. It was the idiotic, chattering laugh of a man full of hideous fear.

"Who are they?" asked Georg, straining his eyes to see what the other man wished he had not seen.

"Wolves." **B**

Applying Your Skills

The Interlopers

LITERARY FOCUS: OMNISCIENT NARRATOR

"The Interlopers" is told to readers by an **omniscient narrator**. Here the narrator knows everything about the characters in the story, from their inner thoughts during the story to their background information and history.

DIRECTIONS: Answer the questions below using complete sentences.

1. This story involves two families that hate each other. What is an advantage in having an omniscient narrator tell this story?
   _____
   _____

2. If the narrator knows how the story will end, why is it kept secret from us?
   _____
   _____

READING FOCUS: DRAWING CONCLUSIONS

DIRECTIONS: Complete the chart by **drawing conclusions** from the details listed below.

Story Details	Conclusions
Georg comments that "people would stare" if he and Ulrich became friends.	
After spotting the approaching wolves, Ulrich releases a "strange laugh."	

VOCABULARY REVIEW

DIRECTIONS: Complete the following sentences with words from the Word Box.

Word Box
- interlopers
- game
- snarled
- condolences

1. Deer and wild turkey are examples of _____.

2. At a funeral, guests offer their _____ to family members of the person who has died.

The Interlopers 91

Preparing to Read

The Cask of Amontillado

Based on the story by Edgar Allan Poe

LITERARY FOCUS: UNRELIABLE NARRATOR

When you read, you usually believe the narrator who is telling the story. However, some stories have an **unreliable narrator**—a narrator you cannot trust. Over the years since Poe wrote this story, people have asked whether the narrator is telling the truth or telling lies. What a narrator does and says is important. The narrator's **voice** (style of speaking), **diction** (word choice), and **tone** (attitude) are also important.

READING FOCUS: DRAWING CONCLUSIONS

When you **draw conclusions**, you pay attention to details in the text. Then you combine those details with your own knowledge to form a new idea about the text.

text + what you know = your conclusion

VOCABULARY

plotted (PLAWT ID) *v.:* planned secretly.

bargain (BAHR GUHN) *n.:* a good deal.

INTO THE STORY

Centuries ago in Italy, early Christians buried their dead in catacombs, which are long underground tunnels. Later, rich families built private catacombs underneath their homes. Dark and cool, these chambers were also useful for storing wine. The wine was kept in containers called casks.

This story is set during Carnival, a time for people to have fun before the Christian season of Lent begins. During Lent, many people eat or drink very little and often give up meat. People celebrate the time before Lent by eating and drinking, wearing costumes, and dancing in the streets.

SKILLS FOCUS

Literary Skills
Understand unreliable narrator.

Reading Skills
Draw conclusions.

The Cask of Amontillado

Based on the Story by Edgar Allan Poe

I put up with Fortunato[1] for years. When he insulted me, however, I decided to get even. I wouldn't threaten him. Instead, I would punish him without getting caught.

I went on smiling at him. He didn't guess that I was smiling at the thought of his destruction. **A**

Fortunato was a man to respect and fear. But he had a weakness: He was proud of his knowledge of wines. I plotted to use Fortunato's pride against him. **B**

One evening during carnival I saw Fortunato. He greeted me with much warmth, for he was drunk. He wore a clown costume and cone-shaped cap with jingling bells. I was very pleased to see him.

I said, "It's lucky we met. I just bought some wine. It's supposed to be amontillado."[2]

"Amontillado? To obtain such a fine wine during carnival—impossible!"

"I have my doubts," I said. "Silly me, I paid the full price. I should have talked to you first, but I was afraid of losing a bargain." **C**

"Amontillado!"

"I have my doubts," I said.

"Amontillado!"

"Since you're busy, I'll go to Luchesi.[3] If anyone knows wine, he does. He'll tell me—"

"Luchesi!" Fortunato snorted. "He's just a phony who pretends to know wine. Let's go to your cellars to have a taste."

"No. The cellars are damp; you'll catch a cold. Besides, you have other plans. Luchesi—" **D**

---

1. **Fortunato** (FAWR TOO NAH TOH).
2. **amontillado** (UH MAHN TEE YAH DOH): a pale type of wine.
3. **Luchesi** (LOO KEH SEE).

A HERE'S HOW

Literary Focus

The **narrator** acts friendly toward a man he plans to punish. This tells me that the narrator is not always honest.

B YOUR TURN

Vocabulary

The word *plotted* can mean "drew a chart" or "planned secretly." Which meaning does it have here?

_____

_____

C HERE'S HOW

Vocabulary

I'm not sure what *bargain* means. Based on what the narrator is saying, though, I think it must be a good deal.

D HERE'S HOW

Reading Focus

The narrator seems worried about Fortunato's health. However, he said earlier that he planned to punish Fortunato. I can **draw conclusions** about the narrator. I think the narrator is not being truthful. He is trying to trick Fortunato here by being nice to him.

The Cask of Amontillado

A YOUR TURN

LITERARY FOCUS
Explain the **unreliable narrator's** hidden reason for mentioning the things below:

- Concern for Fortunato's health

_____
_____
_____
_____

- Luchesi

_____
_____
_____
_____
_____

"I don't have plans. Come," he insisted.

Putting on a black mask, I let him lead me to my palace.

As I expected, the servants had all gone to the carnival. Carrying torches, we went down many stairs to the catacombs. The catacombs were a series of cellars that held the bones of my ancestors, the Montresors.[4] I also used the cellars to store wine.

My friend swayed as he walked; his bells jingled.

"The amontillado," he said.

"It's farther on." I said. "Look; do you see that white web-work on the walls? It is niter, salt deposits left by the dampness.... How long have you had that cough?"

"Ugh! ugh! ugh!—ugh! ugh! ugh!—It's nothing," he said.

"Come," I said. "We'll go back. Your health is important. You are rich, respected. You are happy—as I was once. Besides, there is Luchesi—" **A**

"I won't die of a cough," he said.

"True," I replied. "Here, this wine will keep you warm."

I offered him wine from a bottle that lay in our path.

"I drink to the dead buried here," Fortunato said.

"And I drink to your long life," I replied.

"These vaults are huge," he said as we went on.

"The Montresors were a great family," I answered.

"I forget what your family's coat of arms is."

"The symbols are a human foot crushing a snake. The snake's fangs are stuck in the heel."

"And the motto?" he asked.

"'Nobody attacks me without punishment,'" I replied.

"Good!" he said.

We went farther into the catacombs. I paused.

"The niter!" I said. "We're below the river. The air is _terribly_ damp. Let's return before it's too late. Your cough—!"

"No," he said. "Let's go on. But first, more wine."

I broke open another bottle. He emptied it in one gulp, then made a strange gesture. I looked at him in surprise.

---

4. **Montresors** (MAWN TREH SAWRS).

© Scala/Art Resource, NY

"Aha," he said. "I see you are not a Mason."

"Oh, yes," I said, "Yes, I am."

"You? Impossible! Show me the secret sign," he said.

"It is this," I answered, pulling a mason's tool from my cape. **B**

"You're joking," he said, drawing back. "But let's go on."

As we continued, our torches barely glowed in the bad air. Finally, we entered a small chamber. Bones lined three of its walls. The bones from the fourth wall were piled on the ground. The bare wall revealed an opening that ended in a wall of solid rock.

"The amontillado is inside," I said. "As for Luchesi—"

"He's a fool," said Fortunato. He swayed into the dark opening with me behind him. Bumping into the rock wall, he stopped, confused. Quickly I chained him to the wall. He was too surprised to stop me. I stepped back.

"Move your hand along the wall," I said. "You'll feel the niter. It is *very* damp. Once more let me beg you to return. No? Then I must leave you."

B HERE'S HOW

Reading Focus
Line 63 mentions the word *Mason*. I researched this word to see what it means. The Masons, or Freemasons, are a secret men's club that help each other and the poor. They use secret hand signals to recognize each other. A *mason*, with a small *m*, is someone who builds with stone. The word *mason* seems to be used in these two ways. Judging by his behavior, I am sure Montressor is not a *mason* by trade. I can draw the **conclusion** that his carrying the mason tool will be important later on.

A YOUR TURN

Reading Focus

The narrator enjoys listening to Fortunato's moans. What **conclusions** can you draw about the narrator's personality from this passage?

_____

_____

B YOUR TURN

Literary focus

Why do you think the **narrator** adds "because of the dampness" after saying his heart felt sick? Is he covering up his true feelings, or is he trying to shock us with his coldness? Is this an example of the narrator being **unreliable**? Underline clues that support your response, and then write your answer below.

_____

_____

C HERE'S HOW

Language Coach

A word's **denotation** is the dictionary definition of that word. A word's **connotations** are the feelings that are connected to that word. The dictionary definition of *dampness* is "wetness." So, this is the word's denotation. But, as you know, here *dampness* has other feelings connected to it. Its connotations are different than its denotation.

"The amontillado!" he cried.

"True," I replied, "the amontillado." Under the pile of bones, I found building stones and cement. I began to wall up the opening.

The wine's effect was wearing off. Fortunato's moaning wasn't the cry of a drunken man. I stopped working briefly, listening with satisfaction. **A**

Then the chained man screamed—so loudly that I became worried. But feeling the thick walls of the catacomb, I became calm again. I simply screamed back, longer and louder. Fortunato's screams stopped.

Around midnight, I was almost finished. Then I heard a low laugh that made my hair stand up. It was followed by a sad voice. "Ha! ha! ha!—a very good joke. We'll laugh about it later. Over our wine—he! he! he!"

"The amontillado!" I said.

"He! he! he—yes, the amontillado. But isn't it late? Lady Fortunato will be waiting for me. Let's go."

"Yes," I said, "Let's go."

"For the love of God, Montresor!"

"Yes," I said, "for the love of God!" He didn't answer. I called out, "Fortunato!"

No answer still. I thrust a torch through the last space in the wall and let it fall inside. There came forth in return only the jingling of bells. My heart grew sick—because of the dampness. **B C** I finished sealing up the wall and piled the bones up against it. For half a century no one has bothered them. May he rest in peace.

Applying Your Skills

The Cask of Amontillado

LITERARY FOCUS: UNRELIABLE NARRATOR

A **narrator** can be unreliable in more than one way:

1. He or she may not fully understand what is going on in the story.
2. He or she may not tell us the whole truth.
3. He or she may exaggerate or play with the facts.

DIRECTIONS: Find examples from the selection for any two of the three ways above that Poe's narrator is unreliable. Write the line number of each passage below, followed by your explanation.

1. _____
2. _____

READING FOCUS: DRAWING CONCLUSIONS

DIRECTIONS: Select one detail from the text that you can use to **draw a conclusion** that will help you understand the story. One example is provided below.

Detail: Fortunato is "proud of his knowledge of wines."

Conclusion: Pride can make people do foolish things. The narrator knows this, and he uses Fortunato's pride against him.

Detail: _____

Conclusion: _____
_____

Word Box

plotted
bargain

VOCABULARY REVIEW

1. Using the word **plotted**, write a sentence about the narrator and Fortunato. _____
_____

2. Use the word **bargain** in a sentence about buying a gift.
_____
_____

Preparing to Read

Poe's Final Days
Poe's Death Is Rewritten . . .
If Only Poe Had Succeeded . . .

INFORMATIONAL TEXT FOCUS: SYNTHESIZING SOURCES: DRAWING CONCLUSIONS

When you research a subject, you read many different sources, such as Web sites and newspaper or encyclopedia articles. You then **synthesize** the information, or put the pieces together, to form a big picture. To synthesize your sources:

Find the main ideas: Ask yourself, "What points are the writers making?"

Look for supporting evidence: Pick out facts, statistics, examples, anecdotes (real-life stories), and quotations that support the writer's main ideas.

Compare and contrast: Find the similarities and differences in your sources.

Make connections: Does the information in your sources remind you of anything you already know?

Put it all together: You are now ready to synthesize what you have learned to form one main idea about your sources.

VOCABULARY

Make flashcards for the following words. Write the word on the front and its definition on the back.

insensible (IHN SEHN SUH BUHL) *adj.*: not fully conscious or aware.

imposing (IHM POH ZIHNG) *adj.*: large and impressive looking.

rabid (RAB IHD) *adj.*: having rabies.

symptoms (SIHMP TUHMS) *n.*: signs or indications of a disease.

INTO THE ARTICLE AND LETTERS

Most newspapers have what is called an Op-Ed page. The Op-Ed page is usually found *opposite* the *editorial* page. It may include columns by reporters who work for the paper, articles by people who do not work for the paper, and readers' responses to newspaper articles. These responses are called letters to the editor. You are about to read a newspaper article about the death of Edgar Allan Poe. Then, you will read two letters to the editor that were written after the article. This is an easy way to remember where to find the Op-Ed page.

SKILLS FOCUS

Informational Text Skills: Synthesize information from many different sources.

POE'S FINAL DAYS

from *Edgar A. Poe: Mournful and Never-Ending Remembrance*
by Kenneth Silverman

In the early morning of September 27, a Thursday, Poe began the first leg of his return to the North, setting out from Richmond for Baltimore on the 4 A.M. steamer,[1] with a trunk containing some clothing, books, and manuscripts.

No reliable evidence exists about what happened to or within Poe between that time and October 3, a week later, when a printer named Joseph Walker saw him at Gunner's Hall, a Baltimore tavern, strangely dressed and semiconscious. **A**

It was Election Day for members of Congress, and like other local watering holes[2] the tavern served as a polling place. Poe seemed to Walker "rather the worse for wear" and "in great distress." Apparently flooded with drink, he may also have been ill from exposure. Winds and soaking rains the day before had sent Baltimoreans prematurely hunting up overcoats and seeking charcoal fires for warmth.... **B** Poe managed to tell Walker that he knew Joseph Evans Snodgrass, the Baltimore editor and physician with whom he had often corresponded while living in Philadelphia. As it happened, Walker had worked as a typesetter for Snodgrass's *Saturday Visitor*. He sent Snodgrass a dire note, warning that Poe needed "immediate assistance." **C**

IN OTHER WORDS A week after Edgar Allan Poe left Richmond, Virginia, he was seen at a bar in Baltimore, Maryland, wearing strange clothes. Most people thought Poe was probably drunk, and maybe sick from the bad weather. A man named Joseph Walker found Poe and sent a letter to Joseph Evans Snodgrass, a doctor he and Poe both knew.

1. **steamer** (STEE MUHR): steamship, or ship driven by steam power.
2. **watering holes**: informal for "bars, taverns."

Excerpt (retitled "Poe's Final Days") from *Edgar A. Poe: Mournful and Never-Ending Remembrance* by Kenneth Silverman. Copyright © 1991 by Kenneth Silverman. Reproduced by permission of **HarperCollins Publishers, Inc.**

A HERE'S HOW

Reading Focus

Based on the first two paragraphs and the article title, I think the **main idea** of this article is that something strange happened to Poe just before he died. I will keep reading to see if I am right.

B QUICK CHECK

What was the weather like when Poe went into the tavern?

_____

_____

C HERE'S HOW

Vocabulary

The word *dire* means "urgent" or "very important." The word *immediate* means "right away." These words make it sound like Poe needed help very quickly.

A YOUR TURN

Reading Focus

Underline any **supporting evidence** you can find in this paragraph that backs up Snodgrass' belief that Poe might have been robbed or cheated out of his clothing.

B YOUR TURN

Vocabulary

Look at the word *admitted* in this sentence. Does *admitted* have the same meaning here as it does in the sentence: "Poe *admitted* to close friends that he drank too much?" If not, write the meaning of *admitted* as it is used in line 43 on the lines below.

___

___

___

___

When Snodgrass arrived at Gunner's Hall, he found Poe sitting in an armchair, surrounded by onlookers. Poe had a look of "vacant stupidity." He wore neither vest nor tie, his dingy trousers fit badly, his shirt was crumpled, his cheap hat soiled. Snodgrass thought he must be wearing castoff clothing, having been robbed or cheated of his own. **A** He ordered a room for Poe at the tavern, where he might stay comfortably until his relatives in Baltimore could be notified. Just then, however, one of them arrived—Henry Herring, Poe's uncle by marriage, who somehow had also learned of his condition. A lumber dealer now nearly sixty years old, he had wed Muddy's[3] sister, and spent time with Poe during his early days in Baltimore and later when both families lived in Philadelphia. But he refused now to take over his care, saying that on former occasions, when drunk, Poe had been abusive and ungrateful. Instead, he suggested sending Poe to a hospital. A carriage was called for. Poe had to be carried into it, Snodgrass said—insensible, muttering.

Through the chilly wet streets Poe was driven to the hospital of Washington Medical College, set on the highest ground of Baltimore. An imposing five-story building with vaulted gothic windows, it afforded both public wards and private rooms, advertised as being spacious, well ventilated, and directed by an experienced medical staff. Admitted at five in the afternoon, Poe was given a private room, reportedly in a section reserved for cases involving drunkenness. **B** He was attended by the resident physician, Dr. John J. Moran, who apparently had living quarters in the hospital together with his wife. Moran had received his medical degree from the University of Maryland four years earlier and was now only about twenty-six years old. But he knew the identity of his patient—a "*great* man," he wrote of Poe, to whose "rarely gifted mind are we indebted for many of the brightest thoughts that adorn our literature." He as well as the medical students, nurses, and other physicians—all considered Poe, he said, "an object of unusual regard."

___

3. **Muddy's:** Muddy was Poe's nickname for Maria Clemm, his aunt and mother-in-law. Poe had married his cousin, Virginia Clemm.

According to Moran and his wife, Poe reached the hospital in a stupor,[4] unaware of who or what had brought him there. He remained thus "unconscious" until three o'clock the next morning, when he developed a tremor[5] of the limbs and what Moran called "a busy, but not violent or active delirium."[6] **C** His face was pale and he was drenched in sweat. He talked constantly, Moran said, addressing "spectral[7] and imaginary objects on the walls." **D** **E** Apparently during Poe's delirium, his cousin Neilson Poe came to the hospital, having been contacted by Dr. Moran. A lawyer and journalist involved in Whig politics, Neilson was just Poe's age. In happier circumstances Poe would not have welcomed the visit. Not only had Neilson offered Virginia[8] and Muddy a home apart from him; his cousin also, he believed, envied his literary reputation. **F** Years before he had remarked that he considered "the little dog," as he called Neilson, the "bitterest enemy I have in the world." The physicians anyway thought it inadvisable for Neilson to see Poe at the moment, when "very excitable." Neilson sent some changes of linen and called again the next day, to find Poe's condition improved.

IN OTHER WORDS Snodgrass was going to have Poe sleep at the tavern until his family came to take care of him, but Poe's uncle showed up and said that Poe should go to the hospital. Poe got a room at the hospital and still behaved very strangely. His cousin Neilson came to visit, but the doctors did not think it was a good idea because Poe did not like him. Poe started to get better the next day.

Poe being quieted, Moran began questioning him about his family and about where he lived, but found his answers mostly incoherent. Poe did not know what had become of his trunk or when he had left Richmond, but said he had a wife there, as

---

4. **stupor** (STOO puhr): dull, half-conscious state.
5. **tremor** (TREHM uhr): shaking, especially from a sickness.
6. **delirium** (dih LEER ee uhm): crazy or unusual behavior, often caused by high fever.
7. **spectral** (SPEHK truhl): ghostly; unreal.
8. **Virginia**: Poe's wife, Virginia Clemm. She died of tuberculosis in 1847.

C HERE'S HOW

Language Coach

The word *unconscious* in line 57 means "not aware or awake." An **antonym**, or word with the opposite meaning, for *unconscious* would be the word *lively*.

D HERE'S HOW

Vocabulary

When you write directions on a letter telling where to send it, you are *addressing* the letter. But, I know that Poe is not writing letters here. I think *addressing* means "talking to," which means that Poe is talking to imaginary things on the walls!

E YOUR TURN

Reading Focus

What is the **main idea** of this paragraph so far?

_____
_____
_____

F YOUR TURN

Vocabulary

The article says that Neilson *envied* Poe's "literary reputation," or fame from his writing. What does *envied* mean?

_____
_____

A YOUR TURN

Reading Focus

How does Poe's behavior at the hospital support the **main idea** of this article?

_____

_____

_____

B YOUR TURN

Vocabulary

Using clues from this sentence, circle the best definition for *expired*:
(a) breathed deeply
(b) died
(c) fell asleep

C YOUR TURN

Vocabulary

The article says that many people think that Poe died because of a *lethal* amount of alcohol. What does *lethal* mean?

_____

_____

Moran soon learned was untrue. He said that his "degradation," as Moran characterized it, made him feel like sinking into the ground. Trying to rouse Poe's spirits, Moran told him he wished to contribute in every way to his comfort, and hoped Poe would soon be enjoying the company of his friends. **A**

Then Poe seemed to doze, and Moran left him briefly. On returning he found Poe violently delirious, resisting the efforts of two nurses to keep him in bed. From Moran's description, Poe seems to have raved a full day or more, through Saturday evening, October 6, when he began repeatedly calling out someone's name. It may have been that of a Baltimore family named Reynolds or, more likely, the name of his uncle-in-law Henry Herring. Moran later said that he sent for the Herring family, but that only one of Herring's two daughters came to the hospital. Poe continued deliriously calling the name until three o'clock on Sunday morning. Then his condition changed. Feeble from his exertions he seemed to rest a short time and then, Moran reported, "quietly moving his head he said '*Lord help my poor Soul*' and expired!" **B**

The cause of Poe's death remains in doubt. Moran's account of his profuse perspiration, trembling, and hallucinations indicates delirium tremens, *mania à potu*.[9] Many others who had known Poe, including the professionally trained Dr. Snodgrass, also attributed his death to a lethal amount of alcohol. **C** Moran later vigorously disputed this explanation, however, and some Baltimore newspapers gave the cause of death as "congestion of the brain" or "cerebral inflammation."[10] Although the terms were sometimes used euphemistically[11] in public announcements of deaths from disgraceful causes, such as alcoholism, they may in this case have come from the hospital staff itself. According to

---

9. **delirium tremens, mania à potu:** Delirium tremens is an alcoholic state in which the person sweats a lot, trembles, and sees imaginary things. Mania à potu is a Latin phrase meaning "madness from drinking."
10. **"congestion of the brain" or "cerebral inflammation":** These are terms for sicknesses of the brain caused by injury or infection.
11. **euphemistically** (YOO FUH MIHS TUH KLEE): in a way meant to hide or substitute for something unpleasant or offensive.

Moran, one of its senior physicians diagnosed Poe's condition as encephalitis, a brain inflammation, brought on by "exposure." This explanation is consistent with the prematurely wintry weather at the time, with Snodgrass's account of Poe's partly clad condition, and with Elmira Shelton's recollection that on leaving Richmond Poe already had a fever. **D** Both explanations may have been correct: Poe may have become too drunk to care about protecting himself against the wind and rain. **E**

IN OTHER WORDS Poe was still very confused when Dr. Moran asked him questions. Poe went to sleep, but when he woke up, he tried to get out of bed and he started shouting someone's name. He kept acting like this for a whole day. He rested for a little bit, and then died. No one is sure why he died. The way he was acting made it look like he had been killed by too much alcohol, but Dr. Moran thought it might have been a sickness in Poe's brain caused by the bad weather that killed him. It might be that Poe was very drunk and then got sick because of the weather.

D YOUR TURN

Reading Focus

Why doesn't Moran believe that Poe died of alcohol poisoning? Underline all of the **supporting evidence** in this paragraph.

E YOUR TURN

Reading Focus

In your own words, what is the **main idea** of this article?

_____
_____
_____
_____
_____
_____

Poe's Death Is Rewritten as Case of Rabies, Not Telltale Alcohol

Based on the *New York Times* article, September 15, 1996

A **HERE'S HOW**

Reading Focus
The most important thing I have to do when I read a source is figure out the **main idea**. I think the main idea of this article may be in the title and the first sentence: Edgar Allan Poe died of rabies, not drinking alcohol.

B **HERE'S HOW**

Vocabulary
The word *rabid* sounds a lot like *rabies*. I think *rabid* just means "having rabies."

C **QUICK CHECK**

Who agrees with Dr. Benitez's argument that Poe may have died from rabies?

D **YOUR TURN**

Reading Focus
Underline all the **evidence** you find in this article to support the **main idea**.

Dr. R. Michael Benitez claims that Edgar Allan Poe was falsely accused of drinking himself to death. **A** The doctor says that all of Poe's symptoms point to rabies. Like many rabies victims, Poe was confused, angry, and aggressive, the doctor notes. When he was calm, it was difficult for him to drink water. People with rabies often refuse or fear water because it is painful for them to swallow.

There's no evidence that a rabid animal had bitten Poe. **B** However, rabies victims often don't remember being bitten, and the signs of rabies can take a year to show up. Once the signs appear, patients die in a few days.

A doctor who treats rabies cases in Thailand agrees that Poe showed all the signs of rabies. **C**

Because he believed that people should not drink alcohol, Poe's doctor may have changed the details of Poe's death to teach a lesson about the dangers of alcohol.

Jeff Jerome, who is in charge of the Poe Baltimore House and Museum,[1] said that Poe did not die of alcohol poisoning. He said that Poe was so sensitive to alcohol that a glass of wine made him ill for days. Poe may have had problems in his youth with alcohol, but by the time he was forty Poe almost always avoided alcohol, Jerome said. **D**

---

1. **Poe Baltimore House and Museum:** a house in Baltimore, Maryland, where Poe once lived, now a museum.

"Poe's Death Is Rewritten as Case of Rabies, Not Telltale Alcohol" adapted from *The New York Times*, September 15, 1996. Copyright © 1996 by **The Associated Press**. Retold by Holt, Rinehart and Winston. Reproduced by permission of **The Associated Press**.

IF ONLY POE HAD SUCCEEDED WHEN HE SAID NEVERMORE TO DRINK

Based on the *New York Times* article, September 23, 1996

To the Editor:

Dr. Benitez is wrong to say that rabies, not alcoholism, caused Poe's death. Poe was found drunk and unconscious outside a bar. He died four days later. Dr. Moran's story of Poe's last days appears in a letter to the woman who was both Poe's aunt and mother-in-law. Four people who saw Poe during those four days before his death—Joseph Walker, Joseph Snodgrass, and two relatives—agree that Poe was drunk. In letters to his wife and her mother, Poe wrote often about his periods of heavy drinking. **E**

Dr. Benitez admits the important weakness in his idea: lack of a bite or scratch. In those days, rabies symptoms were easily recognized. **F** If Poe had had any sign of rabies, his doctors would have seen it.

Poe's pet cat, Caterina, showed no sign of rabies. Uninfected, she died of starvation after Poe's death.

There is no need to whitewash the self-destructive behavior of this genius and major American writer. **G**

Burton R. Pollin and Robert E. Benedetto

E YOUR TURN

Reading Focus

This letter to the editor gets right to the point. Underline the **main idea** you find in this paragraph.

F HERE'S HOW

Vocabulary

I have not seen the word *symptoms* before, but the next line starts with "if Poe had any sign of rabies," so I think *symptoms* might mean signs, or indications, of a disease. I checked my dictionary, and I was right!

G HERE'S HOW

Reading Focus

One step in **synthesizing sources** is to compare and contrast the sources. How is the main idea of the previous article similar to or different from this one?

"If Only Poe Had Succeeded When He Said Nevermore to Drink" by Burton R. Pollin adapted from "Editorial Desk" from *The New York Times,* September 23, 1996. Copyright © 1996 by **Burton R. Pollin.** Retold by Holt, Rinehart and Winston. Reproduced by permission of the author.

Skills Practice

Three Readings About Poe's Death

USE A COMPARISON CHART

When you read many sources on a topic, you need to **synthesize the sources**, or fit all the pieces together into one big idea. To do that, you follow these steps: (1) find the main idea; (2) look for supporting evidence; (3) compare and contrast sources; (4) make connections; and (5) put it all together. In the chart below, fill in the boxes with the first four steps for each source. Some have been done for you. Then, synthesize the information you have gathered into one big idea statement.

	Poe's Final Days	Poe's Death Is Rewritten . . .	If Only Poe Had Succeeded . . .
1.	a. Main idea:	b. Main idea:	c. Main idea: Poe died of alcoholism, not rabies.
2.	a. Supporting evidence: Joseph Walker saw Poe at a bar.	b. Supporting evidence: Often, rabies victims do not remember being bitten.	c. Supporting evidence:
3.	a. Compare and contrast:	b. Compare and contrast:	c. Compare and contrast:
4.	a. Make connections:	b. Make connections: I met someone whose relative died of a rabies bite. I was surprised to learn that could still happen these days.	c. Make connections:

Big idea statement: _____

Applying Your Skills

Three Readings on Poe's Death

INFORMATIONAL TEXT FOCUS: SYNTHESIZING SOURCES: DRAWING CONCLUSIONS

DIRECTIONS: Think about the pieces you have read about Poe's death in Baltimore. Now it is *your* turn to decide what happened to Poe! Using the **supporting evidence** from all three selections, write a paragraph on the lines below telling about what you think happened to Poe that night.

_____
_____
_____
_____
_____
_____
_____
_____

VOCABULARY REVIEW

DIRECTIONS: Fill in the blanks with the correct words from the Word Box.

Word Box
- insensible
- imposing
- rabid
- symptoms

1. After being bitten by the _____ dog, James was rushed to the hospital, where he was treated right away.

2. My high school science teacher was a large, _____ man and he frightened many of his students!

3. Poe was completely out of it when he was admitted to the hospital. He was _____, and barely awake.

4. Laura had all of the _____ of the flu, including high fever and a sore throat.

Skills Review

Collection 3

VOCABULARY REVIEW

DIRECTIONS: Write "yes" on the lines if the underlined vocabulary word is used correctly. Write "no" if it is not.

1. Wild animals that are hunted for food, sport, or profit are called <u>game.</u>

   _____

2. It is believed that Edgar Allan Poe drank a <u>portray</u> amount of alcohol, and died in the hospital.

   _____

3. Lisa was so angry that when she replied to Martin, she <u>snarled</u> at him.

   _____

4. Buying three new video games for only $20 was a great <u>distinct</u>.

   _____

5. Without anyone knowing about it, Carey <u>plotted</u> to become the new class president and change the rules.

   _____

6. I knew the dog was <u>rabid</u> because he was foaming at the mouth and had a wild look in his eyes.

   _____

7. An omniscient narrator can <u>portray</u> the feelings of all the characters in the story.

   _____

8. Although Greg visited for only a few days, he left a lasting <u>impression</u> on the community.

   _____

Skills Review

Collection 3

LANGUAGE COACH: ORAL FLUENCY

When you come across unfamiliar words, it is a good idea to first think about how you would pronounce them. Doing so will improve your **oral fluency**. If possible, check pronunciation guides that are provided, or look up the words in a dictionary.

DIRECTIONS: Draw a line to match each word with its correct pronunciation.

portray	RAB IHD
impression	KUHN DOHL UHNS EZ
symptoms	IHM PREHSH UHN
distinct	PAWR TRAY
condolences	DIHS TIHNGKT
rabid	SIHMP TUHMS

ORAL LANGUAGE ACTIVITY

You have read two articles and a letter in which people express their opinions about how Edgar Allan Poe died. Prepare a brief talk, giving your opinion on an issue that you care about. Use at least two of the following phrases in your talk: "*In my opinion . . ., My experience indicates that . . ., It seems that . . ., I agree/disagree that . . .*" Give your talk to the class or to a small group.

Collection 4

Symbolism and Irony

Literary and Academic Vocabulary for Collection 4

LITERARY VOCABULARY

symbol (SIHM BUHL) *n.:* an object, event, person, or animal, to which we have attached special meaning.
In the story, the ship sailing out to sea was a symbol of freedom.

allegory (A LUH GOH REE) *n.:* a story in which the characters, setting, and action stand for something beyond themselves.
I read an allegory in which the characters were named Honesty, Charity, and Hope, and the characters represented the qualities for which they were named.

irony (Y RUH NEE) *n.:* the difference between what we expect and what actually happens.
I spent all day cooking for the party, but when I arrived with my hands full of dishes I realized the party was not until the next night. This is an example of irony.

ACADEMIC VOCABULARY

associate (UH SOH SHEE AYT) *v.:* mentally make a link.
I associate budding trees with the feeling of hope.

imply (IHM PLY) *v.:* suggest; hint at.
Did the writer mean to imply that love never succeeds?

literal (LIHT UHR UHL) *adj.:* based on the ordinary meaning of the actual words.
To get to the truth of a story you sometimes have to look beyond its literal meaning.

ambiguous (AN BIHG YOO UHS) *adj.:* not clearly defined.
The story's ambiguous ending left it up to the reader to determine the outcome.

Preparing to Read

The Scarlet Ibis

By James Hurst

LITERARY FOCUS: SYMBOLS AND THEME

A **symbol** is an object, person, animal, or event that stands for something more than itself. In literature, symbols add deeper levels of meaning to a story. Sometimes a symbol is connected with one of the characters. For example, in "The Scarlet Ibis," you will see similarities between one character and an exotic bird called an ibis. Understanding symbols and their connections to characters can deepen your understanding of a story.

The **theme** is the central idea of a work of literature. Usually, the author does not come right out and tell you what the theme is. When you are looking for the theme, think about all the parts of a work, including symbols. Then make an educated guess about the theme.

READING FOCUS: ANALYZING DETAILS

In most stories, you will find **details** that describe characters, plot, and setting. Some details may seem unimportant at first, but you may find that they have more meaning as you continue to read.

As you read "The Scarlet Ibis," keep track of the details. When you have finished collecting details, review them to see what deeper levels of the story they help reveal. Try making a chart like the one below to help you.

Story Details	Larger Meanings
When the narrator thinks about the past, he remembers someone named Doodle.	This may mean that Doodle is not here anymore.
The family kept a coffin in the barn.	The thought of death was always around.

VOCABULARY

imminent (IHM uh nuhnt) *adj.*: near; about to happen.

iridescent (IHR uh DEHS uhnt) *adj.*: rainbowlike; displaying a shifting range of colors.

infallibility (IHN FAL uh BIHL uh TEE) *n.*: inability to make a mistake.

doggedness (DAWG ihd nihs) *n.*: stubbornness; persistence.

reiterated (REE IHT uh RAY tuhd) *v.*: repeated.

mar (MAHR) *v.*: damage; spoil.

SKILLS FOCUS

Literary Skills Understand symbols; understand theme.

Reading Skills Analyze details.

The Scarlet Ibis

By James Hurst

INTO THE STORY

The title of this story, "The Scarlet Ibis," refers to an exotic tropical bird. The scarlet ibis is a medium-sized bird found mostly in South America. Scarlet ibises tend to travel in flocks. Except for its black wingtips, the scarlet ibis is entirely red. The bird gets its beautiful color from the pigment in the food it eats. As the ibis grows older, its color becomes even more intense. The story "The Scarlet Ibis" takes place in the American South in 1918, the year World War I ended. Although the war is being fought far from the peaceful Southern setting of the story, the characters are aware of the deaths that are happening there.

It was in the clove of seasons, summer was dead but autumn had not yet been born, that the ibis lit in the bleeding tree. The flower garden was stained with rotting brown magnolia petals, and ironweeds grew rank[1] amid the purple phlox. The five o'clocks by the chimney still marked time, but the oriole nest in the elm was untenanted and rocked back and forth like an empty cradle. The last graveyard flowers were blooming, and their smell drifted across the cotton field and through every room of our house, speaking softly the names of our dead. **A**

It's strange that all this is still so clear to me, now that that summer has long since fled and time has had its way. A grindstone stands where the bleeding tree stood, just outside the kitchen door, and now if an oriole sings in the elm, its song seems to die up in the leaves, a silvery dust. The flower garden is prim, the house a gleaming white, and the pale fence across the yard stands straight and spruce. But sometimes (like right now), as I sit in the cool, green-draped parlor, the grindstone begins to

---

A **HERE'S HOW**

Reading Focus

As I read the first paragraph, I notice a lot of **details**. It looks like many of them have something to do with death: summer was dead, magnolia petals were rotting, and the smell of graveyard flowers brought to mind the names of our dead. These details may have a larger meaning. I will keep them in mind as I continue reading the story.

---

1. Something **rank** (RANGK) is thick and wild. Rank can also mean "smelly."

"The Scarlet Ibis" by James R. Hurst from *The Atlantic Monthly,* July 1960. Copyright © 1960 by **James R. Hurst**. Reproduced by permission of the author.

A HERE'S HOW

Literary Focus
The first two paragraphs talk about an ibis, which is a kind of bird, and also introduces a character named Doodle. I wonder if the ibis is going to be a **symbol** for Doodle somehow? I am going to watch for evidence that supports this idea as I read.

B HERE'S HOW

Vocabulary
I am not sure what *shriveled* means. I can picture an old man as being wrinkled, but I am just not sure if "wrinkled" is a good definition for *shriveled*. I checked my dictionary, and it says *shriveled* means "shrunken" and "wrinkled," so I was right.

C YOUR TURN

Reading Focus
As you are **analyzing details**, what larger meaning do you think it might have when the narrator says William Armstrong is a name that "sounds good only on a tombstone"?

_____
_____
_____
_____

© James Randklev/Photographer's Choice/Getty Images

turn, and time with all its changes is ground away—and I remember Doodle. **A**

Doodle was just about the craziest brother a boy ever had. Of course, he wasn't a crazy crazy like old Miss Leedie, who was in love with President Wilson and wrote him a letter every day, but was a nice crazy, like someone you meet in your dreams. He was born when I was six and was, from the outset, a disappointment. He seemed all head, with a tiny body which was red and shriveled like an old man's. **B** Everybody thought he was going to die—everybody except Aunt Nicey, who had delivered him. She said he would live because he was born in a caul[2] and cauls were made from Jesus' nightgown. Daddy had Mr. Heath, the carpenter, build a little mahogany coffin for him. But he didn't die, and when he was three months old, Mama and Daddy decided they might as well name him. They named him William Armstrong, which was like tying a big tail on a small kite. Such a name sounds good only on a tombstone. **C**

---

2. A **caul** (KAWL) is a thin, skinlike material that sometimes covers a baby's head at birth.

114 The Scarlet Ibis

I thought myself pretty smart at many things, like holding my breath, running, jumping, or climbing the vines in Old Woman Swamp, and I wanted more than anything else someone to race to Horsehead Landing, someone to box with, and someone to perch with in the top fork of the great pine behind the barn, where across the fields and swamps you could see the sea. I wanted a brother. But Mama, crying, told me that even if William Armstrong lived, he would never do these things with me. He might not, she sobbed, even be "all there." He might, as long as he lived, lie on the rubber sheet in the center of the bed in the front bedroom where the white marquisette[3] curtains billowed out in the afternoon sea breeze, rustling like palmetto fronds.[4]

It was bad enough having an invalid brother, but having one who possibly was not all there was unbearable, so I began to make plans to kill him by smothering him with a pillow. However, one afternoon as I watched him, my head poked between the iron posts of the foot of the bed, he looked straight at me and grinned. I skipped through the rooms, down the echoing halls, shouting, "Mama, he smiled. He's all there! He's all there!" and he was. **D**

D QUICK CHECK
Why is the narrator so happy that his brother smiled at him?

IN OTHER WORDS The narrator clearly recalls a scene from his childhood—and his younger brother William, who is known as Doodle. When Doodle was born, no one thought he would survive. Even if he did live, he might be mentally and physically disabled. The narrator is very disappointed in his new brother. One day, however, Doodle smiles at him. The narrator realizes that the baby might be mentally aware and healthy after all.

When he was two, if you laid him on his stomach, he began to try to move himself, straining terribly. The doctor said that with his weak heart this strain would probably kill him, but it didn't. Trembling, he'd push himself up, turning first red, then

---

3. **Marquisette** (MAHR kuh ZEHT) is a thin, netlike fabric.
4. **Palmetto fronds** are the fanlike leaves of a palm tree.

The Scarlet Ibis 115

A LITERARY ANALYSIS

What can you learn about Doodle's character from this description of how he learned to crawl?

B HERE'S HOW

Vocabulary

I see in my dictionary that *burden* can mean either "something that is carried" or "something worrisome or oppressive." Even though the narrator carries Doodle in his cart, I think the second meaning makes most sense here.

---

a soft purple, and finally collapse back onto the bed like an old worn-out doll. I can still see Mama watching him, her hand pressed tight across her mouth, her eyes wide and unblinking. But he learned to crawl (it was his third winter), and we brought him out of the front bedroom, putting him on the rug before the fireplace. For the first time he became one of us. **A**

As long as he lay all the time in bed, we called him William Armstrong, even though it was formal and sounded as if we were referring to one of our ancestors, but with his creeping around on the deerskin rug and beginning to talk, something had to be done about his name. It was I who renamed him. When he crawled, he crawled backward, as if he were in reverse and couldn't change gears. If you called him, he'd turn around as if he were going in the other direction, then he'd back right up to you to be picked up. Crawling backward made him look like a doodlebug[5] so I began to call him Doodle, and in time even Mama and Daddy thought it was a better name than William Armstrong. Only Aunt Nicey disagreed. She said caul babies should be treated with special respect since they might turn out to be saints. Renaming my brother was perhaps the kindest thing I ever did for him, because nobody expects much from someone called Doodle.

Although Doodle learned to crawl, he showed no signs of walking, but he wasn't idle. He talked so much that we all quit listening to what he said. It was about this time that Daddy built him a go-cart, and I had to pull him around. At first I just paraded him up and down the piazza,[6] but then he started crying to be taken out into the yard and it ended up by my having to lug him wherever I went. If I so much as picked up my cap, he'd start crying to go with me, and Mama would call from wherever she was, "Take Doodle with you."

He was a burden in many ways. **B** The doctor had said that he mustn't get too excited, too hot, too cold, or too tired and that

---

5. A **doodlebug** (DOO DUHL BUHG) is a type of insect that moves backward.
6. A **piazza** (PEE AZ UH) is a large covered porch.

116   The Scarlet Ibis

he must always be treated gently. A long list of don'ts went with him, all of which I ignored once we got out of the house. To discourage his coming with me, I'd run with him across the ends of the cotton rows and careen him around corners on two wheels. **C** Sometimes I accidentally turned him over, but he never told Mama. His skin was very sensitive, and he had to wear a big straw hat whenever he went out. When the going got rough and he had to cling to the sides of the go-cart, the hat slipped all the way down over his ears. He was a sight. Finally, I could see I was licked. Doodle was my brother, and he was going to cling to me forever, no matter what I did, so I dragged him across the burning cotton field to share with him the only beauty I knew, Old Woman Swamp. I pulled the go-cart through the sawtooth fern, down into the green dimness where the palmetto fronds whispered by the stream. I lifted him out and set him down in the soft rubber grass beside a tall pine. His eyes were round with wonder as he gazed about him, and his little hands began to stroke the rubber grass. Then he began to cry.

"For heaven's sake, what's the matter?" I asked, annoyed.

"It's so pretty," he said. "So pretty, pretty, pretty." **D**

After that day Doodle and I often went down into Old Woman Swamp. I would gather wildflowers, wild violets, honeysuckle, yellow jasmine, snakeflowers, and waterlilies, and with wire grass we'd weave them into necklaces and crowns. We'd bedeck ourselves with our handiwork and loll about thus beautified, beyond the touch of the everyday world. Then when the slanted rays of the sun burned orange in the tops of the pines, we'd drop our jewels into the stream and watch them float away toward the sea.

IN OTHER WORDS The baby does not die. With great effort, he learns to crawl. Because of his awkward movements, the narrator calls the baby Doodle. The narrator has to take his brother along wherever he goes. At first he is unhappy, but then he takes him to a beautiful swamp. Doodle loves it there, and they return often and spend time there together.

C YOUR TURN

Vocabulary

In line 96, the narrator says he would *careen* Doodle "around corners on two wheels." What part of speech is *careen*? By looking at the sentence, what do you think the word means?

_____

_____

D HERE'S HOW

Reading Focus

I am **analyzing details** about Doodle's reaction to going to the swamp. He reacts with his eyes, his hands, by crying, and by saying how pretty it is. I think the larger meaning is that Doodle loves life and the world around him.

The Scarlet Ibis

A YOUR TURN

Vocabulary

Read lines 125–127 to find clues that might give away the meaning of the word *casket*. What do you think a synonym, or word with the same meaning, might be for *casket*?

_____
_____

B YOUR TURN

Vocabulary

Use a dictionary to find the meaning of *sullenly*. Why do you think Doodle answered *sullenly*?

_____
_____
_____
_____

C LITERARY ANALYSIS

Why do you think Doodle is afraid of being left alone with the coffin? How does his fear of the coffin here connect to his almost dying when he was very young?

_____
_____
_____
_____

There is within me (and with sadness I have watched it in others) a knot of cruelty borne by the stream of love, much as our blood sometimes bears the seed of our destruction, and at times I was mean to Doodle. One day I took him up to the barn loft and showed him his casket, telling him how we all had believed he would die. **A** It was covered with a film of Paris green[7] sprinkled to kill the rats, and screech owls had built a nest inside it.

Doodle studied the mahogany box for a long time, then 130 said, "It's not mine."

"It is," I said. "And before I'll help you down from the loft, you're going to have to touch it."

"I won't touch it," he said sullenly. **B**

"Then I'll leave you here by yourself," I threatened, and made as if I were going down.

Doodle was frightened of being left. "Don't go leave me, Brother," he cried, and he leaned toward the coffin. His hand, trembling, reached out, and when he touched the casket, he screamed. **C** A screech owl flapped out of the box into our faces, 140 scaring us and covering us with Paris green. Doodle was paralyzed, so I put him on my shoulder and carried him down the ladder, and even when we were outside in the bright sunshine, he clung to me, crying, "Don't leave me. Don't leave me."

IN OTHER WORDS One day the narrator does a mean thing to his brother. He shows Doodle the casket that was made for him when he was a baby. He forces Doodle to touch it by threatening to leave him alone. The idea of being left alone frightens Doodle terribly.

When Doodle was five years old, I was embarrassed at having a brother of that age who couldn't walk, so I set out to teach him. We were down in Old Woman Swamp and it was spring and the sick-sweet smell of bay flowers hung everywhere like a mournful song. "I'm going to teach you to walk, Doodle," I said.

---

7. **Paris green** is a poisonous green powder used to kill insects.

He was sitting comfortably on the soft grass, leaning back against the pine. "Why?" he asked.

I hadn't expected such an answer. "So I won't have to haul you around all the time."

"I can't walk, Brother," he said.

"Who says so?" I demanded.

"Mama, the doctor—everybody."

"Oh, you can walk," I said, and I took him by the arms and stood him up. He collapsed onto the grass like a half-empty flour sack. It was as if he had no bones in his little legs.

"Don't hurt me, Brother," he warned.

"Shut up. I'm not going to hurt you. I'm going to teach you to walk." I heaved him up again, and again he collapsed.

This time he did not lift his face up out of the rubber grass. "I just can't do it. Let's make honeysuckle wreaths."

"Oh yes you can, Doodle," I said. "All you got to do is try. Now come on," and I hauled him up once more.

It seemed so hopeless from the beginning that it's a miracle I didn't give up. But all of us must have something or someone to be proud of, and Doodle had become mine. I did not know then that pride is a wonderful, terrible thing, a seed that bears two vines, life and death. Every day that summer we went to the pine beside the stream of Old Woman Swamp, and I put him on his feet at least a hundred times each afternoon. Occasionally I too became discouraged because it didn't seem as if he was trying, and I would say, "Doodle, don't you *want* to learn to walk?"

He'd nod his head, and I'd say, "Well, if you don't keep trying, you'll never learn." Then I'd paint for him a picture of us as old men, white-haired, him with a long white beard and me still pulling him around in the go-cart. This never failed to make him try again.

Finally, one day, after many weeks of practicing, he stood alone for a few seconds. When he fell, I grabbed him in my arms and hugged him, our laughter pealing through the swamp like a ringing bell. Now we knew it could be done. Hope no longer hid in the dark palmetto thicket but perched like a cardinal in the

---

D YOUR TURN

Literary Focus

From what you have read so far, which do you think might be a **theme** of this story?
a) Sick children never get better.
b) Pride and cruelty hurt the ones we love the most.
c) Little brothers cause nothing but trouble.

A HERE'S HOW

Vocabulary

I looked up *imminent* in the dictionary, and the definition said "near, or about to happen." Using that definition, I can restate the phrase "With success so *imminent*" in my own words. I think the phrase means this: Because we were very close to Doodle learning to walk.

B YOUR TURN

Vocabulary

Knowing what you do about the narrator's and Doodle's surprise, what do you think the word *spectacular* means? Write your definition below and check your answer in a dictionary.

_____

_____

---

lacy toothbrush tree, brilliantly visible. "Yes, yes," I cried, and he cried it too, and the grass beneath us was soft and the smell of the swamp was sweet.

With success so imminent, we decided not to tell anyone until he could actually walk. **A** Each day, barring rain, we sneaked into Old Woman Swamp, and by cotton-picking time Doodle was ready to show what he could do. He still wasn't able to walk far, but we could wait no longer. Keeping a nice secret is very hard to do, like holding your breath. We chose to reveal all on October eighth, Doodle's sixth birthday, and for weeks ahead we mooned around the house, promising everybody a most spectacular surprise. **B** Aunt Nicey said that, after so much talk, if we produced anything less tremendous than the Resurrection,[8] she was going to be disappointed.

At breakfast on our chosen day, when Mama, Daddy, and Aunt Nicey were in the dining room, I brought Doodle to the door in the go-cart just as usual and had them turn their backs, making them cross their hearts and hope to die if they peeked. I helped Doodle up, and when he was standing alone I let them look. There wasn't a sound as Doodle walked slowly across the room and sat down at his place at the table. Then Mama began to cry and ran over to him, hugging him and kissing him. Daddy hugged him too, so I went to Aunt Nicey, who was thanks-praying in the doorway, and began to waltz her around. We danced together quite well until she came down on my big toe with her brogans,[9] hurting me so badly I thought I was crippled for life.

Doodle told them it was I who had taught him to walk, so everyone wanted to hug me, and I began to cry.

"What are you crying for?" asked Daddy, but I couldn't answer. They did not know that I did it for myself; that pride, whose slave I was, spoke to me louder than all their voices; and

---

8. The **Resurrection** refers to the Christian belief in the rising of Jesus from the dead after his burial.
9. **Brogans** (BROH guhnz) are heavy ankle-high shoes.

120 The Scarlet Ibis

© Christie's Images/The Bridgeman Art Library International

that Doodle walked only because I was ashamed of having a crippled brother. **C**

IN OTHER WORDS The narrator is embarrassed about Doodle and decides to teach him to walk. It takes a long time for Doodle to learn, but they keep the plan a secret until he turns six. Then Doodle walks in front of the whole family, who are amazed and happy. The narrator is not happy, though. He realizes that he helped Doodle only because of his own negative feelings about his brother.

220 Within a few months Doodle had learned to walk well and his go-cart was put up in the barn loft (it's still there) beside his little mahogany coffin. Now, when we roamed off together, resting often, we never turned back until our destination had been reached, and to help pass the time, we took up lying. **D** From the beginning Doodle was a terrible liar, and he got me in the habit. Had anyone stopped to listen to us, we would have been sent off to Dix Hill.

C **QUICK CHECK**

Why does the narrator cry when Doodle shows he can walk?

_____
_____
_____
_____

D **HERE'S HOW**

Vocabulary

In line 221 the two brothers *roamed* together. Since Doodle's cart is put away, I think *roamed* must mean "walked." I checked my dictionary and I was on the right track. *Roamed* means "wandered," or "went from place to place without a direction."

The Scarlet Ibis 121

A YOUR TURN

Vocabulary

Something *iridescent* is like a rainbow. It shows an ever-changing range of different colors. What is being described as *iridescent* in lines 233–236?

_____

_____

B YOUR TURN

Language Coach

Practicing the pronunciations of new words can improve your **oral fluency**. On the line below, write out the separate syllables in the word *infallibility*. Practice pronouncing this word until you feel confident using it in conversation.

_____

My lies were scary, involved, and usually pointless, but Doodle's were twice as crazy. People in his stories all had wings and flew wherever they wanted to go. His favorite lie was about 230 a boy named Peter who had a pet peacock with a ten-foot tail. Peter wore a golden robe that glittered so brightly that when he walked through the sunflowers they turned away from the sun to face him. When Peter was ready to go to sleep, the peacock spread his magnificent tail, enfolding the boy gently like a closing go-to-sleep flower, burying him in the gloriously iridescent, rustling vortex.[10] **A** Yes, I must admit it. Doodle could beat me lying.

Doodle and I spent lots of time thinking about our future. We decided that when we were grown, we'd live in Old Woman 240 Swamp and pick dog's-tongue[11] for a living. Beside the stream, he planned, we'd build us a house of whispering leaves and the swamp birds would be our chickens. All day long (when we weren't gathering dog's-tongue) we'd swing through the cypresses on the rope vines, and if it rained we'd huddle beneath an umbrella tree and play stickfrog. Mama and Daddy could come and live with us if they wanted to. He even came up with the idea that he could marry Mama and I could marry Daddy. Of course, I was old enough to know this wouldn't work out, but the picture he painted was so beautiful and serene that all I could do was 250 whisper yes, yes.

IN OTHER WORDS Doodle and the narrator spent a lot of time together in the swamp. They told each other fantastic stories and made plans for the future.

Once I had succeeded in teaching Doodle to walk, I began to believe in my own infallibility and I prepared a terrific development program for him, unknown to Mama and Daddy, of course. **B** I would teach him to run, to swim, to climb trees, and to fight. He, too, now believed in my infallibility, so we set the

---

10. A **vortex** (VAWR tehks) is something similar to a whirlpool.
11. **Dog's-tongue** is another name for wild vanilla.

122 The Scarlet Ibis

deadline for these accomplishments less than a year away, when, it had been decided, Doodle could start to school.

That winter we didn't make much progress, for I was in school and Doodle suffered from one bad cold after another. But when spring came, rich and warm, we raised our sights again. Success lay at the end of summer like a pot of gold, and our campaign got off to a good start. On hot days, Doodle and I went down to Horsehead Landing, and I gave him swimming lessons or showed him how to row a boat. Sometimes we descended into the cool greenness of Old Woman Swamp and climbed the rope vines or boxed scientifically beneath the pine where he had learned to walk. Promise hung about us like leaves, and wherever we looked, ferns unfurled and birds broke into song.

That summer, the summer of 1918, was blighted.[12] In May and June there was no rain and the crops withered, curled up, then died under the thirsty sun. One morning in July a hurricane came out of the east, tipping over the oaks in the yard and splitting the limbs of the elm trees. That afternoon it roared back out of the west, blew the fallen oaks around, snapping their roots and tearing them out of the earth like a hawk at the entrails[13] of a chicken. Cotton bolls were wrenched from the stalks and lay like green walnuts in the valleys between the rows, while the cornfield leaned over uniformly so that the tassels touched the ground. Doodle and I followed Daddy out into the cotton field, where he stood, shoulders sagging, surveying the ruin. When his chin sank down onto his chest, we were frightened, and Doodle slipped his hand into mine. **C** Suddenly Daddy straightened his shoulders, raised a giant knuckly fist, and with a voice that seemed to rumble out of the earth itself began cursing heaven, hell, the weather, and the Republican party.[14] Doodle and I, prodding each other and giggling, went back to the house, knowing that everything would be all right.

---

12. Something that is **blighted** (BLY TIHD) cannot grow. It suffers from conditions that destroy or prevent growth.
13. **Entrails** (EHN TRAYLZ) are guts or other inner organs of the body.
14. At this time most southern farmers were loyal Democrats and opposed the **Republican party**.

C YOUR TURN

Reading Focus

Analyze the details in lines 271–282. Then state what the author is getting at by including those details.

_____
_____
_____
_____

The Scarlet Ibis 123

A HERE'S HOW

Reading Focus

This is the second time the story has mentioned the **detail** that the seasons are changing. I remember from the beginning of the story that summer is ending and autumn is beginning. I know that when summer ends, flowers and gardens die and leaves fall off the trees. This may have a larger meaning that death and dying are important to the story.

And during that summer, strange names were heard through the house: Château-Thierry, Amiens, Soissons, and in her blessing at the supper table, Mama once said, "And bless the Pearsons, whose boy Joe was lost in Belleau Wood."[15]

IN OTHER WORDS After Doodle learns to walk, the narrator wants to teach him more things. In the summer, he starts teaching his little brother to swim. That summer was a bad time. A terrible storm destroyed the crops, and many men were dying overseas in World War I.

So we came to that clove of seasons. **A** School was only a few weeks away, and Doodle was far behind schedule. He could barely clear the ground when climbing up the rope vines, and his swimming was certainly not passable. We decided to double our efforts, to make that last drive and reach our pot of gold. I made him swim until he turned blue and row until he couldn't lift an oar. Wherever we went, I purposely walked fast, and although he kept up, his face turned red and his eyes became glazed. Once, he could go no further, so he collapsed on the ground and began to cry.

"Aw, come on, Doodle," I urged. "You can do it. Do you want to be different from everybody else when you start school?"

"Does it make any difference?"

"It certainly does," I said. "Now, come on," and I helped him up.

As we slipped through the dog days,[16] Doodle began to look feverish, and Mama felt his forehead, asking him if he felt ill. At night he didn't sleep well, and sometimes he had nightmares, crying out until I touched him and said, "Wake up, Doodle. Wake up."

---

15. **Château-Thierry** (SHA TOH TEE ER EE), **Amiens** (AH MYAN), **Soissons** (SEAH SUHN), and **Belleau** (BEH LOH) **Wood** were all World War I battle sites in France.
16. The **dog days** are hot days in July and August. They are named after the Dog Star (Sirius), which rises and sets with the sun during this period of the year.

124 The Scarlet Ibis

IN OTHER WORDS It is now the time the narrator remembered at the beginning of the story. The seasons are changing. Doodle is working hard to get stronger, but he is not doing well. He looks sick and has bad dreams at night.

It was Saturday noon, just a few days before school was to start. I should have already admitted defeat, but my pride wouldn't let me. **B** The excitement of our program had now been gone for weeks, but still we kept on with a tired doggedness. **C** It was too late to turn back, for we had both wandered too far into a net of expectations and had left no crumbs behind.

Daddy, Mama, Doodle, and I were seated at the dining-room table having lunch. It was a hot day, with all the windows and doors open in case a breeze should come. In the kitchen Aunt Nicey was humming softly. After a long silence, Daddy spoke. "It's so calm, I wouldn't be surprised if we had a storm this afternoon."

"I haven't heard a rain frog," said Mama, who believed in signs, as she served the bread around the table.

"I did," declared Doodle. "Down in the swamp."

"He didn't," I said contrarily.

"You did, eh?" said Daddy, ignoring my denial.

"I certainly did," Doodle reiterated, scowling at me over the top of his iced-tea glass, and we were quiet again. **D**

Suddenly, from out in the yard came a strange croaking noise. Doodle stopped eating, with a piece of bread poised ready for his mouth, his eyes popped round like two blue buttons. "What's that?" he whispered.

I jumped up, knocking over my chair, and had reached the door when Mama called, "Pick up the chair, sit down again, and say excuse me."

B **LITERARY ANALYSIS**

How us the narrator's pride affecting Doodle's training?

_____
_____
_____
_____

C **YOUR TURN**

Vocabulary

The brothers keep working with *doggedness* even though they are tired and no longer excited. Which of these meanings best fits *doggedness* as it is used in this sentence?
A) having to do with the dog days of summer
B) stubbornness
C) enthusiasm

D **HERE'S HOW**

Vocabulary

I am not sure what the word *reiterated* means, but I think I can figure it out. Doodle already said that he heard a rain frog in the swamp. When he *reiterated* that statement, he said it again. So I think *reiterated* probably means "to repeat something or say it again."

The Scarlet Ibis **125**

A HERE'S HOW

Reading Focus

I notice that in line 340, there is a **detail** of the setting that may be important. There is a "bleeding tree." The description of the tree as "bleeding" makes me wonder if someone is going to get hurt.

B YOUR TURN

Literary Focus

What **symbol** from the beginning of the story appears again at this point?

© age fotostock/SuperStock

By the time I had done this, Doodle had excused himself and had slipped out into the yard. He was looking up into the bleeding tree. **A** "It's a great big red bird!" he called. **B**

The bird croaked loudly again, and Mama and Daddy came out into the yard. We shaded our eyes with our hands against the hazy glare of the sun and peered up through the still leaves. On the topmost branch a bird the size of a chicken, with scarlet feathers and long legs, was perched precariously. Its wings hung down loosely, and as we watched, a feather dropped away and floated slowly down through the green leaves.

"It's not even frightened of us," Mama said.

"It looks tired," Daddy added. "Or maybe sick."

Doodle's hands were clasped at his throat, and I had never seen him stand still so long. "What is it?" he asked.

Daddy shook his head. "I don't know, maybe it's—"

At that moment the bird began to flutter, but the wings were uncoordinated, and amid much flapping and a spray of flying feathers, it tumbled down, bumping through the limbs of the bleeding tree and landing at our feet with a thud. Its long, graceful neck jerked twice into an S, then straightened out, and the bird was still. A white veil came over the eyes, and the long white beak unhinged. Its legs were crossed and its clawlike feet were delicately curved at rest. Even death did not mar its grace, for it lay on the earth like a broken vase of red flowers, and we stood around it, awed by its exotic beauty. **C**

"It's dead," Mama said.

"What is it?" Doodle repeated.

"Go bring me the bird book," said Daddy.

I ran into the house and brought back the bird book. As we watched, Daddy thumbed through its pages. "It's a scarlet ibis," he said, pointing to a picture. "It lives in the tropics—South America to Florida. A storm must have brought it here." **D**

Sadly, we all looked back at the bird. A scarlet ibis! How many miles it had traveled to die like this, in *our* yard, beneath the bleeding tree.

IN OTHER WORDS The family's Saturday lunch is interrupted by a strange noise. It is a beautiful and unusual red bird that has landed in a tree outside. As they watch it, the bird falls to the ground and dies. They look it up in a book and find that it is a scarlet ibis from very far away.

"Let's finish lunch," Mama said, nudging us back toward the dining room.

"I'm not hungry," said Doodle, and he knelt down beside the ibis.

"We've got peach cobbler for dessert," Mama tempted from the doorway.

Doodle remained kneeling. "I'm going to bury him." **E**

"Don't you dare touch him," Mama warned. "There's no telling what disease he might have had."

"All right," said Doodle. "I won't."

Daddy, Mama, and I went back to the dining-room table, but we watched Doodle through the open door. He took out a piece of string from his pocket and, without touching the ibis, looped one end around its neck. Slowly, while singing softly "Shall We Gather at the River," he carried the bird around to the

---

C YOUR TURN

Vocabulary

To *mar* something means to damage or spoil it. According to lines 360–362, what might have been expected to *mar* the ibis's beauty?

_____

_____

D QUICK CHECK

What is unusual about finding a scarlet ibis in the yard?

_____

_____

_____

_____

E LITERARY ANALYSIS

Why do you think Doodle feels so strongly about the ibis? Is there a connection between Doodle's own life and struggles and what the bird may have gone through?

_____

_____

_____

_____

The Scarlet Ibis 127

A YOUR TURN

Reading Focus
Underline **details** in lines 394–401 that suggest that Doodle is still upset.

B QUICK CHECK

Why do the brothers go to Horsehead Landing in lines 404–407?

_____
_____
_____

front yard and dug a hole in the flower garden, next to the petunia bed. Now we were watching him through the front window, but he didn't know it. His awkwardness at digging the hole with a shovel whose handle was twice as long as he was made us laugh, and we covered our mouths with our hands so he wouldn't hear.

When Doodle came into the dining room, he found us seriously eating our cobbler. He was pale and lingered just inside the screen door. "Did you get the scarlet ibis buried?" asked Daddy.

Doodle didn't speak but nodded his head.

"Go wash your hands, and then you can have some peach cobbler," said Mama.

"I'm not hungry," he said. **A**

"Dead birds is bad luck," said Aunt Nicey, poking her head from the kitchen door. "Specially *red* dead birds!"

IN OTHER WORDS Doodle is upset at the death of the ibis. He refuses to finish his lunch and insists on burying it. No one else seems to feel the same way or helps him.

As soon as I had finished eating, Doodle and I hurried off to Horsehead Landing. Time was short, and Doodle still had a long way to go if he was going to keep up with the other boys when he started school. **B** The sun, gilded with the yellow cast of autumn, still burned fiercely, but the dark green woods through which we passed were shady and cool. When we reached the landing, Doodle said he was too tired to swim, so we got into a skiff and floated down the creek with the tide. Far off in the marsh a rail was scolding, and over on the beach locusts were singing in the myrtle trees. Doodle did not speak and kept his head turned away, letting one hand trail limply in the water.

After we had drifted a long way, I put the oars in place and made Doodle row back against the tide. Black clouds began to gather in the southwest, and he kept watching them, trying to pull the oars a little faster. When we reached Horsehead Landing,

128 The Scarlet Ibis

lightning was playing across half the sky and thunder roared out, hiding even the sound of the sea. The sun disappeared and darkness descended, almost like night. Flocks of marsh crows flew by, heading inland to their roosting trees, and two egrets, squawking, arose from the oyster-rock shallows and careened away.

Doodle was both tired and frightened, and when he stepped from the skiff he collapsed onto the mud, sending an armada[17] of fiddler crabs rustling off into the marsh grass. I helped him up, and as he wiped the mud off his trousers, he smiled at me ashamedly. He had failed and we both knew it, so we started back home, racing the storm. We never spoke (what are the words that can solder[18] cracked pride?), but I knew he was watching me, watching for a sign of mercy. The lightning was near now, and from fear he walked so close behind me he kept stepping on my heels. The faster I walked, the faster he walked, so I began to run. The rain was coming, roaring through the pines, and then, like a bursting Roman candle, a gum tree ahead of us was shattered by a bolt of lightning. When the deafening peal of thunder had died, and in the moment before the rain arrived, I heard Doodle, who had fallen behind, cry out, "Brother, Brother, don't leave me! Don't leave me!" **C**

YOUR TURN

Reading Focus
What **details** about the setting appear in this paragraph? What larger meaning do you think they might have?

IN OTHER WORDS Doodle is tired, but he goes out on the water with his brother and practices rowing. By the time they reach shore, Doodle is completely exhausted, and a terrible storm is beginning. The brothers run for home, but Doodle falls behind and becomes frightened.

The knowledge that Doodle's and my plans had come to naught was bitter, and that streak of cruelty within me awakened. I ran as fast as I could, leaving him far behind with a wall of rain dividing us. The drops stung my face like nettles, and the wind

---

17. An **armada** (AHR MAH DUH) is a group. *Armada* is generally used to mean a fleet, or group, of warships.
18. To **solder** (SOD UHR) means to patch or repair something. Solder is a mixture of metals melted and used to repair metal parts.

The Scarlet Ibis **129**

> **A** **HERE'S HOW**
>
> **Literary Focus**
>
> If I compare the description of Doodle here to the description of the ibis, there are many similarities. The red color, the long neck, and the bent knees all are like the ibis. This makes me even more sure that the ibis is a **symbol** of Doodle in this story.

> **B** **YOUR TURN**
>
> **Literary Focus**
>
> Think about everything you know about the story, including **symbols**. Is the following statement a **theme** for this story? Write Yes or No on the line that follows it.
> *We should be careful to protect and be kind to the special lives we encounter, because it is easy to lose them if we are careless or cruel.*
>
> _____

flared the wet, glistening leaves of the bordering trees. Soon I could hear his voice no more.

I hadn't run too far before I became tired, and the flood of childish spite evanesced[19] as well. I stopped and waited for Doodle. The sound of rain was everywhere, but the wind had died and it fell straight down in parallel paths like ropes hanging from the sky. As I waited, I peered through the downpour, but no one came. Finally I went back and found him huddled beneath a red nightshade bush beside the road. He was sitting on the ground, his face buried in his arms, which were resting on his drawn-up knees. "Let's go, Doodle," I said.

He didn't answer, so I placed my hand on his forehead and lifted his head. Limply, he fell backward onto the earth. He had been bleeding from the mouth, and his neck and the front of his shirt were stained a brilliant red.

"Doodle! Doodle!" I cried, shaking him, but there was no answer but the ropy rain. He lay very awkwardly, with his head thrown far back, making his vermilion[20] neck appear unusually long and slim. His little legs, bent sharply at the knees, had never before seemed so fragile, so thin. **A**

I began to weep, and the tear-blurred vision in red before me looked very familiar. "Doodle!" I screamed above the pounding storm, and threw my body to the earth above his. For a long, long time, it seemed forever, I lay there crying, sheltering my fallen scarlet ibis from the heresy[21] of rain. **B**

> **IN OTHER WORDS** The narrator is upset about Doodle's weakness. He feels mean and runs too fast for his younger brother to catch up. When Doodle does not appear, the narrator eventually returns to look for him. The narrator finds the little boy curled under a bush. Doodle does not move. He is covered in blood. It seems that he has died. The narrator cries and holds his brother, whom he calls his scarlet ibis.

---

19. **Evanesced** (EHV uh NEHST) means faded away or disappeared.
20. **Vermilion** (VUHR MIHL yuhn) is a bright red color.
21. Here, **heresy** (HEHR uh see) refers to mockery. In general, heresy usually means "denial of what is commonly believed to be true" or "rejection of a church's teaching."

Applying Your Skills

The Scarlet Ibis

LITERARY FOCUS: SYMBOLS AND THEME

DIRECTIONS: Below, write an explanation in your own words of how the scarlet ibis is a **symbol** for Doodle in the story.

_____
_____
_____

READING FOCUS: ANALYZING DETAILS

DIRECTIONS: Each **detail** below is matched with a larger meaning. Decide if that larger meaning belongs with the detail. If the detail and meaning match, put a check mark on the line. If the detail and meaning do not match, put an X on the line.

Detail	Meaning
Mama told me that William Armstrong would never run and jump with me. He might never be healthy.	Sick people are not worth caring about. They are just a burden on others. _____
I wanted him to stop asking to come with me. So I'd run with him across cotton rows and careen him around corners on two wheels.	Doodle's brother does not always treat him with the care he deserves. _____
The war had begun. In her blessing at the supper table, Mama once said, "And bless the Pearsons, whose boy Joe was lost in Belleau Wood."	The war does not matter at all to families in this story. _____

Word Box

imminent
iridescent
infallibility
doggedness
reiterated
mar

VOCABULARY REVIEW

DIRECTIONS: Answer the questions below.

1. When do characters in this story show _doggedness_? _____
_____

2. Early in the story the narrator has a feeling of _infallibility_. Is he actually _infallible_?
_____

The Scarlet Ibis   131

Preparing to Read

The Gift of the Magi

Based on the story by O. Henry

LITERARY FOCUS: SITUATIONAL IRONY

What would you think of a movie that was completely predictable? You would probably think it was pretty boring. Stories by good writers are often very *unpredictable*. When something happens that is the opposite of what you expected, it is called **situational irony**. Situational irony reminds us that many things in life turn out differently from what we expect.

READING FOCUS: ANALYZING DETAILS

To bring stories to life, writers carefully choose **details** to make characters, settings, and events seem more real. The writer can use these details to *show* rather than *tell*. For example, a writer may describe an apple as being red and shiny. This *shows* you what the apple looks like, as opposed to just *telling* you.

VOCABULARY

Look for these words and their context as you read the selection.

stingy (STIHN JEE) *adj.:* too careful with money; cheap.

expenses (IHK SPEHS SIHZ) *n.:* costs.

collected (KUH LEHK TIHD) *v.:* regained control of.

INTO THE STORY

O. Henry's real name was William Sydney Porter. He worked as a bank teller in Austin, Texas, until he was accused of stealing $1,000 from the bank. Porter was arrested, tried, and sentenced to five years in prison. No one knows whether he really stole the money. Porter served three years of his sentence, and he wrote more than a dozen stories while in prison. He left prison in 1901 and moved to New York. He wrote about New York City and the people who lived there until his death in 1910.

In this story, the Magi from the title are the "three wise men" from the Bible. According to the Bible, these three men brought gifts to the baby Jesus. These gifts are traditionally seen as the very first Christmas presents.

SKILLS FOCUS

Literary Skills
Understand situational irony.

Reading Skills
Analyze details.

The Gift of the Magi

Based on the story by O. Henry

Della had saved one dollar and eighty-seven cents. That was all. And sixty cents of it was in pennies. She had saved the pennies one and two at a time by bargaining with the grocer, the vegetable seller, and the butcher to lower their prices. At times, her cheeks had burned with shame, for she was certain these sellers thought she was stingy. **A** She counted her money three times. One dollar and eighty-seven cents. And the next day was Christmas. **B**

Della decided there was nothing she could do except flop down on the shabby little couch and cry. So she did.

Della and her husband lived in a furnished apartment costing $8 per week. It didn't exactly look like the home of a beggar, but it had no extras, either.

In the entrance hall below, there was a letterbox that a letter couldn't fit in and a doorbell that didn't ring. There was also a card with the name *"Mr. James Dillingham Young"* on it.

For a short time, Mr. James Dillingham Young had done well for himself, making $30 per week.[1] Now, his pay had shrunk to $20. With his pay cut, he'd lost his sense of place in the outside world. But whenever he came home, he was joyously greeted and hugged by his wife, Della. Which was all very good.

Della finished her crying and dried her cheeks. She stood by the window and looked out dully at a gray cat walking a gray fence in a gray backyard. **C** Tomorrow would be Christmas Day, and after all her saving, she had only $1.87 to buy Jim a present. There were always more expenses than she thought. She had spent many happy hours planning a gift for him, something fine and rare and perfect, something worthy of her special Jim.

Suddenly Della turned from the window and looked at herself in the tall, old mirror. Her eyes were shining brightly, but

---

1. **$30 per week:** equal to over $600 today.

A HERE'S HOW

Vocabulary

I do not know what the word *stingy* means. I see that Della's cheeks "burned with shame" for bargaining to get a lower price. Because Della was embarrassed, I think that *stingy* means "too careful with money," or "cheap."

B HERE'S HOW

Reading Focus

I see in the first paragraph that Della is very careful to save her money and not spend more than she has to. By **analyzing details**, the author shows me that Della really wants to save up some money. I will be sure to pay close attention to see what she is saving her money for.

C HERE'S HOW

Language Coach

I know that adding the suffix *-y* to the adjective *dull* creates the adverb *dully*. This alternate word form is called a **word derivation**.

The Gift of the Magi 133

A   YOUR TURN

Vocabulary

The word *collected* in line 40 can mean "gathered together" or "regained control of." What meaning does it have here?

_____

_____

B   LITERARY ANALYSIS

Pause at line 41. How does Della's selling her hair connect to her being careful to save money earlier in the story?

---

her face had lost its color within twenty seconds. Quickly she pulled down her hair and let it fall loosely around her.

Jim and Della were proud of two things, Jim's gold watch, which had been his father's and his grandfather's, and Della's hair. Della's beautiful, shiny hair now fell below her knees. A few of her tears splashed on the worn carpet.

But she put on her coat and hat and, with a brilliant sparkle still in her eyes, hurried out. She stopped at a shop with a sign that read "Madame Sofronie. Hair Goods of All Kinds." Della ran
40   up the flight of stairs. Panting, she collected herself and said to Madame Sofronie, "Will you buy my hair?" **A B**

"Let's have a look at it," said Madame.

Della let down her beautiful hair.

Madame lifted the mass of hair. "Twenty dollars," she said.

"Give it to me quickly," said Della.

© Harris Museum and Art Gallery, Preston, Lancashire, UK/Bridgeman Art Library

134   The Gift of the Magi

For two hours, Della searched for Jim's present. At last she found a platinum fob chain,[2] worthy of The Watch. It was like Jim—quiet and valuable.

She paid twenty-one dollars. With that chain, instead of the old leather strap he used now, Jim could proudly check the time in public.

At home, Della worked with her curling iron. After forty minutes, her head was covered with tiny curls. She studied herself in the mirror. "If Jim doesn't kill me right away," she said to herself, "he'll say I look like a chorus girl. But what could I do with a dollar and eighty-seven cents!"

When she heard him on the stairs, her face turned white for a minute. She whispered, "Please, God, make him think I am still pretty."

The door opened and Jim entered. His eyes fixed on Della. He did not show anger, surprise, disapproval, or horror. He had an expression she could not read.

Della went to hug him.

"Jim, darling," she cried, "don't look at me that way. I sold my hair because I couldn't have lived without giving you a Christmas present. It'll grow. You won't mind, will you?"

"You've cut your hair?" asked Jim.

"Cut it off and sold it. Don't you like me just as well, anyhow? I'm me without my hair."

"You say your hair is gone?" he said. He seemed stunned.

"It's sold. It's Christmas Eve. Be good to me, because I sold it for you. I love you dearly."

Jim came out of his trance and hugged Della.

"Don't mind me, Dell," he said. "You could cut or shave your hair any way you like and I wouldn't love you less. But if you unwrap that package, you may see why I was so surprised."

Della tore at the paper and string. She screamed for joy and then began crying. Jim rose to comfort her.

He had given her The Combs—the set of combs, side and back, that Della had wanted for a long, long time. They would

---

2. **fob chain:** short chain meant to be attached to a pocket watch.

YOUR TURN

Reading Focus

Analyze details in lines 60–70. Describe Jim's reaction to Della's haircut. What is the author showing you here?

A HERE'S HOW

Literary Focus

This must be what is called an **ironic situation**. Della really did not expect Jim to buy her the combs for her hair. This twist in the story caught me by surprise, too.

B HERE'S HOW

Literary Focus

Take another look at lines 91–101. Circle the sentence in this passage that provides the second **ironic situation** in the story.

have been perfect in her long hair. She had longed for them without ever believing she'd own them. And now they were hers, but the beautiful hair to wear them in was gone. **A**

She smiled at Jim. "My hair grows fast!"

And then Della cried, "Oh, oh!"

Jim hadn't seen his beautiful present yet. She held it out to him eagerly.

"Isn't it a dandy, Jim? You'll have to look at the time one hundred times a day now. Give me your watch. I want to see how the fob looks on it."

Jim didn't hand over the watch. "Dell," he said, "let's put away our Christmas presents. They're too nice to use right now. I sold the watch to get the money to buy your combs."

The Magi,[3] as you know, were wise men. They brought gifts to the baby Jesus. They were the first people to give Christmas presents. They were wise, and probably so were their gifts. Here you have read the story of two foolish children in an apartment. They unwisely gave up the greatest treasures of their house for each other. But of all who give and receive gifts, those like these two are wisest. Everywhere they are the wisest. They are the Magi. **B**

© Andrew Sadler/Alamy

---

3. **Magi** (MAY jy).

Applying Your Skills

The Gift of the Magi

LITERARY FOCUS: SITUATIONAL IRONY

DIRECTIONS: With **situational irony**, events turn out to be the opposite of what you may have expected. Authors use irony to surprise the reader. Write "Yes" after each quotation that contributed to the story's situational irony. Write "No" after each quotation if it did not.

1. Della, lines 71–72: "Be good to me, because I sold [my hair] for you." _____
2. Della, line 84: "My hair grows fast!" _____
3. Jim, line 93: "I sold the watch to get the money to buy your combs." _____

READING FOCUS: ANALYZING DETAILS

DIRECTIONS: Review the story and analyze, or examine and think about, its **details**. Notice in the chart below how one detail from the story has been analyzed. Complete the chart by selecting two more details O. Henry uses to offer deeper insights into his story. Then, analyze your details.

Story Details	Analysis of Details
Della looks out the window "dully at a gray cat walking a gray fence in a gray backyard."	Rather than just saying Della is sad, O. Henry uses vivid details to describe her dreary surroundings.
1.	
2.	

VOCABULARY REVIEW

Word Box
- stingy
- expenses
- collected

DIRECTIONS: Fill in each blank space with the correct vocabulary word from the Word Box.

1. Jim was in shock when he first saw Della's haircut, but he eventually _____ himself.
2. Della was not _____ when she spent over twenty dollars on Jim's present.
3. Jim's wages were barely enough to cover their living _____.

Preparing to Read

Three Readings from Einstein

INFORMATIONAL TEXT FOCUS: SYNTHESIZING SOURCES: WORKS BY ONE AUTHOR

When you read several works by the same author, it is helpful to **synthesize** sources. This means that you look for ways to **connect** the pieces together. When you **synthesize**, you use information from different sources to better understand an author's views. As you read these selections written by Albert Einstein, ask yourself:

- What is the author's purpose, or goal, in writing?
- How would I **compare** and **contrast** (or see what is the same and different in) what the writer is saying in each piece?
- How can I relate the ideas in each piece to what I already know about the author?

As you read, it may also be helpful to **paraphrase** the texts, or restate the author's ideas in your own words.

VOCABULARY

goodwill (GUD WIHL) *n.*: kind feeling.

radical (RAD UH KUHL) *adj.*: extreme; thorough.

INTO THE SELECTIONS

Albert Einstein (1879–1955) is one of the most important scientists in history. Einstein believed strongly in peace. However, in the years building up to World War II, he understood the dangers the world faced. He was born in Germany, but left in 1933 to come to the United States and escape the Nazi Party.

In 1939, Einstein wrote a letter to U.S. President Franklin D. Roosevelt, warning him that a powerful bomb could be developed from nuclear energy. Many people believed that Germany was already working on such an atomic bomb. Einstein helped the United States work to create an atomic bomb before any other country.

On August 6, 1945, the United States dropped the first atomic bomb ever to be used in a war. The target was Hiroshima, Japan. The use of this new weapon led to the end of World War II. The bomb killed thousands of people. Many others died later from illness caused by the bomb.

SKILLS FOCUS

Informational Text Skills
Synthesize content from several works by a single author dealing with a single issue.

WEAPONS OF THE SPIRIT

Based on an interview with George Sylvester Viereck from *Einstein on Peace* by Albert Einstein

It may not be possible to teach our children to stop fighting. I wouldn't even want people to stop fighting completely. Men should continue to fight, but only for the most important things. We should not have wars for prejudice and greed. People should fight with weapons of the spirit, not guns and tanks. **A**

Think of what a world we could build if the power we used for war was used instead to make life better! Just one tenth of the energy and money spent fighting in World War II would help people in every country to have better jobs, better homes, and better lives.

We must be prepared to make the same sacrifices for peace that we make for war. There is nothing that is more important or closer to my heart.

Nothing that I can do or say will change the universe. But maybe, by saying what I believe, I can help the greatest of all causes—goodwill among men and peace on earth. **B**

—1931

A HERE'S HOW

Reading Focus

I can relate what I read here to what I already learned about Einstein. I remember he believed in peace. In lines 2–4 he says people should not have wars for the wrong reasons. This may be an important point to help me understand his views.

B YOUR TURN

Vocabulary

Einstein calls *goodwill* among men the "greatest of all causes." The word *goodwill* is made up of two different smaller words. Draw a line between the two smaller words that are joined together in *goodwill*. Then, based on this and its use in the sentence, write a definition for *goodwill*.

_____
_____
_____

From "Einstein's Interview with George Sylvester Viereck" from *Einstein on Peace*, edited by Otto Nathan and Heinz Norden. Copyright © 1960 by Otto Nathan. Reproduced by permission of **The Albert Einstein Archives, the Hebrew University of Jerusalem, Israel.**

Letter to President Roosevelt, 1939

Based on the letter by Albert Einstein

A QUICK CHECK

Who is the "sir" addressed here?

_____
_____

B HERE'S HOW

Language Coach

My teacher says that the word *radium* came from the Latin word *radius*, meaning a "ray." *Radium* is defined as "a highly radioactive chemical element," so it sends out rays, and its Latin **word origin** makes sense.

C YOUR TURN

Reading Focus

How does the opening of this letter **contrast**, or differ, from the first paragraph of "Weapons of the Spirit," the previous selection?

_____
_____
_____

"Letter to President Roosevelt" from *Dr. Einstein's Warning to President Roosevelt* by Albert Einstein. Copyright © 1939 by Albert Einstein. Reproduced by permission of **The Albert Einstein Archives, The Hebrew University of Jerusalem, Israel.**

Sir: **A**

Some recent scientific work leads me to believe that uranium may become a new and important source of energy in the immediate future. Your administration needs to pay attention, and, if necessary, act quickly. I believe, therefore, that it is my duty to call your attention to the following facts and recommendations:

In the last four months it has become more likely that, very soon, a nuclear chain reaction could be set up in a large mass of uranium. Huge amounts of power and large quantities of new radium-like elements would be created. **B** This new possibility might also lead to the building of a new type of extremely powerful bombs. A single bomb of this type, delivered by boat and exploded in a port, could destroy the entire port and some of the surrounding area. Such bombs might be too heavy to be transported by air, however. **C**

The United States does not have much high-quality uranium. There is some good ore in Canada and Czechoslovakia. The most important source of uranium is the Belgian Congo.

You may want to start contact between the Administration and the physicists working on this project. If you give the task to someone you trust, he could keep different government departments informed. He could also recommend ways that the United States could get more uranium. He could raise private funds to speed up experimental work. He could also seek the help from industrial labs, which have the necessary equipment.

I understand Germany has stopped the sale of uranium from the Czechoslovakian mines. This may be because the German Under-Secretary of State is involved in uranium research taking place in Berlin.

Yours very truly,
Albert Einstein

On the Abolition of the Threat of War

from *Ideas and Opinions* by Albert Einstein

My part in producing the atomic bomb consisted in a single act: I signed a letter to President Roosevelt, pressing the need for experiments on a large scale in order to explore the possibilities for the production of an atomic bomb.

I was fully aware of the terrible danger to mankind in case this attempt succeeded. But the likelihood that the Germans were working on the same problem with a chance of succeeding forced me to this step. I could do nothing else although I have always been a convinced pacifist. To my mind, to kill in war is not a whit better than to commit ordinary murder. **D**

As long, however, as the nations are not resolved to abolish[1] war through common actions and to solve their conflicts and protect their interests by peaceful decisions on a legal basis, they feel compelled to prepare for war. They feel obliged to prepare all possible means, even the most detestable ones, so as not to be left behind in the general armament race.[2] This road necessarily leads to war, a war which under the present conditions means universal destruction.

IN OTHER WORDS Even though I wrote President Roosevelt a letter encouraging the production of the first atomic bomb, I am against war. The atomic bomb is a dangerous weapon, but it would have been more dangerous if the Germans had created one first. While I believe that nations should solve their problems peacefully, they seem more eager to prepare for war. But constantly creating more powerful weapons will eventually lead to our destruction.

---

1. **abolish** (UH BOL IHSH): put an end to. *Abolition* is the noun form of this word.
2. **armament race:** rivalry between hostile nations to build up larger and larger stores of weapons.

D YOUR TURN

Reading Focus
Thinking about the author's **purpose** can help you **synthesize** works by the same author. What **purpose** or goal do you think the author has in writing lines 5–10?

> **A** **HERE'S HOW**
>
> **Reading Focus**
> I can **compare and contrast** sources by the same author to help me **synthesize**. In lines 20–21 Einstein talks about abolishing, or eliminating, war completely. This is similar to the views he expresses about war and peace in "Weapons of the Spirit." In "Weapons of the Spirit," though, he says men should only fight for the most important things.
>
> **B** **LITERARY ANALYSIS**
>
> In this paragraph, Einstein holds up Mohandas Gandhi, a man who led a movement of nonviolent protest, as a role model. What does Einstein hope people will achieve using Gandhi's methods?
>
> _____
> _____
> _____
> _____

20 Under these circumstances the fight against means has no chance of success. Only the radical abolition of wars and of the threat of war can help. **A** This is what one has to work for. One has to be resolved not to let himself be forced to actions that run counter to this goal. This is a severe demand on an individual who is conscious[3] of his dependence on society. But it is not an impossible demand.

Gandhi,[4] the greatest political genius of our time, has pointed the way. He has shown of what sacrifices people are capable once they have found the right way. His work for the liberation of India is a living testimony[5] to the fact that a will governed by firm conviction is stronger than a seemingly invincible material power.[6] **B**

—1952

IN OTHER WORDS Our only chance of breaking this cycle is by getting rid of war completely. Everyone must work toward this goal, which will be difficult, but not impossible. The fact that Gandhi freed India from Great Britain through nonviolent means is proof that peace is possible. His example should be our inspiration.

---

3. **conscious** (KON SHUHS): aware.
4. **Ghandi** (GAHN DEE): Mohandas Gandhi (1869–1948) led the struggle for India's independence from Britain. He practiced the use of non-violent protest to achieve political goals.
5. **testimony** (TEHS TUH MOH NEE): evidence; proof.
6. **invincible material power:** here, an unconquerable nation.

Applying Your Skills

Three Readings from Einstein

INFORMATIONAL TEXT FOCUS: SUMMARIZING SOURCES: WORKS BY ONE AUTHOR

You have been learning about how to **synthesize** sources. You use tools like considering the author's purpose and **comparing and contrasting** sources. You can also relate ideas in the writing to what you already know about the author. Taken together, you can use these tools to get a better idea of how the author feels about particular issues. Consider the selections you have read by Einstein and his overall point of view.

DIRECTIONS: In all three of the works by Albert Einstein, he talks about the issues of war and peace. On the lines below, use what you have learned about synthesizing sources to answer the questions in your own words.

1. How does Einstein feel about war in general?
   _____
   _____

2. Why did Einstein feel it was important for the United States to work on an atomic bomb?
   _____
   _____

3. What did Einstein feel were the possible negative, or bad, results of creating nuclear weapons?
   _____
   _____

4. What would you say was Einstein's biggest hope for the future?
   _____
   _____

Word Box
goodwill
radical

VOCABULARY REVIEW

DIRECTIONS: Fill in the blanks with words from the Word Box.

1. Einstein believed that people should show _____ to others.

2. Getting rid of war completely is a _____ idea.

Three Readings from Einstein   143

Skills Review

Collection 4

VOCABULARY REVIEW

DIRECTIONS: Write the letter of the definition in the second column that best matches each word in the first column.

1. goodwill _____
2. imply _____
3. ambiguous _____
4. reiterated _____
5. mar _____
6. associate _____
7. literal _____
8. imminent _____
9. infallibility _____
10. doggedness _____
11. radical _____
12. roamed _____
13. iridescent _____

a. to damage or spoil
b. about to happen
c. based on the ordinary meaning of the actual words
d. inability to make a mistake
e. kind feeling
f. mentally make a link
g. extreme
h. stubborness
i. not clearly defined
j. repeated
k. suggest; hint at
l. colorful; rainbowlike
m. wandered without a particular direction

Skills Review

Collection 4

LANGUAGE COACH: WORD ORIGINS

Recognizing Latin **origins** of English words can help you better understand meanings.

DIRECTIONS: The Latin word *radix* means "root." Study the list of new words below. Then circle the <u>two</u> words that you think come from the Latin root word *radix*.

eradicate (IH RAD UH KAYT) *v.:* get rid of

phenomenon (FUH NOM UH NON) *n.:* extraordinary thing

conceivable (KUHN SEE VUH BUHL) *adj.:* able to be understood or imagined

radical (RAHD UH KUHL) *adj.:* extreme

mar (MAHR) *v.:* damage, spoil

WRITING ACTIVITY

Think about how writers use animals, things, or objects as **symbols** for something else in a story. Use an example of a symbol that was used in one of the stories in this collection. Did the symbol add to your understanding of the story? Explain your answer.

Review **145**

Collection 5

Form and Style

View on Mississippi River, Ferdinand Reichardt,
©Minnesota Historical Society/Corbis

Literary and Academic Vocabulary for Collection 5

LITERARY VOCABULARY

personal essay (PUHR SUH NUHL ES SAY) *n.:* writing about any topic; reveals a lot about the writer's personality.

"The Grandfather" is a personal essay by Gary Soto about his childhood.

autobiography (AW TOH BY AWG RUH FEE) *n.:* a full-length work that tells the story of the writer's life.

When I read her autobiography, I learned that she had grown up in Cuba and had come to the United States as an adult.

style (STYL) *n.:* how an author writes, usually shown through his or her choice of words.

The author's style included hard words and sentences, but the story was still really funny.

tone (TOHN) *n.:* a writer's attitude toward a subject, character, or the audience.

The author used a sarcastic tone that let me know she was not serious.

ACADEMIC VOCABULARY

appeal (UH PEEL) *v.:* attract, interest.

She played many different songs at the party to try to appeal to different people.

attitude (AT UH TOOD) *n.:* a way of thinking, acting, or feeling.

She has a different attitude about the issue than her husband does.

establish (EHS TAB LIHSH) *v.:* to set up; create.

The author used her childhood memories to help establish her tone.

enhance (EHN HANS) *v.:* make greater; improve.

Allowing a fruit to ripen fully will enhance its flavor.

Preparing to Read

Cub Pilot on the Mississippi
Based on the autobiography by Mark Twain

LITERARY FOCUS: STYLE AND TONE

Style and tone are tools that a writer uses to get his or her point across. An author's **style** relates to his or her:

- **diction**, or choice of words (do they seem formal, or funny, or direct?)
- use of images (does the language create a picture?)

An author's **tone** includes:

- attitude (is the writer sad, angry, happy, or sarcastic?)
- voice (can you tell if the writer is old or young, tired or energetic?)

As you read this selection by Mark Twain, make notes to yourself about his choice of words. In the chart below, write words from the text that seem formal, funny, and direct.

Formal	Funny	Direct

READING FOCUS: READING ALOUD AND PARAPHRASING

Reading text aloud can help you "hear" the writer's style and tone. To **paraphrase** means to restate in your own words. Paraphrasing can help you understand the writer's meaning. You can also compare the style and tone of the original to the style and tone of the words you used.

VOCABULARY

Look for these words as you read the selection.

apprenticeship (UH PREHN TIH SHIHP) *n.:* a period of training for a job by working under someone who is an expert.

dread (DREHD) *n.:* great fear or uneasiness.

unaware (UHN UH WAYR) *adj.:* not knowing or realizing.

trembled (TREHM BUHLD) *v.:* shook, sometimes with fear or cold.

SKILLS FOCUS

Literary Skills Understand elements of style, including diction and tone.

Reading Skills Read aloud and paraphrase.

Cub Pilot on the Mississippi

Based on the autobiography by Mark Twain

INTO THE STORY

Mark Twain's real name was Samuel Clemens. He held many jobs before becoming a famous writer. "Cub Pilot on the Mississippi" is a true story written by Mark Twain about his own life. When he was 22, he began working as a cub pilot on a steamboat. A cub pilot is an assistant to the pilot. (A pilot steers the ship.) As you read, keep in mind that the author is writing events as he remembers them. Although it is a true story, it is influenced by his point of view.

When I was a boy growing up on the Mississippi River, the only job my friends and I ever wanted was to work on a steamboat[1]. Sometimes we had other ideas, but they passed quickly. When a circus came to town, we all wanted to be clowns. Now and then we hoped that, if we were good, God would permit us to be pirates. **A** These ideas faded, but the wish to work on a steamboat always remained.

Some of my friends did get jobs on steamboats on the river, as engineers, barkeepers, and pilots. Pilot was the best job and came with a large salary. Some of us, though, could not get on the river—our parents would not let us. So I ran away. I said I never would come home again until I was a pilot.

During the two and a half years of my apprenticeship, I worked with many kinds of people and on many kinds of steamboats. **B** This helped me to be a writer. I got to know

---

1. A **steamboat** (STEEM BOHT) is a type of boat usually used on rivers. In the 1800s, many steamboats traveled the rivers of our country carrying people and goods.

A HERE'S HOW

Literary Focus

I am looking for clues to the author's **style** and **tone** as I read. In lines 4–6, the author talks about how he and his friends wanted to be clowns and pirates. This makes me think that Twain has a sense of humor. He also remembers what it was like to be a young boy.

B HERE'S HOW

Vocabulary

In line 13, the author talks about his *apprenticeship*. I know he spent more than two years on steamboats learning from pilots. I checked the meaning of *apprenticeship* in my dictionary. It means "a period of learning a job by working under someone skilled at it."

Cub Pilot on the Mississippi 149

A HERE'S HOW

Reading Focus

I know that **paraphrasing**, or restating in my own words, can help me to understand meaning. In line 20, the author uses the phrase "my soul became lead in my body." I can paraphrase this as "I got really scared."

B HERE'S HOW

Language Coach

When Twain says *wheel* in line 22, I think he means a "steering wheel." *Wheel* must be **jargon**, or specialized vocabulary, for steamboat workers.

C YOUR TURN

Vocabulary

The author says that he always started his work with *dread*. Considering what you have read about his boss, the pilot named Brown, which of the following words seems like the best definition for *dread*: joy, fear, or confusion?

---

about all the different types of people that there are in the world or in any kind of story.

The person I remember most often is Brown. He was an ugly, mean bully. No matter how good a time I was having, my 20 soul became lead in my body the moment I got near him. **A**

I still remember the first time I met Brown. He was the pilot, so he was at the wheel of the boat. **B** I waited, but he did not look around. There was silence for ten minutes; then, my new boss turned and looked me over. After what seemed like a long time, he asked, "What's your name?"

I told him. He repeated it after me. But he never used my name again. He always called "Here!" when he wanted me.

"Where was you born?"

"In Florida, Missouri."

30 He kept asking questions about my family until he had to turn back to his work.

When he turned to me again, what a change! His face was as red as fire. He yelled, "Here!—You going to sit there all day?"

I stood and apologized—"I have had no orders, sir."

"You've had no ORDERS! My, how fine we are! We must have ORDERS! Our father was a GENTLEMAN—and we've been to SCHOOL. WE are a gentleman, TOO, and got to have ORDERS! What you standing there for? Take that ice down to the officers!"

40 The moment I got back, Brown said, "Here! What was you doing down there all this time?"

"I couldn't find the room," I told him.

"Likely story! Fill up the stove."

He watched me like a cat. Then he shouted, "Put down that shovel—ain't even got sense enough to fill up a stove!"

This went on for months. I always started my work with dread. **C** I often wanted to kill Brown, but a cub had to take everything his boss gave.

Later, I got into serious trouble. Brown was steering. My 50 younger brother appeared on deck, and shouted to Brown to stop in about a mile. Brown did not reply. But that was his way.

He never spoke to people if he didn't think they were important. The wind was blowing and I thought he probably had not heard the order.

We went sailing by the stopping point. The captain came on deck, and said, "Turn the boat around. Didn't Henry tell you to land here?"

"NO, sir!"

"I sent him up to do it."

"He did come up, but he never said anything."

"Didn't YOU hear him?" the captain asked me.

Of course I didn't want to be mixed up in this, but I said, "Yes, sir."

Brown said, "Shut your mouth! you never heard anything of the kind." **D**

An hour later, Henry came up, unaware of what had been going on. **E** Brown began, "Here! why didn't you tell me we'd got to land at that stop?"

"I did tell you, Mr. Brown."

"It's a lie!"

I said, "You lie, yourself. He did tell you."

Brown looked at me in surprise, then he shouted to me, "I'll deal with you in a minute!" then to Henry, "And you get out!"

Henry was just outside the door when Brown picked up a ten-pound lump of coal and aimed at him. I picked up a heavy stool and hit Brown with it so hard it knocked him flat. **F**

I had committed the worst crime—I had hit a pilot! I was sure I was going to jail, so I decided I might as well hit him for as long I wanted. Finally he jumped up and ran to the wheel. All this time, the steamboat had been speeding down the river with no pilot to steer it! By luck alone, the boat was still steering straight down the middle of Eagle Bend.

Brown ordered me to get out. But I was not afraid of him now. The noise of our fight had brought everybody to the deck, and I trembled when I saw the captain. **G** He was usually very kind, but I was sure he would be angry with me.

D YOUR TURN

Reading Focus

Reading aloud can help you hear the writer's use of **style** and **tone**. Read lines 55–65 aloud. Pay special attention to who is speaking in each line and how the character talks. Write a **C** next to lines spoken by the captain. Write a **B** next to lines spoken by Brown. Write an **N** next to lines spoken by the narrator. Is there a difference in the **diction** and tone of each character?

E HERE'S HOW

Vocabulary

The word *unaware* sounds familiar, but I want to make sure I understand its meaning. The root word seems to be "aware." When I am aware of something, I know about it. The prefix *un-* means "not." So, I think, Henry being *unaware* means he does not know what has been going on.

F QUICK CHECK

Why did the narrator hit Brown?

G YOUR TURN

Vocabulary

Think about the word *trembled* in context. Is it a noun, adjective, or verb? What do you think it means? Use your dictionary to double-check your answers.

Cub Pilot on the Mississippi

A **YOUR TURN**

Literary Focus

Mark Twain uses images as part of his **style** to help get his meaning across. Re-read lines 107–108 and describe how the captain feels about Brown's beating. Why will the captain only show his feelings behind a closed door? How does Twain's style here help us better understand the captain?

_____
_____
_____
_____
_____
_____

The captain stood in silence a moment or two, then said, "Follow me."

He led the way to his room. We were alone, now. He closed all the doors. Then he said, "So you have been fighting Mr. Brown? Do you know that that is very serious?"

"Yes, sir."

"Are you aware that this boat was going down the river for five whole minutes with no one at the wheel?"

"Yes, sir."

"Did you strike him first?"

"Yes, sir."

"What with?"

"A stool, sir."

"Did you do anything further?"

"Pounded him, sir."

"I'm glad of it! Now never tell anyone that I said that. You are guilty of a great crime; and don't you ever be guilty of it again on this boat. BUT—wait for him when he gets off the boat! Give him a good beating, do you hear?! Now go—and not a word of this to anybody."

I slid out and I heard him laughing to himself after I had closed his door. **A**

Brown went to the captain and demanded that I be fired. "I won't even stay on the same boat with him. One of us has got to go."

"Very well," said the captain to Brown, "let it be you."

152 Cub Pilot on the Mississippi

Applying Your Skills

Cub Pilot on the Mississippi

LITERARY FOCUS: STYLE AND TONE

DIRECTIONS: In "Cub Pilot on the Mississippi," Mark Twain uses **style** and **tone** to help the reader understand how he felt about the character named Brown. What feeling or picture do you get about Brown from each of the three sentences below?

1. "His face was as red as fire." _____
2. "He never spoke to people if he didn't think they were important." _____
3. "Henry was just outside the door when Brown picked up a ten-pound lump of coal and aimed at him." _____
4. "I always started my work with dread. I often wanted to kill Brown, but a cub had to take everything his boss gave." _____

READING FOCUS: READING ALOUD AND PARAPHRASING

DIRECTIONS: Below are several sentences from the selection you just read. First, read each sentence aloud to yourself or to a partner. Then, complete the second column of the chart by **paraphrasing** the sentence. The first line has been completed as an example.

Sentence	In my own words
"Now and then we hoped that, if we were good, God would permit us to be pirates."	Once in a while we wished that if everything went perfectly we would get the best job of being pirates.
"No matter how good a time I was having, my soul became lead in my body the moment I got near him."	
"We must have ORDERS! Our father was a GENTLEMAN—and we've been to SCHOOL. WE are a gentleman, TOO, and got to have ORDERS!"	
"I slid out and I heard him laughing to himself after I had closed his door."	

Cub Pilot on the Mississippi   153

Preparing to Read

The Grandfather
Based on the personal essay by Gary Soto

LITERARY FOCUS: STYLE AND IMAGERY

Style is one of the terms we use when we talk about *how* an author writes. Style refers to the many ways writers use language. If two people write about the same event, the words they choose and the kinds of sentences they create will make the description different. For example:

I went to the grocery store today.

is different than

When I woke up on this beautiful sunny morning, I was so hungry for peaches that I had to walk to the nearest market right away.

A big part of writing style is **imagery**, or words that make us feel like our senses are involved in the story. If you feel as if you can see, hear, touch, or taste what the writer is talking about, it is because he or she is using imagery.

READING FOCUS: MAKING GENERALIZATIONS

A **generalization** is a broad statement based on details. For example, we could say: "Reading helps us learn more about ourselves." We could support this generalization by naming and describing stories and books we have read and what we have learned about ourselves from each one. To make a generalization, focus on these steps:

- Look for details in the text.
- Think about what the details tell you when taken together.
- Create a broad statement based on the details.

VOCABULARY

Both of the following words describe foods. Write a sentence using each word, and try to use **imagery** in each sentence.

avocado (AH VUH CAH DOH) *n.*: a fruit with a dark green or purple skin and soft, light green flesh.

chile (CHIH LEE) OR (CHEE LAY) *n.*: a hot pepper often used as a seasoning.

SKILLS FOCUS

Literary Skills
Understand and analyze elements of style; understand imagery.

Reading Skills
Make generalizations about a text.

THE GRANDFATHER

Based on the personal essay by Gary Soto

> **INTO THE PERSONAL ESSAY**
> The following selection is a personal essay. Personal essays are usually written in the first person and show the author's thoughts and feelings. Author Gary Soto wrote "The Grandfather" based on memories of his own grandfather. Soto's grandfather came from Mexico to the United States. He worked hard and saved the little money he had for his family. One way he did this was by growing his own fruit instead of buying it at the store. In this essay, Soto remembers what he learned about life from his grandfather.

Grandfather believed that having a tree with strong roots was like having money. He kept his money hidden behind pictures, tucked into the sofa, or his shoes, or in his soft brown wallet marked with the word "MEXICO." He had left Mexico and come to Fresno[1] years ago and worked for thirty years at Sun Maid Raisin.

After work, he sat in the backyard under the trees. He had fruit trees, including a lemon tree and two orange trees. His favorite tree was the avocado, which he had started in a jar from a seed. **A** It rarely grew fruit, though. He blamed life in the city and said that in Mexico buildings were shorter. You could see the moon at night, and the stars were clear there. **B**

When the avocado tree was first planted, I could leap over it. I kicked my legs over the top branch and screamed because I thought I was flying. Grandpa would scold, "Hijo,[2] what's the matter with you? You're gonna break it."

By the third year, the tree was as tall as I. I sat beneath its shade, scratching words in the dirt with a stick.

---

1. **Fresno** (FREHZ NOH): city in central California.
2. **Hijo** (EE HOH): Spanish for "child" or "son."

"The Grandfather" adapted from *A Summer Life* by Gary Soto (Dell 1991). Copyright © 1990 by University Press of New England. Retold by Holt, Rinehart and Winston. Reproduced by permission of **University Press of New England** and electronic format by permission of **Gary Soto**.

A **HERE'S HOW**

Vocabulary
The *avocado* in line 9 must be a fruit tree. I am not sure what an *avocado* looks or tastes like. I looked up *avocado* in a dictionary. I learned that the fruit from the *avocado* tree has a dark green or purple skin and a soft, light green inside.

B **HERE'S HOW**

Reading Focus
Lines 10–12 have a lot of details about the grandfather's memories. From reading these details, I think I can make the **generalization** that there are many things about Mexico the grandfather still misses after many years.

A YOUR TURN

Vocabulary

Chile is another food-related word. Underline an adjective in line 30 that describes what *chile* tastes like. Then, circle the best description of a *chile* from the choices below:
—a hot seasoning
—a bitter liquid
—a sweet fruit

B LITERARY ANALYSIS

How does the tree growing taller connect to the grandfather's family growing larger in number?

_____
_____
_____

C YOUR TURN

Literary Focus

Read lines 34–37 and think about the **imagery** the author uses. Try to picture the tree with a thick trunk and high branches. Do you think it is important that, even with the wind blowing, the big old tree "hugged the ground?" What else in this story does the tree make you think of, and why?

_____
_____
_____
_____

© Ron Giling/Peter Arnold, Inc.

A tree was money. If a lemon cost seven cents, then Grandfather saved lots of money when his lemon tree had heavy yellow fruit. And winter brought oranges, juicy and large as softballs. Apricots he got from his son, who was wisely planting his own trees.

But his favorite tree was the avocado because it offered hope and the promise of more in later years. After ten years, the first avocado hung on a branch, but the meat was spotted with black. Five years later, another avocado grew, larger than the first and good to eat. Grandfather sprinkled it with salt and a lot of chile.

"It's good," he said, and let me taste.

I took a big bite. The spicy chile made me run for a drink from the garden hose. **A**

After twenty years, the tree began to have a lot of fruit. Although Grandfather complained about how long it took, he loved that tree. It grew, as did his family. **B** When he died, all his sons standing on each other's shoulders could not reach the highest branches. The wind could move the branches, but the thick, strong trunk hugged the ground. **C**

Applying Your Skills

The Grandfather

LITERARY FOCUS: STYLE AND IMAGERY

DIRECTIONS: The author of "The Grandfather" uses a lot of **imagery** to help the reader experience events the way he remembers them. In the sentences below, underline the words that involve your senses of seeing, hearing, tasting, touching, or feeling.

1. He kept his money hidden behind pictures, tucked into the sofa or his shoes, or in his soft brown wallet marked with the word "MEXICO."

2. I kicked my legs over the top branch and screamed because I thought I was flying.

3. And winter brought oranges, juicy and large as softballs.

4. After ten years, the first avocado hung on a branch, but the meat was spotted with black.

READING FOCUS: MAKING GENERALIZATIONS

DIRECTIONS: What details from the story support the **generalization** written in the center circle, below? Write those details in the connecting circles.

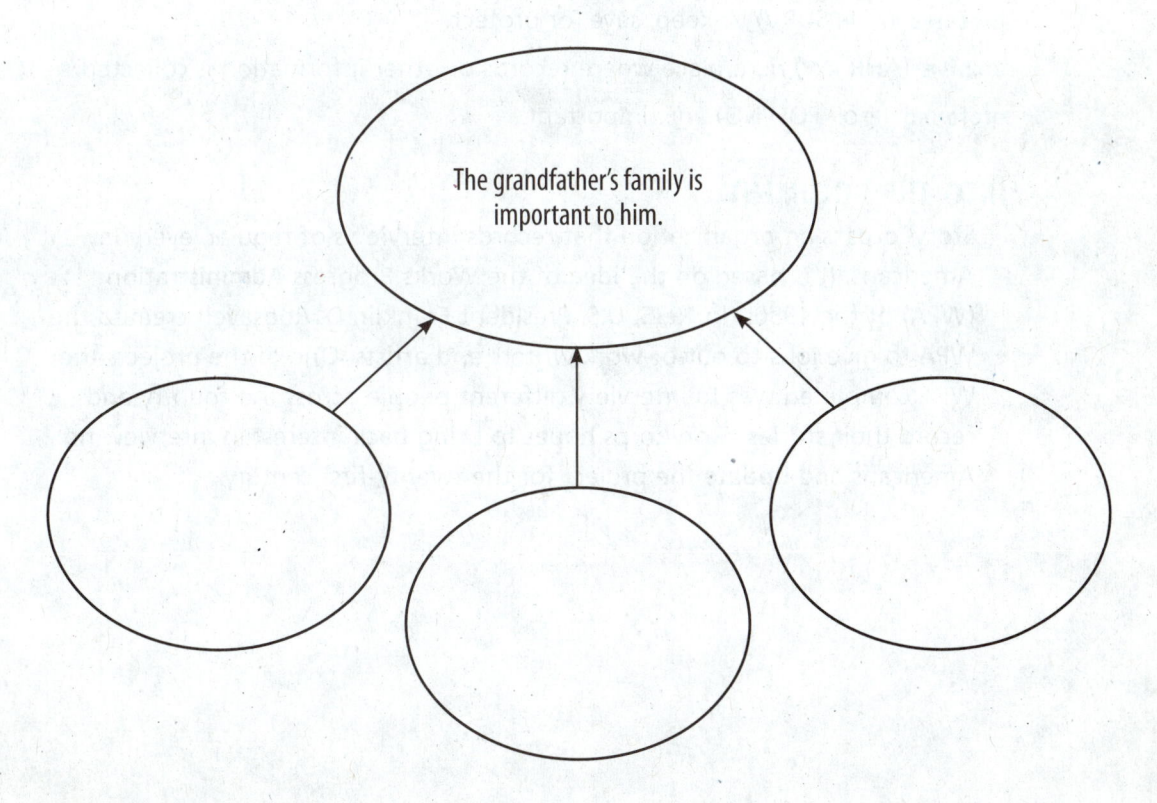

(Center circle: The grandfather's family is important to him. Three empty circles connect to it.)

The Grandfather 157

Preparing to Read

About StoryCorps

Based on the document "About StoryCorps"

INFORMATIONAL TEXT FOCUS: STRUCTURE AND FORMAT

When you read informational texts, the **structure** and **format** of the writing can help you better understand what you are reading.

When you look at structure, look for:

- <u>Sections</u>: Are there headings dividing the text into shorter sections? Quickly scan the headings to see what each section will be about.

When you look at format, look for:

- <u>Words or phrases in bold or italic</u>: Do these words have a special meaning or importance?
- <u>Illustrations</u>: Are there drawings, photos, charts, or other artwork on the page? How do these relate to the text?

VOCABULARY

Work with a partner to practice using these words in complete sentences.

preserve (PRUH SURV) *v.:* keep, save, or protect.

archive (AHR KYV) *n.:* a place where records or other information is collected.

profound (PROH FOWND) *adj.:* important.

INTO THE DOCUMENT

StoryCorps is an organization that records interviews of regular, everyday Americans. It is based on the idea of the Works Progress Administration (WPA) of the 1930s. In 1935, U.S. President Franklin D. Roosevelt created the WPA to give jobs to out-of-work writers and artists. One of the projects the WPA completed was to interview different people across the country and record their stories. StoryCorps hopes to bring back interest in interviewing Americans and update the project for the twenty-first century.

SKILLS FOCUS

Informational Text Skills
Analyze structure and format to better understand informational texts.

158 About StoryCorps

ABOUT STORYCORPS

Based on the document "About StoryCorps"

StoryCorps   A

StoryCorps is a national project to help people record each others' stories.

We're here to help you interview your grandmother, your uncle, the lady who works down the block—anyone whose story you want to hear and preserve.   B

To start, we're building recording studios across the country, called StoryBooths. You can use StoryBooths to record interviews with the help of our trained staff. Our first StoryBooth opened in New York City's Grand Central Terminal train station
10 on October 23, 2003. A second StoryBooth opened in Lower Manhattan, another part of New York City, on July 12, 2005. We also have two traveling recording studios, called MobileBooths. They started driving across the country on May 19, 2005.

We've tried to make the experience as simple as possible. We help you decide what questions to ask. We handle the recording. At the end of an hour, you get a copy of your interview on CD. Since we want to make sure your story lives on, we'll also add your interview to the StoryCorps Archive, at the Library of Congress in Washington DC.   C

From "About Story Corps" (slightly adapted) from *StoryCorps*. Reproduced by permission of Sound Portraits Productions, Inc.

A | HERE'S HOW

Reading Focus

I want to think about the **structure** of this article as I read. I notice there are two headings in this document. I think since the first one is just "StoryCorps," that section will give me general information about what StoryCorps is and what the article will be about. The second section, under the heading "Our Vision," probably has more to do with what StoryCorps wants or hopes to do.

B | HERE'S HOW

Vocabulary

Preserve is a word that can have more than one meaning. As a noun, it can mean a kind of fruit jam or jelly. As a verb, it means "to save or protect." It is obvious that here, *preserve* means "to save or protect."

C | HERE'S HOW

Vocabulary

The word *archive* in line 18 is part of a name, but I think I have seen it before. If I remember correctly, an *archive* is a place where information is collected. This definition makes sense, since in this sentence it has to do with a library.

A QUICK CHECK

What hope, or goal, does StoryCorps have for the 21st century?

_____
_____
_____

B YOUR TURN

Vocabulary

Line 28 talks about how interviews can have a *profound* impact. Keep reading through line 31. Based on the kinds of changes the paragraph describes, what do you think *profound* means?

_____
_____
_____

C YOUR TURN

Reading Focus

The words in italic font are an example of a special **format**. On the lines below, explain why you think these three questions were made to look different from the rest of the text.

_____
_____
_____
_____

Our Vision

20   Our project is based on the example of the Works Progress Administration (WPA) of the 1930s.[1] The WPA recorded interviews with everyday Americans across the country. These recordings remain the most important collection of American voices gathered in our country's history. We hope that StoryCorps will build and expand on that work in the 21st century. **A**

We've found that the process of interviewing a friend, neighbor, or family member can have a profound impact on both the interviewer and the person being interviewed. We've seen
30   people change, friendships grow, and families understand each other better. Listening, after all, is an act of love. **B**

A StoryCorps interview is a chance to ask the questions that you've never asked. *How did you come to this country? How did you and mom meet? How did Uncle Harry get the nickname "Twinkles?"* **C**

© Andrew Holbrooke/Corbis

---
1. **The Works Progress Administration,** or WPA, was a government agency created by President Roosevelt in 1935.

Applying Your Skills

About StoryCorps

INFORMATIONAL TEXT FOCUS: STRUCTURE AND FORMAT

DIRECTIONS: Look at the following pieces of information taken from "About StoryCorps." Think about the **structure** of the selection you just read. Decide whether each of the following pieces of information comes from the first section, "StoryCorps," or the second section, "Our Vision." Write each piece of information under its correct section heading in the chart below.

- You can record an interview in a StoryBooth.
- The idea of StoryCorps is based on the WPA.
- Interviewing a friend or family member can create big changes for people.
- StoryCorps is a national project.
- MobileBooths are traveling studios.
- StoryCorps gives you the chance to ask questions you have never asked.

StoryCorps	Our Vision

DIRECTIONS: In the list below, put a check mark next to any element that has to do with the **format** of a selection.

1. there are photographs on a page _____
2. the author's choice of words _____
3. the use of bold or italics _____
4. the humor in the text _____

Word Box

preserve
archive
profound

VOCABULARY REVIEW

DIRECTIONS: Fill in the blanks with the correct word from the Word Box. One of the words will not be used.

1. Old photographs are stored in the _____.
2. The captain's speech had a _____ impact on his men.

Skills Review

Collection 5

VOCABULARY REVIEW

DIRECTIONS: For each sentence below, choose the word from the Word Box at left that best fills in each blank.

Word Box

apprenticeship
establish
dread
unaware
trembled
avocado
chile
preserve
appeal
archive
profound

1. I was so scared of the horror movie that I _____ in my seat.

2. She had missed the first ten minutes of class and so she was _____ that we were going to have a quiz at the end of the period.

3. The spicy _____ was the last ingredient I added to the recipe.

4. The librarian told me that the document I was looking for was available in the _____.

5. A feeling of _____ filled me as I realized that I would have to face the bully who had been bothering me.

6. The last chapter revealed a _____ truth about the importance of family.

7. I tried to _____ all of the photographs since I knew I would want them to last for many years.

8. He sliced the green _____ and sprinkled the pieces with salt and pepper to eat before dinner.

9. She learned to be a good mechanic by completing an _____ with someone who knew cars inside and out.

10. The children's author tried to select topics that would _____ to her young audience.

11. By frequently participating in class discussions, I hoped to _____ myself as a dedicated student.

Skills Review

Collection 5

LANGUAGE COACH: ONOMATOPOEIA

Onomatopoeia (AH NAH MAH TUH PEE YAH) is the use of a word whose sounds imitate or tell you its meaning. For example, "Moo" is the word for the sound a cow makes. When something "clicks" into place, the sound it makes is "click." So, the sound and the meaning are the same. Can you think of other words that are examples of onomatopoeia?

DIRECTIONS: Circle the word in each sentence that is an example of onomatopoeia.

1. The water gurgled out of the hose and into the rosebush.
2. At dawn, I heard the cock-a-doodle-doo of the rooster.
3. When I got very close to the kitten, I could hear her meow.
4. The buzz near my ear let me know the bee was close.
5. At the end of the fireworks show, a loud ka-boom filled the air.

WRITING ACTIVITY

The goal of a **summary** is to give readers a short view of a piece of writing they might not have read. Choose one of the selections you just read, "Cub Pilot on the Mississippi," "The Grandfather," or "About StoryCorps." Write a three- or four-sentence summary of the selection you have chosen. Be sure to state the main idea of the selection in your first sentence. Add two or three additional sentences to cover the major ideas or points the writer used to support the main idea.

_____
_____
_____
_____

Collection 6

Persuasion

Literary and Academic Vocabulary for Collection 6

LITERARY VOCABULARY

argument (AHR GYOO MUNT) *n.:* a writer's main point of view.
   The author's argument in favor of more money for the public library led me to agree with him.

structure (STRUHK CHUR) *n.:* the organization a writer uses to make a point.
   Sometimes the headings or questions and answers in an article help you to see the writer's organization, or structure.

pro (PROH) *n.:* argument for something.
   The only pro about the new class president is that she got us healthy snacks in the cafeteria.

con (KAHN) *n.:* argument against something.
   The biggest con for your book is that it is just too long.

ACADEMIC VOCABULARY

influence (IHN FLOO UHNS) *v.:* to persuade or affect someone.
   A strong speech can influence people to take action.

counter (KOWN TUHR) *v.:* to say something against or opposing another statement.
   His writings counter the argument that the public library should get more money.

valid (VAL IHD) *adj.:* supported by facts; true.
   I know the statement is valid because it is based on facts.

verify (VEHR UH FY) *v.:* prove something to be true.
   You can verify a fact by looking it up in a good resource, like an encyclopedia.

Preparing to Read

Cinderella's Stepsisters
Based on the speech by Toni Morrison

LITERARY FOCUS: ARGUMENT: INTENT AND TONE

A writer's **intent** is his or her purpose or goal. When you are reading for the author's intent, ask yourself: What is the reason the author is writing this? What does he or she want me to take away from this text? When you read an argument, for example, the author's intent will be to try to convince you of her way of thinking.

The author's **tone** is the attitude he or she expresses toward the audience, reader, or subject. As you read an argument, think about the author's tone—is he or she angry, sad, serious, respectful, or disrespectful?

An author may use different tools to express the intent and tone of her argument. In the speech you are about to read, Toni Morrison uses the story of Cinderella and her stepsisters as an **analogy** for the relationships between women in the modern world. An analogy is a kind of comparison. It can help explain something unfamiliar by comparing it to a familiar example.

READING FOCUS: QUESTIONING

An argument is one kind of persuasive writing—writing meant to convince you of something. When you read an argument or another kind of persuasive writing, it may help you to ask **questions**. You can even use the questions to challenge the author's point of view. For example, you might ask:

- Why is the author making this point?
- Do I agree with her?
- What might the other side of this argument be?

VOCABULARY

With a partner, practice using each of the words below in complete sentences.

unsettling (UHN SEHT LIHNG), *adj.:* upsetting or worrying.

oppression (UH PREH SHUHN), *n.:* unfair or cruel use of power.

function (FUHNK SHUHN), *n.:* the purpose for which something exists.

SKILLS FOCUS

Literary Skills
Identify and understand the relationship between writers' intent, tone, and use of tools like analogy.

Reading Skills
Ask questions about the text.

CINDERELLA'S STEPSISTERS

Based on the speech by Toni Morrison

INTO THE SPEECH
In the 1960s and 1970s, women fought to gain the same rights and opportunities as men. This was the beginning of the women's rights movement. The movement has succeeded in giving many women new opportunities—and power—in the world. In 1979, Toni Morrison gave a speech at the graduation ceremony of Barnard College. Barnard College is an all-women's college in New York City. The graduates grew up during the first decades of the women's rights movement.

Let me begin by asking you to remember. Once-upon-a-time, you first heard, or read, or saw "Cinderella." **A** What is unsettling about that fairy tale is that it is the story of a family—or even a world—of women who abuse another woman. **B** It is Cinderella's stepsisters who interest me. How terrible it must have been for those young girls to grow up watching and imitating their mother who kept another girl as a slave.

I am curious about the stepsisters after the story ends. Unlike what most of us have read or heard, the stepsisters were not ugly, clumsy, stupid girls with huge feet. The original story describes them as "beautiful and fair in appearance." When we first meet them they are beautiful, elegant, powerful women. But having watched and participated in the abuse of another woman, will they be any less cruel? Will they treat their own children or even their mother the same way?

This is a modern problem, too. In the past, women have taken advantage of their power over other women in a "masculine" manner. Soon you will be in a position to do the very same thing. You may be rich or poor. You may come from an educated family or an uneducated one. But once you have become educated at Barnard College, you will be like the stepsisters. You will have their power. **C**

A **HERE'S HOW**

Reading Focus
I have a **question**. Why is the author starting this speech with a once-upon-a-time story? As I go on, I will try to note how the story of "Cinderella" will relate to this story.

B **HERE'S HOW**

Vocabulary
The author uses the word *unsettling* to describe the Cinderella story. By using context clues, I can tell that *unsettling* means "upsetting."

C **HERE'S HOW**

Literary Focus
Toni Morrison is making an **analogy** here. She compares the power that Cinderella's stepsisters have to the power the graduates now have.

"Cinderella's Stepsisters" by Toni Morrison from *Ms. Magazine*, September, 1979. Copyright © 1979 by **Toni Morrison**. Reproduced by permission of the author.

A **YOUR TURN**

Reading Focus
What **questions** do you have about the speech so far? Write them below.

_____
_____
_____

B **YOUR TURN**

Literary Focus
How would you describe the author's **tone** in lines 30–36?

_____
_____

C **YOUR TURN**

Vocabulary
The word *function* can mean "a big event or party," "the purpose for which something is used," "a mathematical expression," or "a computer action." Which meaning makes the most sense as the word is used in line 43?

_____
_____

I want not to *ask* you but to *tell* you not to participate in the oppression of your sisters. Mothers who abuse their children are women. Another woman has to be willing to stop them. Mothers who set fire to school buses are women. Another woman has to stop them. Women who stop other women from getting better jobs are women. Another woman must help the victims of this problem. **A** **B**

I am worried about all the ways women hurt other women. You are the women who will decide who will succeed and who will fail. You may even decide who deserves to live and who does not. As educated women, you need to be able to tell the difference between having this power and having the right to use it.

I am suggesting that we pay as much attention to helping others as to helping ourselves. You are moving in the direction of freedom, and the function of freedom is to free somebody else. **C** As you achieve your goals, you should discover that there is something just as important as you are. That just-as-important thing may be other women, just like Cinderella—or your stepsister.

Don't make choices based only on your safety. Nothing is safe. It is not safe to have a child. It is not safe to challenge the way things are done. It is not safe to choose work that has not been done before. There will always be someone there to stop you. But in working toward your highest personal goals, don't take away the safety of your stepsister. In gaining power that you deserve, don't allow it to enslave your stepsisters. Let your power come from that place in you that is caring.

Women's rights is not only an idea; it is also something personal. It is not only about "us"; it is also about me and you. Just the two of us.

168 Cinderella's Stepsisters

Applying Your Skills

Cinderella's Stepsisters

LITERARY FOCUS: ARGUMENT: INTENT AND TONE

DIRECTIONS: In this speech, Toni Morrison makes an **analogy** between Cinderella's stepsisters and women today. How are the stepsisters and women today similar?

_____
_____
_____

READING FOCUS: QUESTIONING

DIRECTIONS: Reread the selection. This time, practice asking **questions** of the author. Write your questions in the chart below. Then, record your answers. An example of a question has been included for you.

Questions	Answers
1. Do I agree with Toni Morrison?	1.
2.	2.
3.	3.

VOCABULARY REVIEW

DIRECTIONS: Use the correct words from the Word Box to fill in the blanks in the paragraph below.

Word Box
- unsettling
- oppression
- function

Toni Morrison's speech is meant to encourage educated young women to use their power wisely and to help other women. Morrison is upset by the _____ of some women by other women. Morrison finds this kind of abuse _____. The author asks the young graduates to share their freedom with others.

Preparing to Read

Two Articles on Kaavya Viswanathan

INFORMATIONAL TEXT FOCUS: EVALUATING ARGUMENTS

Some texts will show you both sides of an **argument**—the **pro** (argument for) and the **con** (argument against). How can you decide which argument makes the most sense to you? Ask yourself these questions:

- What is the **claim** (what is the author asking you to believe)?
- What facts and examples does the author use to support the claim?
- Is the argument **logical**—does it make sense?
- Does the author stay focused on the issues, or does he or she attack the character of people who do not agree with him or her?

VOCABULARY

Work with a partner to practice using these words in complete sentences.

unconscious (UHN KAHN SHUHS) *adj.:* not knowing or not aware

plagiarism (PLAY JUH RIHZ UHM) *n.:* the use of someone else's words or ideas as one's own

controversy (KAHN TRUH VUHR SEE) *n.:* a discussion in which people have opposing views

feat (FEET) *n.:* an achievement or a remarkable act

syndrome (SIHN DROHM) *n.:* a disorder or disease defined by a group of specific symptoms

INTO THE ARTICLES

Kaavya Viswanathan was a Harvard student who published a book and became famous at a young age. In 2006, it was discovered that she had copied parts of her book from someone else's work. People disagreed about whether or not she had meant to do it. Many people wrote about the situation—including on the Internet in journals, blogs, and online publications.

SKILLS FOCUS

Informational Text Skills
Evaluate arguments.

Kaavya Viswanathan: Unconscious Copycat or Plagiarist?

Based on the blog by Sandhya Nankani

Friday, April 28, 2006

Plagiarism is no joke. If you are found guilty of it, you can fail a class or be expelled from school. In 2003, *New York Times* reporter Jayson Blair lost his job after he admitted to copying other people's writing and faking reports. **A**

In 2006, the person everyone was talking about was Kaavya Viswanathan.

The Harvard student was given $500,000 by the publishing company Little, Brown to write a novel about a high school senior who tries to become popular and get into Harvard.

10 The book was called *How Opal Mehta Got Kissed, Got Wild, and Got a Life.*

In February, I read the book with interest. It's not every day that such a young writer is discovered. Kaavya was only 17 when she got her book deal. My friend Pooja read the book too. There were a few things about it that bothered us, but we decided that any 19-year-old who could write a 250+-page novel deserved to be complimented. **B** We wondered what other readers would think.

Neither Pooja nor I expected what happened next.

20 Last Sunday, *The Harvard Crimson* newspaper reported that Kaavya had plagiarized over 40 sections from two novels by author Megan McCafferty.

In an email on Monday, Kaavya said that she had been a fan of McCafferty's books since high school and had read them 3 or 4 times. Kaavya said that she had copied McCafferty's style without realizing it. Many did not believe her.

A HERE'S HOW

Reading Focus
It is important to look at facts when you **evaluate arguments**. Here, the author claims that plagiarism is very serious. The author supports this claim with the information about Jayson Blair.

B QUICK CHECK

How did the author and her friend feel about Viswanathan's book after they read it?

_____
_____
_____
_____

Slightly adapted from "Kaavya Viswanathan: Unconscious Copycat or Plagiarist?" by Sandhya Nankani from *WORD: Official Blog of READ® and WRITING® magazines,* Friday, April 28, 2006. Retold by Holt, Rinehart and Winston. Reproduced by permission of **Weekly Reader Corporation.**

A YOUR TURN

Language Coach

Look carefully at these words from this page: publisher, reprint, admitted, unsold. Do you recognize any **word parts**, or smaller words, inside these words? Circle the word parts in the list above.

B HERE'S HOW

Vocabulary

I need to think about the word *unconscious*. I know that sometimes *unconscious* can mean "not awake," like from an injury. Here I think it means something else. It sounds like an "unconscious copycat" is the opposite of an "intentional plagiarist." I know *intentional* means "on purpose," so I think *unconscious* means "not knowing," or "not aware."

C HERE'S HOW

Reading Focus

The author says that it is not always easy to write something original. I think she is **arguing** that Kaavya was telling the truth when she said she did not mean to plagiarize. I am not sure I agree with this **pro argument**. I will continue reading to see what facts and examples support the author's **claim**.

On Tuesday Kaavya's publisher said that they would reprint the book with changes and a note about McCafferty.

On Wednesday Kaavya admitted that a company called 17th Street Media Productions had helped her create the story. She added that she "had a photographic memory."

Thursday: The publisher asked stores to stop selling the book and to return unsold copies to the publisher for their money back. **A**

Is this the end of Kaavya's story? Will everyone forget about her by next Friday? I'm not sure.

This controversy does not seem so clear to me. Is Kaavya an intentional plagiarist or an unconscious copycat? **B** What role did 17th Street Media Productions play? If Kaavya knew about the similarity to McCafferty's 49 sections, did she think it was OK because she was changing the words, names, and places around?

As writers—whether we are writing for fun, for school, or for money—we have a responsibility to our readers and to ourselves. That responsibility is to select each word with care and to do our best to offer original thoughts and words to the world.

That task is not always easy. **C** Many times I have written something and thought, "Hmmm, that sounds familiar. Did someone else say that?" As a writer, I need to be responsible for looking it up, checking to see whether that is true. If I find that my words sound a lot like someone else's, I need to go back and delete and rewrite.

Of course, there are some things that there just aren't too many ways of saying:

Her name was Lucy. She lived in a house

She was named Lucy. In a house she lived.

Lucy was her name. She resided in a house.

If you rewrite something like that or write a fact that's well known—"There are 12 months in a year"—that's not plagiarism. Plagiarism is copying someone else's writing without saying where it came from. Plagiarism is different from liking a writer and learning from his or her style.

You see why this situation is so complicated? A lot of people are saying, "Aha! Kaavya got caught. Serves her right!" I don't think this is the lesson of this story. Instead, we should use Kaavya's experience to remind us of the importance of carefully choosing our words. When it comes to writing, there's nothing better than writing in our own voices. **D**

When Kaavya's book has disappeared from bookshelves and her life has returned to normal, I hope that she will ask herself: What is my original writing voice? I wish her good luck in finding it. From what I've seen so far, it is a voice that shines with humor. **E**

D YOUR TURN

Reading Focus
The author tells what we should learn from Kaavya's experience in lines 62–66. **Evaluate** this **argument**. Do you agree with the author, or is there another lesson here?

E YOUR TURN

Reading Focus
What is the author's main **argument** in this selection? Do you think it is **logical**?

Kaavya Syndrome

Based on the online article by Joshua Foer

April 27, 2006

Kaavya Viswanathan has an excuse. In this morning's *New York Times*, the author explained how she plagiarized more than 29 passages from the books of Megan McCafferty without knowing or meaning to do so. Viswanathan said she has a photographic memory.[1]

This seems like a good opportunity to clear up the greatest myth about human memory. Lots of people claim to have a photographic memory, but nobody actually does. **A**

Well, maybe one person.

In 1970, a scientist named Charles Stromeyer III studied a Harvard student named Elizabeth. Stromeyer showed Elizabeth's right eye a pattern of 10,000 dots. A day later, he showed her left eye a different dot pattern. Her brain combined the two patterns to make a new picture. Elizabeth seemed to offer the first proof that photographic memory is possible. But then Stromeyer married her, and she was never tested again. **B** These tests were later questioned because Stromeyer married his test subject.

In 1979, a researcher named John Merritt placed a photographic memory test in magazines and newspapers around the country. About 1 million people took the test. Only 30 wrote in with the right answer. Merritt visited 15 of them. However, not one of them could do what Elizabeth had.

Many people have excellent memories. They just can't take "photographs" with their brain and remember them perfectly. Kim Peek was the basis for a character in the movie *Rain Man* and is said to have memorized every page of more than 9,000 books. No one has seriously tested whether this is

---

A HERE'S HOW

Reading Focus

The writer makes the **claim** that no one has a photographic memory. I will look to see what facts he uses to support his claim.

B QUICK CHECK

Reread lines 10–16. What did scientific tests of Elizabeth Stromeyer try to prove? How many times was she tested?

---

1. Someone with a **photographic memory** is said to take a mental picture of everything he or she sees and can remember each thing exactly.

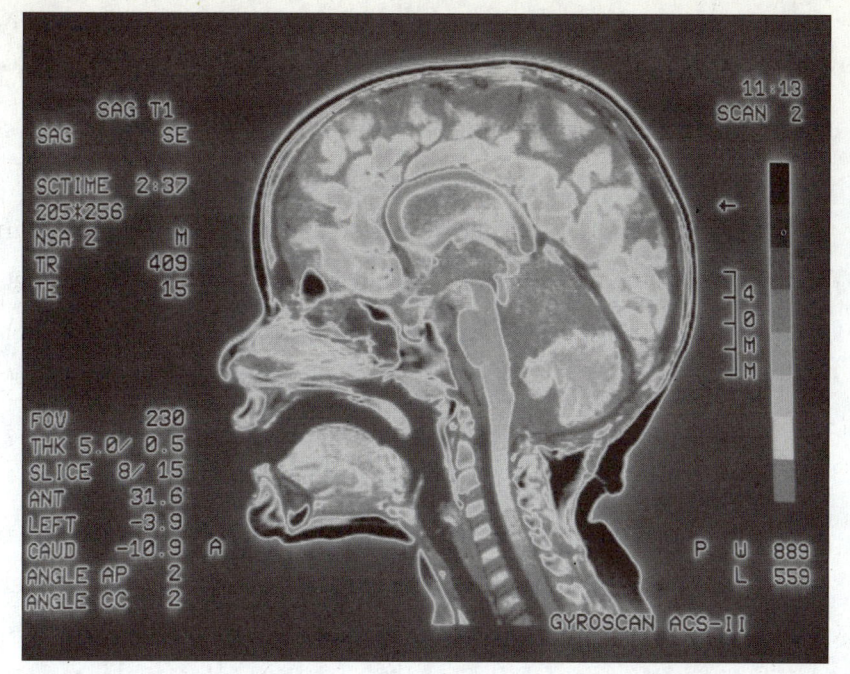

© age fotostock/SuperStock

C HERE'S HOW

Language Coach
I have underlined two words in which I recognize **word parts**—or smaller words.

D YOUR TURN

Reading Focus
At the beginning of the article, the author makes the **claim** that no one has a photographic memory. What are two facts the author uses in lines 32–42 to support this claim?

_____
_____
_____
_____
_____

true, however. **C** A man named Stephen Wiltshire has been called the "human camera." He can draw a scene after looking
30   at it for just a few seconds. But even he doesn't have a truly photographic memory. His mind doesn't work like a photocopier. He changes some details.

In every case except Elizabeth's where someone has claimed to have a photographic memory, there has always been another explanation. The writer Truman Capote famously claimed to have a perfect memory of people's speech. He never took notes or used a tape recorder, but I think his memory claims were used to hide the fact that he would later make up people's words in his writing. A Russian journalist called S was studied for thirty
40   years by psychologist A.R. Luria. Although S was famous for his memory, he did not have a photographic memory. Rather, he seemed to have learned a system that allowed him to memorize certain kinds of information. **D**

Viswanathan is not the first person to claim that her memory is to blame for her plagiarism. Famous musician George Harrison said he never intended to steal the melody of the Chiffons' "He's So Fine" when he wrote "My Sweet Lord."

Kaavya Syndrome   175

A HERE'S HOW

Vocabulary

The word *feat* sounds like the word "feet" but I know it has a different spelling and a different meaning. The meaning that fits into the context of this sentence is "achievement."

B LITERARY ANALYSIS

How does the quotation from Helen Keller in lines 51–55 help support the author's point?

_____
_____
_____

C YOUR TURN

Reading Focus

Evaluate the author's **argument**. Do you agree or disagree with his **claim** that Kaavya does not have a photographic memory? Why or why not?

_____
_____
_____

D HERE'S HOW

Vocabulary

The word *syndrome* was also used in the title of this article. Here, I see that the author defines it as a "disorder." I will look up the word in the dictionary to learn more about this kind of disorder.

He just forgot he'd ever heard it. And young Helen Keller[2] used parts of Margaret Canby's "The Frost Fairies" in her story "The Frost King." Canby herself said, "I do not see how any one can be so unkind as to call it a plagiarism; it is a wonderful feat of memory." **A** But Keller was terrified of doing the same thing again. "I have ever since been tortured by the fear that what I write is not my own," she wrote. "It is certain that I cannot always distinguish my own thoughts from those I read, because what I read becomes the very substance[3] of my mind." **B**

Psychologists have studied this kind of unknowing plagiarism. In one study, researchers had people play the word game Boggle against a computer. Afterward, the players were asked to list the words they had found during the game. The researchers found that the players often claimed words found by the computer as their own. But it's hard to figure out how this kind of mistake could lead to unknowingly stealing 29 different passages. **C**

Then again, maybe Viswanathan really does have a photographic memory. She could be the first (or second). Earlier this year, a group of researchers published an article about a woman who can remember every day of her life. Such people weren't supposed to exist. Her case totally changes everything we thought we knew about human memory. The scientists even had to make up a new name for her disorder, or syndrome. **D** If Viswanathan's story is true, I know a few scientists who'd probably like to meet her. She might even be able to get a syndrome named after her.

---

2. **Helen Keller** was an American author and educator. She was blind and deaf—she could not see or hear.
3. When Helen Keller used the word **substance**, she meant that what she read became a natural part of her thinking.

Kaavya Syndrome

Applying Your Skills

Two Articles on Kaavya Viswanathan

INFORMATIONAL TEXT FOCUS: EVALUATING ARGUMENTS

DIRECTIONS: Now that you have read two opposing **arguments** on the Kaavya Viswanathan story, compare and contrast the authors' arguments by completing the chart below.

	Nankani's blog	Foer's article
Author's claim		
Examples or facts		
Make sense?		
Personal attack?		
Do I agree?		

VOCABULARY REVIEW

DIRECTIONS: Complete each of the sentences below with the best choice from the Word Box.

Word Box
- unconscious
- plagiarism
- controversy
- feat
- syndrome

1. The young woman was _____ that her words had upset her parents.
2. A _____ is marked by a particular group of symptoms.
3. The journalist lost his job because he committed _____ instead of doing his own reporting.
4. The gymnast performed an amazing _____ of flexibility.
5. Should the proposed new law pass? Many people disagree, and newspapers have been covering the _____ all week.

Skills Review

Collection 6

VOCABULARY REVIEW

DIRECTIONS: Read each sentence below. Then choose the letter of the word that best fits in the blank.

1. The article was in favor of the new skyscraper downtown, so it was a _____ argument.

    a. pro   **b.** program   **c.** pronoun

2. The article helped _____ my opinion about the issue.

    a. structure   **b.** feat   **c.** argument

3. The horror movie was so _____ that I couldn't sleep at all the night after I saw it.

    a. unconscious   **b.** unsettling   **c.** unfair

4. Before I write the report, I am going to _____ the facts by checking them in the encyclopedia.

    a. verify   **b.** counter   **c.** feat

5. All my friends are talking about the _____ over the new television show, which some people find really offensive.

    a. con   **b.** constant   **c.** controversy

6. The _____ of an argument is usually to convince you that the author's opinion is correct.

    a. plagiarism   **b.** syndrome   **c.** function

Skills Review

Collection 6

LANGUAGE COACH: SYNONYMS AND ANTONYMS

A **synonym** is a word that has the same or almost the same meaning as another word. For example, a synonym for *small* is *tiny*. An **antonym** is a word that has the opposite meaning of another word. For example, an antonym for *right* is *wrong*.

DIRECTIONS: Look at the word pairs, below. On the blank line, write **synonyms** if the words have similar meanings, or **antonyms** if the words have opposite meanings.

1. tall / short _____
2. unsettling / upsetting _____
3. con / against _____
4. valid / false _____
5. verify / prove _____
6. high / low _____
7. late / early _____
8. pro / for _____
9. feat / achievement _____
10. above / below _____

ORAL LANGUAGE ACTIVITY

DIRECTIONS: With a partner, discuss the arguments you have read about Kaavya Viswanathan's plagiarism. Then prepare and participate in a short debate. One of you should argue, like Nankini, that Kaavya's plagiarism was not her fault. The other partner should argue, like Foer, that Kaavya must be lying. Use evidence from the articles to support your argument.

Collection 7

Poetry

M.C. Escher's "Rippled Surface" © 2007 The M.C. Escher Company—The Netherlands. All rights reserved.

Literary and Academic Vocabulary for Collection 7

LITERARY VOCABULARY

ballad (BA LUHD) *n.:* a song that tells a story using a steady rhythm, strong rhymes, and repetition.
When you hear a ballad, you usually start to know when the refrain, or repeated words or lines, will come next.

image (IH MUHJ) *n.:* a word or phrase that appeals to one or more of our five senses.
The image of the sunny beach was so strong, I thought I could see the ocean, hear the waves, and smell the salty air.

simile (SIHM UH LEE) *n.:* a comparison of two different things using a word such as *like*, *as*, or *than*.
Mike used a simile when he said "Hearing that song is like flying."

metaphor (MEHT UH FAWR) *n.:* a comparison of two different things without the use of a word such as *like*, *as*, or *than*.
Betsy's metaphor made me laugh when she said "You are a pig!"

ACADEMIC VOCABULARY

nuances (NOO AHNS IHZ) *n.:* shades of meaning or feeling.
I had to read the poem a second time for the nuances to become clear.

associate (UH SOH SHEE AYT) *v.:* connect in thought.
A poet might associate the moon with love.

evoke (EE VOHK) *v.:* bring a memory or feeling to mind.
Pine trees might evoke memories of winter.

elaborate (EE LAB UH RAYT) *v.:* go into greater detail about something.
The second and third parts of the poem elaborate on the ideas of the first part.

Preparing to Read

A Blessing

By James Wright

LITERARY FOCUS: IMAGERY AND THEME

Poets often use words that excite our feelings and our imaginations. One of the ways they do this is by using **imagery**—words that appeal to our senses. If you are reading a poem and you think that you can *see, hear, taste, touch,* or *feel* what the poet is writing about, that is because the poet is using imagery.

As you read this poem, think about what meanings and feelings are suggested by the imagery. Then, think about how the imagery helps support the poem's **theme**, or central idea.

READING FOCUS: ANALYZING DETAILS

The **details** of a poem include more than just the details in the poem's story. There are many details that have to do with how a poem is created and presented. For example:

- Does the poet choose to use simple or complex words?
- Does the poem rhyme?
- Are all the lines the same length?

As you read a poem, it may be helpful to make notes for yourself about these kinds of details.

VOCABULARY

Work with a friend to practice using these words in complete sentences.

twilight (TWY LYT) *n.:* soft light just after sunset.

bounds (BOWNDZ) *v.:* leaps or springs forward.

nuzzled (NUHZ UHLD) *v.:* rubbed gently with the face.

caress (KUH REHS) *v.:* touch gently in an affectionate manner.

INTO THE POEM

James Wright often wrote about the places in his life, including Minnesota, where he taught college. "A Blessing," which takes place in Rochester, Minnesota, is a poem famous for its imagery and its theme of hope. Wright once called it "a love poem." The poem focuses on two small horses and their meeting with two men near a crowded highway. As you read, think about what Wright may have meant when he called "A Blessing" a love poem.

SKILLS FOCUS

Literary Skills Understand theme; understand imagery.

Reading Skills Analyze details.

A Blessing

By James Wright

Just off the highway to Rochester, Minnesota,
Twilight bounds softly forth on the grass,
And the eyes of those two Indian ponies
Darken with kindness. **A** **B**
They have come gladly out of the willows
To welcome my friend and me.
We step over the barbed wire into the pasture
Where they have been grazing[1] all day, alone.
They ripple tensely, they can hardly contain their happiness
10   That we have come. **C**
They bow shyly as wet swans. They love each other.
There is no loneliness like theirs. **D**
At home once more,
They begin munching the young tufts[2] of spring in the darkness.
I would like to hold the slenderer[3] one in my arms,
For she has walked over to me

---

1. Horses that are **grazing** (GRAY SIHNG) are eating the grass in the field.
2. **Tufts** (TUHFTS) of grass are small clumps or bunches that are smaller at the roots and bigger on top.
3. The **slenderer** (SLEHN DUHR UHR) horse is smaller or narrower.

"A Blessing" from *Collected Poems* by James Wright. Copyright © 1963, 1971 by James Wright. Reproduced by permission of **Wesleyan University Press, www.wesleyan.edu/wespress**.

A HERE'S HOW

Vocabulary

I think *bounds* has several meanings. It can mean "limits," "encloses" or it can mean "leaps forward." In line 2, I think "leaps forward" makes the most sense.

B YOUR TURN

Language Coach

The prefix *twi–* is from Middle English and means "two." Circle the word in line 2 that **originated** partially from this Middle English root.

C YOUR TURN

Literary Focus

Underline the words through line 10 that use **imagery**—language that appeals to your senses.

D HERE'S HOW

Reading Focus

As I read, I want to **analyze details** about the poem. It does not rhyme. The lines are mostly the same length, but not exactly. The words are mostly simple. There is a lot of imagery.

A YOUR TURN

Vocabulary

In line 17, one horse *nuzzled* the speaker's left hand. Use a dictionary to help you find a synonym, or word with a similar meaning, for *nuzzled*.

_____

_____

B QUICK CHECK

How does the speaker feel about the horses?

_____

_____

_____

And nuzzled my left hand. **A**
She is black and white,
Her mane falls wild on her forehead,
20 And the light breeze moves me to caress her long ear
That is delicate as the skin over a girl's wrist.
Suddenly I realize
That if I stepped out of my body I would break
Into blossom.

IN OTHER WORDS On the side of the highway near Rochester, Minnesota, evening is beginning. Two small horses come out from behind the trees. They seem kind and welcoming. My friend and I step over the wire fence to be close to them. They have been alone all day and their energy shows how happy they are to see us. Seeing them together makes me think about love and about loneliness. The smaller horse comes over and touches my left hand with her mouth. I would like to hug her. **B** She is black and white. Her mane falls over her forehead. I feel the breeze and I move to rub the horse's ear. Her delicate skin makes me think of a young girl's. This meeting with the horses has brought the hope of spring, of life, into my body. I feel free, like a flower ready to blossom.

184   A Blessing

Applying Your Skills

A Blessing

LITERARY FOCUS: IMAGERY AND THEME

DIRECTIONS: Use the map below to explore the **imagery** in "A Blessing." Each circle includes a line from the poem. Write which of your senses the line appeals to: *see*, *hear*, *taste*, *touch*, or *feel*. If the line appeals to more than one sense, write down all of them.

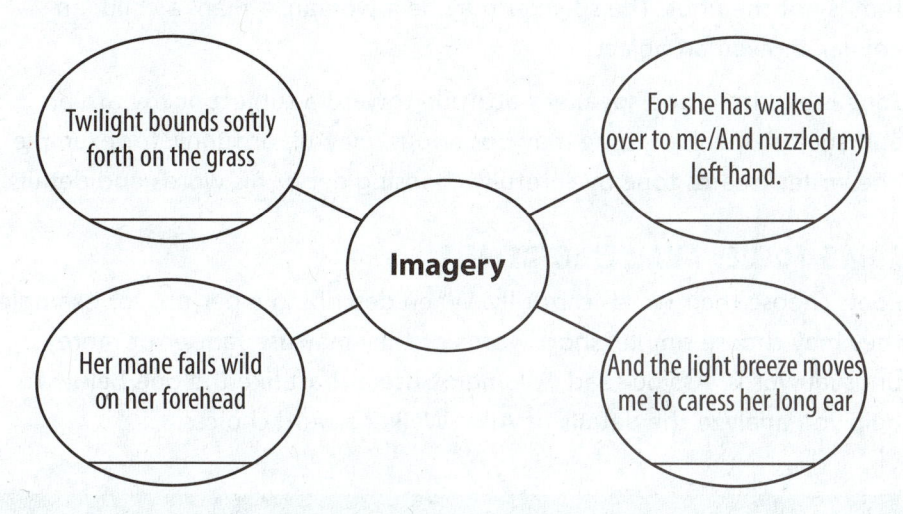

- Twilight bounds softly forth on the grass
- For she has walked over to me/And nuzzled my left hand.
- Her mane falls wild on her forehead
- And the light breeze moves me to caress her long ear

(Imagery)

READING FOCUS: ANALYZING DETAILS

DIRECTIONS: Think about the **details** of how "A Blessing" is written. Then answer the questions below.

1. How do you think the poem might affect you differently if it rhymed?

   _____
   _____
   _____

2. Why do you think the poet chose to use mostly simple words, rather than very complex ones, to describe the scene?

   _____
   _____
   _____

VOCABULARY REVIEW

DIRECTIONS: Write a sentence about the action in "A Blessing" using the vocabulary words *twilight* and *nuzzled*.

_____

Preparing to Read

Women

By Alice Walker

LITERARY FOCUS: SPEAKER AND TONE

The voice that talks to us in a poem is called the **speaker**. Sometimes the speaker is the same person as the poet, but often the speaker is a character that is not the poet. The speaker may be a woman, a man, a child, an animal, or even an object.

Tone is a writer's or a speaker's attitude toward a subject or toward an audience. A speaker's tone may be serious, playful, or funny, for example. The writer creates tone by carefully choosing her or his words and details.

READING FOCUS: ANALYZING DETAILS

Poets choose their words carefully. When describing a person, for example, they may choose simple, short words or they may use fancier or more unusual words. As you read "Women," use a chart like the one below to help you **analyze the details** of Alice Walker's word choices.

Words/Phrases from Poem	My Thoughts
"My mama's generation"	The speaker seems affectionate toward her mother; she uses the word "mama," not the more formal "mother."

VOCABULARY

As you read "Women," circle these words and consider their meanings.

generation (JEHN UHR AY SHUHN) *n.:* a group of individuals living at the same time.

stout (STOWT) *n.:* determined; forceful.

battered (BAT UHRD) *v.:* wore down with hard blows.

SKILLS FOCUS

Literary Skills
Understand speaker; understand tone.

Reading Skills
Analyze details.

186 Women

WOMEN

By Alice Walker

INTO THE POEM

Alice Walker writes poems, novels, short stories, and essays. She says that she wrote "Women" for her mother, who worked as a maid. Walker calls her mother and her teachers the most important influences in her life. Her teachers, she says, "saved me from feeling alone, from worrying that the world I was stretching to find might not even exist." As you read "Women," think about why women like Walker's mother and teachers made such an impression on her.

They were women then
My mama's generation **A**
Husky of voice—stout of
Step
5   With fists as well as
Hands **B**
How they battered **C** down
Doors
And ironed
10 Starched white
Shirts
How they led
Armies
Headragged[1] generals **D**
15 Across mined[2]
Fields

---

1. Women described as **headragged** (HEHD RAHG UHD) are wearing kerchiefs or cloths tied around their hair.
2. Fields that are **mined** (MYND) have explosives buried under the ground, just waiting to go off when someone steps on them.

"Women" from *Revolutionary Petunias & Other Poems* by Alice Walker. Copyright © 1970 and renewed © 1998 by Alice Walker. Reproduced by permission of **Harcourt, Inc.** and electronic format by permission of **The Wendy Weil Agency, Inc.** This material may not be reproduced in any form or by any means without the prior written permission of the publisher.

A HERE'S HOW

Vocabulary

I have heard the word *generation* before. I think it means "a group of individuals living at the same time." The speaker is talking about the group of women who lived when her mother did.

B HERE'S HOW

Literary Focus

The **tone** of this poem so far seems to be serious and respectful. The speaker uses words that make the women she knew sound very strong.

C YOUR TURN

Vocabulary

In lines 7–8, the women "battered down doors." What do you think *battered* means in this context?

_____
_____
_____

D HERE'S HOW

Language Coach

My teacher says that the word *generals* comes from the Latin **root word** *generis*. Some other English words with this Latin root are *generous* and *generic*.

> **A** **HERE'S HOW**
>
> **Reading Focus**
> The speaker uses words like *armies*, *generals*, *mines*, and *ditches* to describe the actions of the women she is discussing. If I **analyze details**, I can see that these words make me think of war. In some ways, I guess, these women were fighting a war for more opportunities.
>
> **B** **YOUR TURN**
>
> **Literary Focus**
> Describe what you have learned about the poem's **speaker**. Is the speaker a man, woman, child, or animal? What else do you know?
>
> _____
> _____
> _____
> _____
> _____
> _____
> _____

Booby-trapped[3]
Ditches
To discover books
20 Desks
A place for us **A**
How they knew what we
Must know **B**
Without knowing a page
25 Of it
Themselves.

IN OTHER WORDS The women who are my mother's age are very strong. You can tell by the way they talk and the way they walk. They fought for new opportunities for women. They did this while still taking care of their families and homes. Many people did not agree with them. But these women believed in the importance of education. Although many of them did not go to college, they wanted to make sure their daughters would do so. These women had not been allowed to learn as much as they wanted. But they could see how more education and more opportunities would make better lives for the women who came next.

3. When something is **booby-trapped** (BOO BEE TRAHPT), it has a trap or explosive connected to something ordinary looking.

188 Women

Applying Your Skills

Women

LITERARY FOCUS: SPEAKER AND TONE

DIRECTIONS: Now that you have read "Women" and thought about its **speaker**, consider its **tone**. Read the list of words below. Which ones best describe the tone of the poem? Circle those words.

grateful   questioning   funny   angry   serious   unsure   impressed

READING FOCUS: ANALYZING DETAILS

DIRECTIONS: The chart below will help you **analyze details** in the poem "Women." The chart lists words or phrases from the poem and asks for your reaction to those words or phrases. Fill in the "my thoughts" column for each word or phrase listed.

Words/Phrases from Poem	My Thoughts
My mama's generation	The speaker seems affectionate toward her mother; she uses the word "mama," not the more formal "mother."
Stout of step	
With fists	
Starched white shirts	
A place for us	

Word Box

generation
stout
battered

VOCABULARY REVIEW

DIRECTIONS: Select the words from the Word Box that best complete each sentence. Write your answers on the blank lines.

1. The police _____ down the door to the room where the criminal was hiding.

2. My grandfather's _____ grew up in a very different era.

Preparing to Read

I Wandered Lonely as a Cloud

By William Wordsworth

LITERARY FOCUS: RHYTHM AND METER

The musical quality in poems comes from repetition, or **rhythm**. Some poets create rhythm by arranging the words so that the lines repeat a regular pattern of stressed and unstressed syllables. This kind of regular pattern is called **meter**. When you **scan** a poem, you mark the stressed syllables with the symbol ′ and the unstressed syllables with the symbol ˘. This is how you would scan the first line of William Wordsworth's famous poem:

˘ ′ ˘ ′ ˘ ˘ ′ ˘ ′
I wandered lonely as a cloud

READING FOCUS: READING ALOUD

When you are trying to find the meter in a poem, you put extra emphasis on the stressed syllables. But that is not how you read a poem when you want to get the meaning across. Here are some tips for **reading** poetry **aloud**:

- Most poems are written in sentences. Look for punctuation telling you where the sentences begin and end.
- Do not stop at the end of a line if there is no period, question mark, or exclamation point. Pause only briefly for commas, semicolons, and dashes.

VOCABULARY

Look for these words and their context as you read the selection.

sprightly (SPRYT LEE) *adj.*: lively; full of spirit.

glee (GLEE) *n.*: great delight.

pensive (PEHN SIHV) *adj.*: dreamily thoughtful.

solitude (SOL UH TOOD) *n.*: state of being alone.

INTO THE POEM

This poem captures a special moment that happened over two hundred years ago—on April 15, 1802. We know the exact date because another person was there at the time. The poet's sister, Dorothy, captured the very same scene in her journal.

SKILLS FOCUS

Literary Skills Understand rhythm and meter.

Reading Skills Read aloud; break down texts.

I Wandered Lonely as a Cloud

By William Wordsworth

© A. Curtis/Alamy

I wandered lonely as a cloud
That floats on high o'er vales[1] and hills,
When all at once I saw a crowd,
A host, of golden daffodils,
Beside the lake, beneath the trees,
Fluttering and dancing in the breeze. **A** **B**

IN OTHER WORDS I was out walking one day, feeling lonely—like a cloud floating high above the valleys and hills. Suddenly, next to a lake and under some trees, I saw a field of yellow daffodils. As they fluttered in the breeze, they seemed to me to be like a crowd of people dancing.

Continuous as the stars that shine
And twinkle on the Milky Way,
They stretched in never-ending line

---

1. **vales** (VAYLZ): valleys.

A HERE'S HOW

Literary Focus

I scanned all the lines in the first stanza (lines 1–6), and they all have the same regular **meter**. The only variation is the first word in line 6. You would never stress the *ter* in *Fluttering*. I know poets do not always follow the meter exactly, and this variation adds to the "fluttery" quality of the daffodils.

B HERE'S HOW

Vocabulary

I have never seen the word *host* used like it is in line 4. Since *host* is set off by commas right after the word *crowd*, I think *host* and *crowd* must mean the same thing.

A **HERE'S HOW**

Reading Focus

I see that lines 7–12 are one sentence. When **reading aloud**, I will not pause after lines without punctuation—lines 7 and 9.

B **HERE'S HOW**

Language Coach

I know that the word *glee* means "great delight." I also know that its **connotations**, or feelings that a word suggests, are feelings of joy and happiness.

C **YOUR TURN**

Reading Focus

Read this stanza **aloud**. Does doing so change your impression of the poem?

_____
_____
_____
_____

D **YOUR TURN**

Literary Focus

Use the scanning symbols demonstrated on the Preparing to Read page to mark the stressed and unstressed syllables of the last line of the poem. Put your marks on the poem, right above the line. Is the **meter** in the last line of the poem the same as the meter in the first line?

_____

10   Along the margin of a bay;
　　　Ten thousand saw I at a glance,
　　　Tossing their heads in sprightly dance. **A**

IN OTHER WORDS The flowers seemed to be endless, like the stars that twinkle in the Milky Way galaxy. They stretched endlessly along the shore of the lake. I could see ten thousand with just a short look.

　　　The waves beside them danced, but they
　　　Outdid the sparkling waves in glee; **B**
15   A poet could not but be gay,
　　　In such a jocund[2] company;
　　　I gazed—and gazed—but little thought
　　　What wealth the show to me had brought.

IN OTHER WORDS The waves from the lake also seemed like they were dancing, but as sparkling and beautiful as the waves were, the daffodils outdid them. I couldn't help but be happy, amid such a happy group. I watched them for a long time, but I didn't really think of how much the sight of these daffodils would mean to me someday.

　　　For oft[3], when on my couch I lie
20   In vacant or in pensive mood,
　　　They flash upon that inward eye
　　　Which is the bliss of solitude;
　　　And then my heart with pleasure fills,
　　　And dances with the daffodils. **C D**

IN OTHER WORDS Now, when I am lying on my couch, thinking mindlessly or even thinking deep, sad thoughts, the vision of those daffodils appears to me. I see them in my mind's eye, which is one of the joys of being alone. Then, my heart fills with pleasure, and it feels as if it is with the daffodils, dancing beside the lake.

2.　**jocund** (JAHK UHND): merry.
3.　**oft** (AWFT): shortened form of *often*.

Applying Your Skills

I Wandered Lonely as a Cloud

LITERARY FOCUS: RHYTHM AND METER

DIRECTIONS: Review the explanation of the poem's **meter** on the Preparing to Read page. Then try writing your own lines of poetry! You can write about any subject you want, but try to use the same meter as "I Wandered Lonely as a Cloud."

_____
_____
_____
_____

READING FOCUS: READING ALOUD

DIRECTIONS: To improve your **reading aloud** of the first stanza, mark each stressed and unstressed syllable. Remember to use the symbol ´ for stressed syllables, and ˘ for unstressed syllables.

I wandered lonely as a cloud

That floats on high o'er vales and hills,

When all at once I saw a crowd,

A host, of golden daffodils,

Beside the lake, beneath the trees,

Fluttering and dancing in the breeze.

VOCABULARY REVIEW

DIRECTIONS: Write "Yes" after each sentence if the vocabulary word is being used correctly. Write "No" if it is not being used incorrectly.

Word Box
sprightly
glee
pensive
solitude

1. I **glee** the smell of daffodils; they're so fragrant. _____
2. I felt **pensive** relaxing in the field, just thinking about things and daydreaming. _____
3. After being surrounded by people all the time, it felt good to be alone for once; the **solitude** was a nice change. _____

I Wandered Lonely as a Cloud   193

Preparing to Read

Legal Alien

By Pat Mora

LITERARY FOCUS: SPEAKER, WORD PLAY, AND PARALLEL STRUCTURES

Poets can imagine anyone or anything as their **speaker**, or the voice talking to us in a poem. The speaker is often the poet, but not always. A poet, for example, may choose to speak from a different point of view, or **persona**.

Whoever the speaker is, the poet carefully chooses his or her words to best express their meaning. Sometimes, the poet uses **word play**—drawing on words' multiple meanings, experimenting with sounds, or pairing two words that would not normally go together. As you read, also look for Mora's use of **parallel structure**, or similar sentence patterns, and think about its impact on the poem.

READING FOCUS: ANALYZING DETAILS

To fully appreciate a poem, you should read it several times. The first reading can be just for enjoyment. In the second reading you can focus on understanding the poem. In the third reading of a poem, you can **analyze the details**. In doing so, you might look for deeper meaning in the poem, and think about how the poem is put together.

VOCABULARY

fluent (FLOO IHNT) *adj.:* capable of using a language easily and correctly.

inferior (IHN FEE REE UHR) *adj.:* of little or less importance or value.

discomfort (DIHS CUHM FUHRT) *n.:* uneasiness.

INTO THE POEM

Poet Pat Mora was born on the border of Mexico and El Paso, Texas. Raised in a Mexican-American family, she grew up learning to speak and read in both English and Spanish. Her poetry reflects her personal life, blending Hispanic culture into American society. She sees the differences between people as less important than the ties of culture they share—living, loving, working, marrying, raising children, and growing old.

SKILLS FOCUS

Literary Skills Understand speaker; understand diction; understand parallel structures.

Reading Skills Analyze details.

LEGAL ALIEN/EXTRANJERA LEGAL

By Pat Mora

Bi-lingual, Bi-cultural,[1] **A**
able to slip from "How's life?"
to "*Me'stan volviendo loca*,"[2]
able to sit in a paneled
    office
drafting memos in smooth
    English,
able to order in fluent
    Spanish
10 at a Mexican restaurant, **B**
American but hyphenated,[3] **C**
viewed by Anglos[4] as perhaps
    exotic,
perhaps inferior, definitely
    different, **D**
viewed by Mexicans as
    alien[5]
(their eyes say, "You may
    speak
20 Spanish but you're not like
    me"),
an American to Mexicans
a Mexican to Americans

Bi-lingüe, bi-cultural,
capaz de deslizarse de "*How's life?*"
a "*Me'stan volviendo loca*,"
capaz de ocupar un despacho
    bien apuntado,
redactando memorandums en
    inglés liso,
capaz de ordenar la cena en
    español fluido
en restaurante mexicano,
americana pero con guión,
vista por los anglos como
    exótica,
quizás inferior, obviamente
    distinta,
vista por mexicanos como
    extranjera
(sus ojos dicen "Hablas
    español
pero no eres como
    yo"),
americana para mexicanos
mexicana para americanos

---

1. **Bi-lingual** (BY LIHNG WUHL) means "able to use two languages," and **bi-cultural** (BY KUHL CHUHR UHL) means "of two different cultures."
2. *Me'stan volviendo loca* (MEH STAHN VOHL VEE EHN DOH LOH KAH) is a Spanish phrase meaning "They're driving me crazy."
3. **Hyphenated** (HY FIHN AYT EHD) means "joined by a punctuation mark called a hyphen (a short dash)." Parts of words or word compounds are hyphenated. Sometimes the compound Mexican-American is hyphenated.
4. **Anglos** (AN GLOHS) is a word used to mean "white, non-Hispanic residents of the United States."
5. The word **alien** (AY LEE UHN) can mean "different" or "foreign."

"Legal Alien" and "Extranjera legal" from *Chants* by Pat Mora. Copyright © 1984 by Pat Mora. Published by **Arte Público Press–University of Houston, Houston, TX, 1985, 2000.** Reproduced by permission of the publisher.

A HERE'S HOW

Language Coach

I see that in the first line of her poem, Mora uses the **prefix** *bi-*, meaning "two," in the words *bi-lingual* and *bi-cultural*. Although these words are not usually hyphenated, Mora separates the word parts. I think this helps to show her feeling of living in two different worlds.

B HERE'S HOW

Literary Focus

I know that the **speaker** in poems is not always the poet. But based on what I read about Mora's background, it seems that she is describing herself in this poem.

C YOUR TURN

Literary Focus

Hyphenated means "joined by a punctuation mark." How does Mora use the word *hyphenated* in line 11 as an example of **word play**?

D HERE'S HOW

Vocabulary

I think the word *inferior* has a negative meaning based on the context. My dictionary says *inferior* means "less important" or "less valuable." That is not a way I would want someone to see me.

A **YOUR TURN**

Language Coach

In line 29, draw a line between the parts of the word *discomfort* like this: dis/comfort. The **prefix** *dis-* means "not." Write what you think *discomfort* means below.

_____

_____

B **YOUR TURN**

Reading Focus

You have read the poem once. Now read it again, and look for clues about the poem's deeper meaning as you **analyze details**. Is the speaker comfortable or uncomfortable with the way people treat her? Explain your answer.

_____

_____

_____

_____

_____

a handy token
25 sliding back and forth
    between the fringes[6] of both
        worlds
    by smiling
    by masking[7] the discomfort **A**
30 of being pre-judged
    Bi-laterally.[8] **B**

una ficha servible
pasando de un lado al otro
de los márgenes de dos
    mundos
sonriéndome
disfrazando la incomodidad
del pre-juicio
bi-lateralmente.

IN OTHER WORDS I speak two languages and I live in two cultures. There are some people in my life I speak to in English, and others I speak to in Spanish. In some ways I do not really fit in with either group of people. English-speaking Americans think I'm different, or even less intelligent than they are. Mexicans also think I'm different. Each group sees me as part of the other group. I can smile and talk in either world. But it is always uncomfortable for me to know I'm being judged by everyone around me.

---

6. Here, the word **fringes** (FRIHN jehz) means "edges."
7. **Masking** (MASK ihng) means "covering up or hiding," as someone would hide behind a mask.
8. **Bi-laterally** (by LAT uhr uhl lee) means "by two sides." Mora has added a hyphen to this word.

196 Legal Alien/Extranjera legal

Applying Your Skills

Legal Alien/Extranjera legal

LITERARY FOCUS: SPEAKER, WORD PLAY, AND PARALLEL STRUCTURES

DIRECTIONS: What have you learned about the **speaker** of this poem? Complete the exercise below by writing four phrases that describe her based on your readings of the poem.

1. _____
2. _____
3. _____
4. _____

READING FOCUS: ANALYZING DETAILS

DIRECTIONS: Use the chart below to record some notes about each time you read "Legal Alien." Write down what you gained from each reading. Did you notice different **details** with each reading?

Legal Alien/Extranjera legal		
First reading (enjoyment)	**Second reading (understanding)**	**Third reading (analyze details)**

VOCABULARY REVIEW

DIRECTIONS: Write a few sentences describing the speaker in "Legal Alien." Use at least two of these three vocabulary words: *fluent*, *inferior*, and *discomfort*.

_____
_____
_____

Preparing to Read

The History Behind the Ballad/ Ballad of Birmingham/ 4 Little Girls

LITERARY FOCUS: HISTORICAL ACCOUNTS ACROSS GENRES

Writers can choose many different ways to respond to a **historical account**, or event. The writing form they choose (poem or article, for example) reflects their purpose for writing. For example, a historian who wants to explain what really happened might write a nonfiction book full of research and facts. A poet who wants to focus more on the emotional effect of the event might write a **ballad**—a poem that tells a story, using rhythm, rhyme, and repetition. A film critic might watch a documentary (a factual film) about the same event and offer his own opinions about the movie and the period of history it illustrates.

READING FOCUS: COMPARING MESSAGES IN DIFFERENT FORMS

When comparing different works inspired by the same historical event, ask yourself, "Why did the writer choose this **form**?" Think about how the form shaped each writer's style. For example, a poet who writes a ballad will shape ideas using rhyme and rhythm. A historian, meanwhile, will focus more on telling a story using facts and quotes.

SKILLS FOCUS

Literary Skills Analyze historical context; understand the characteristics of a ballad.

Reading Skills Compare historical accounts across genres.

VOCABULARY

debris (DEH BREE) *n.:* the remains of something broken or destroyed.

sacred (SAY KREHD) *adj.:* dedicated to religious use.

clawed (KLAWD) *v.:* dug, scraped, or scratched.

racism (RAY SIH ZUHM) *n.:* prejudice against people of a particular race.

contributions (KAHN TRIHB YOO SHUNS) *n.:* things that are given to a shared cause.

The History Behind the Ballad

Based on the excerpt from *Parting of the Waters*, by Taylor Branch

INTO THE HISTORICAL ACCOUNT

The author of the following piece, Taylor Branch, is a historian. He has written several books about the civil rights movement in the United States in the 1960s. One of his books, *Parting the Waters*, won the important Pulitzer Prize. Below is an excerpt from that book, talking about the events of a particular Sunday in Alabama in 1963.

That Sunday was the Youth Day at the Sixteenth Street Baptist Church. For this one day each year, young people would run the main church service for the adults. Mamie H. Grier was in charge of the Sunday school. She stopped in the basement ladies' room. Four young girls had left Bible classes early and were talking there. All four were dressed in white for their special day. **A** Grier asked the girls to hurry upstairs. Then she went to her own Sunday-school class. During the lesson, a loud earthquake shook the church. Pieces of debris fell into the classroom. **B** Grier's first thought was that it sounded like a parade. Maxine McNair, a school teacher next to her, was the first one to speak. "Oh my goodness!' she said. She and Grier ran out of the classroom, but the stairs down to the basement were blocked. The large stone staircase on the outside of the building was gone. When the women got outside they heard moans and sirens. A church member shouted to Grier that her husband had already gone to the hospital in the first ambulance. McNair searched for her only child until finally she found her own father, crying. She screamed, "Daddy, I can't find Denise!" The man helplessly replied, "She's dead, baby. I've got one of her shoes." He held a girl's white dress shoe. The look on his daughter's face made him scream out, "I'd like to blow the whole town up!" **C**

A YOUR TURN

Literary Focus

In analyzing **historical accounts** in different forms, notice how the form reflects the author's purpose. Underline three facts you have read so far. What do the factual details tell you about this author's purpose?

_____
_____
_____

B YOUR TURN

Vocabulary

From the context of the sentence in which it appears, what do you think the word *debris* means?

_____
_____
_____

C HERE'S HOW

Reading Focus

The writer uses quotes which really make me feel the fear and anger of McNair and her father. This writer seems to be using the historical nonfiction **form** of writing very well.

Excerpt [retitled "The History behind the Ballad"] from *Parting the Waters: America in the King Years, 1956-63* by Taylor Branch. Copyright © 1988 by Taylor Branch. Reproduced by permission of **Simon & Schuster Adult Publishing Group**.

Ballad of Birmingham (On the bombing of a church in Birmingham, Alabama, 1963)

By Dudley Randall

A YOUR TURN

Reading Focus

This is the second account you have read about this event. You can compare messages in different **forms**. How do the rhyme and rhythm of this ballad affect you differently than facts and nonfiction details did in the historical account you read earlier?

_____
_____
_____
_____

B QUICK CHECK

Why does the mother tell her daughter not to attend the Freedom March?

_____
_____
_____

INTO THE POEM

Tragic events made the headlines on September 15, 1963. During the struggle for civil rights for African Americans, a bomb exploded in a church in Birmingham, Alabama. Four girls were killed. In this ballad, Dudley Randall uses poetry to shine a light on the dark feelings raised by this tragedy.

"Mother dear, may I go downtown
Instead of out to play,
And march the streets of Birmingham
In a Freedom March[1] today?" **A**

5   "No, baby, no, you may not go,
For the dogs are fierce and wild,
And clubs and hoses, guns and jails
Aren't good for a little child." **B**

IN OTHER WORDS A daughter asks her mother if she can go to a march in downtown Birmingham, Alabama, to support equal rights for African Americans. The mother does not want the daughter to go because she is afraid the police may be violent toward the people at the march.

---

1. A **Freedom March** (FREE DUHM MAHRCH) was a gathering of people who walked, carried signs, and otherwise protested against laws that discriminated against African Americans.

"Ballad of Birmingham" from *Cities Burning* by Dudley Randall. Copyright © 1968 by Broadside Press. Reproduced by permission of the publisher.

200   Ballad of Birmingham

"But, mother, I won't be alone.
10   Other children will go with me,
And march the streets of Birmingham
To make our country free."

"No, baby, no, you may not go,
For I fear those guns will fire.
15   But you may go to church instead
And sing in the children's choir." **C**

IN OTHER WORDS The daughter argues that she should join the others who are fighting prejudice, and that she will be safe in the crowd. The mother repeats that the daughter may not go. Instead, the mother wants the daughter to go to church and sing in the choir.

She has combed and brushed her
night-dark hair,
And bathed rose-petal sweet,[2]
20   And drawn white gloves on her small brown hands,
And white shoes on her feet.

The mother smiled to know her child
Was in the sacred place,
But that smile was the last smile
25   To come upon her face. **D E**

IN OTHER WORDS The daughter obeys her mother and gets dressed up to go to church. The mother feels safe knowing her daughter is going to church instead of to the march.

For when she heard the explosion,
Her eyes grew wet and wild.
She raced through the streets of Birmingham
Calling for her child. **F**

---

2. The term **rose-petal sweet** (ROHZ PEHT UHL SWEET) describes the effect of adding rose petals to bath water, so that the water smells sweet like roses.

C   HERE'S HOW

Reading Focus

I think the writer chose this **form** for a reason. I know that the ballad form is used to express feelings. The nonfiction form is used to present facts. I think the author chose this ballad form to focus on people's feelings about what happened.

D   YOUR TURN

Vocabulary

Do you think that *sacred* in line 23 means 1) afraid or 2) for religious use?

_____

E   LITERARY ANALYSIS

Re-read this stanza. Given the message of the last line, what do you think is going to happen next?

_____
_____
_____
_____

F   YOUR TURN

Literary Focus

This author uses a **ballad** to help express his meaning. Underline words in lines 26–29 of the ballad that express emotion.

Ballad of Birmingham   201

A **HERE'S HOW**

Vocabulary

I know that a *claw* is a sharp nail that certain animals have. Here, a person *clawed*. I think the word here means the mother used her hands to dig.

Courtesy of The Birmingham Public Library Archives, Neg. [85.1.20]

30 She clawed through bits of glass and brick,
Then lifted out a shoe. **A**
"O, here's the shoe my baby wore,
But, baby, where are you?"

IN OTHER WORDS The mother hears a bomb go off and runs to the church looking for her daughter. The mother sees the church has been destroyed. Her daughter has died in the one place the mother thought would be safest. Only one of her daughter's shoes is left.

202 Ballad of Birmingham

4 LITTLE GIRLS

Based on the review by Roger Ebert

INTO THE MOVIE REVIEW
Film director Spike Lee noted that there are "a lot of young people, both black and white, that really don't know about the civil rights struggle and civil rights movement." In 1997, Lee helped more people become aware of this struggle by making a movie called "4 Little Girls." It is a documentary film about the bombing in Birmingham in 1963. Roger Ebert, who wrote the piece you are about to read, is a film critic who has written more than fifteen books about movies. In this essay, Ebert offers his opinions not only on Spike Lee's movie, but also on the event itself.

Spike Lee's "4 Little Girls" tells the story of the Birmingham, Alabama, church bombing of Sept. 15, 1963. Four young members of the choir died in the explosion. One was 11 years old. The other three were 14. This bombing drew people's attention to the civil rights movement. America could no longer ignore racism. **B**

The little girls had gone to church early. We can imagine them meeting their friends in the room destroyed by the bomb. We can see this picture in our minds because Spike Lee's movie, in a way, brings the girls back to life. Lee uses photographs, old home movies, and the memories of families and friends about the four girls. **C**

Not long after seeing "4 Little Girls," I heard a report on the radio from a woman named Charlayne Hunter-Gault. In 1961, she was the first black woman to attend the University of Georgia. Today she is a reporter for a major national radio program. In 1963, Carole Robertson was a Girl Scout who had earned many badges. Because she was killed that day, we will never know what would have happened in her life.

The four little girls never got to grow up. Their lives were stolen, and so were their contributions to our lives. **D** I believe

---

B YOUR TURN

Vocabulary

Circle the best definition for *racism*: 1) prejudice against people of another race, or 2) violence against young people.

C HERE'S HOW

Reading Focus

I want to compare how this same event is presented in different **forms**. In lines 8–11, Ebert talks about a picture in his mind. I got this same picture from the history and the poem. But this review talks about the power of film to actually *show* the girls. This ability to show powerful images is one reason movies are good for exploring a story.

D HERE'S HOW

Vocabulary

Ebert says the four little girls' *contributions* were stolen from us. I think their *contributions* are what they would have given to all of us. My dictionary shows that I am correct.

Roger Ebert's review *of 4 Little Girls* by Spike Lee, from *Chicago Sun Times*, October 24, 1997. Copyright © 1997 by Roger Ebert. Reproduced by permission of **Universal Press Syndicate**.

> **A** **HERE'S HOW**
>
> **Literary Focus**
> This paragraph gives another good example of how writers can approach a **historical account**. Here Ebert tells us quotes from Denise's father. Including these quotes makes the story much more powerful.
>
> **B** **YOUR TURN**
>
> **Reading Focus**
> This paragraph gives some examples of how a filmmaker can use his **form** to tell a story. Underline words in this paragraph that show how Lee uses film to re-create the day of the bombing.
>
> **C** **LITERARY ANALYSIS**
> Use your own words to re-state the sentence: The hatred shown by the bomb made all the speeches against civil rights sound as ugly as they really were.
>
> _____
> _____
> _____
> _____
> _____

that Denise McNair, who was 11 when she died, would have made a difference in the world. Her parents, Chris and Maxine McNair, speak about her in the film. They remember Denise as a special child.

Chris McNair talks of a day when he took Denise to downtown Birmingham. The smell of onions frying at a restaurant made her hungry. "That night I knew I had to tell her she couldn't have that sandwich because she was black,"[1] he recalls. "That couldn't have been any less painful than seeing her with a rock smashed into her head." **A**

Lee's film re-creates the day of the bombing through news films, photographs, and the reports of people who were there. He also shows other events of the civil rights movement in the South that happened around the same time. **B**

Birmingham police officer Bull Connor is seen directing other officers to stop civil rights marchers. The governor of Alabama, George Wallace, promises to stop black students from entering any Alabama public school. After Sept. 15, 1963, everything changed. The hatred shown by the bomb made all the speeches against civil rights sound as ugly as they really were. **C**

---

1. Restaurants in the southern United States were segregated, which means that service to whites and service to African Americans was separate. Some restaurants did not serve African Americans at all.

Spike Lee says he has wanted to make this film since 1983, when he read a *New York Times Magazine* article by Howell Raines about the bombing. "He wrote me asking permission back then," Chris McNair said. "That was before he had made any of his films." It is perhaps good that Lee waited, because he is a better filmmaker now. Also, as time passed the courts found a man named Robert Chambliss ("Dynamite Bob") guilty of the bombing. Raines said Chambliss was the worst racist he had ever seen. **D**

The other victims were Addle Mae Collins and Cynthia Wesley, both 14. In the movie, we see the girls' bodies. Why does Lee show them? To show racism for what it really is. In the film, a white Birmingham policeman tells a black minister after the bombing, "I really didn't believe they would go this far." The policeman was a Klansman,[2] the movie says. But in using the word "they" he separates himself from the crime. Others also wanted to separate themselves from racism after the bombing. Soon even Governor Wallace was apologizing for his behavior and trying to show himself as a different man.

There is mostly sadness and regret in "4 Little Girls," but there is also anger underneath, as there should be. **E**

D QUICK CHECK

When did Spike Lee first want to make a film of this incident?

___

E YOUR TURN

Reading Focus

Ebert is using the **form** of a film review for a purpose. What does he want you to know, overall, about the movie "4 Little Girls"?

___

---

2. A **Klansman** (KLANS MAN) refers to a member of the Ku Klux Klan, a group that was founded on the belief that whites are better than all other groups, and that has acted violently towards non-whites.

Skills Practice

The History Behind the Ballad/ Ballad of Birmingham/ 4 Little Girls

USE A COMPARISON CHART

DIRECTIONS: You have read three works inspired by the same **historical event**. Each was written in a different **form**. Use the comparison chart below to compare and contrast each form of writing. Include your thoughts on how each text made you feel.

Title/Form of writing	Strengths of this form	Impact of this work
The History Behind the Ballad/ historical account		
Ballad of Birmingham/ballad		
4 Little Girls/movie review		

Applying Your Skills

The History Behind the Ballad/ Ballad of Birmingham/ 4 Little Girls

LITERARY FOCUS: HISTORICAL ACCOUNTS ACROSS GENRES

DIRECTIONS: One way to compare **historical accounts** in different forms is to think about different parts of each account. Look over the three texts again and underline the sentence from each that you find to be the most powerful. Then write that sentence in the chart below.

Historical Account	
Ballad	
Movie Review	

READING FOCUS: COMPARING MESSAGES IN DIFFERENT FORMS

DIRECTIONS: Each of the texts you read used a different **form** to describe the same event. Suppose you were going to write something about the four girls killed in the Birmingham church bombing. What form of writing would you use? Explain why you would use this form.

_____
_____

VOCABULARY REVIEW

DIRECTIONS: Each of the three accounts you read discusses *racism* and the bombing of the church in Birmingham. Below, write a few sentences in your own words about the meaning of the word *racism* and how it affected the events you have been learning about.

_____
_____

Preparing to Read

FBI Art Crime Team/Collection Is Found to Contain Stolen Rockwell Art

INFORMATIONAL TEXT FOCUS: GENERATING RESEARCH QUESTIONS

When you **research**, or study, a topic, your goal is to gain more specific, in-depth knowledge. Doing research is largely a question-and-answer process. You start by thinking about what you already know about the subject. Then you ask questions about it, and do research to answer those questions.

Asking good questions is the key to doing research that will lead to interesting results. When you create questions for your research, try to stay focused on your topic. Ask only questions that will help you find out what you want to know. A great way to get started is to ask the *5W-How?* questions.

- **Who** was involved?
- **What** happened?
- **When** and **where** did it happen?
- **Why** and **how** did it happen?

VOCABULARY

inception (IHN SEHP SHUHN) *n.:* start of something; beginning.

ceremonial (SEHR UH MOH NEE UHL) *adj.:* having to do with a rite or ceremony.

recovered (REE KUH VUHRD) *v.:* got back; regained.

rare (RAYR) *adj.:* uncommon; an unusually good example of its kind.

inspected (IHN SPEHK TIHD) *v.:* viewed closely; examined.

INTO THE WEB PAGE AND NEWSPAPER ARTICLE

The Federal Bureau of Investigation, or FBI, is an agency of the United States government that works to solve crimes. You are about to read about a special division of the F.B.I. that works to solve crimes having to do with art works. The first selection is from their Web site. The words on the left make up a *menu* of *links*—if you were on your computer, you could click on one of those phrases to find out more information about that subject.

Informational Text Skills
Generate research questions to guide reading; generate relevant, interesting, and researchable questions.

208 FBI Art Crime Team/Collection Is Found to Contain Stolen Rockwell Art

Read with a Purpose Read these two selections to learn what the FBI Art Crime Team does.

Federal Bureau of Investigation

HOME | SITE MAP | FAQ's

About Us
Art Theft Program Home
Criminal Investigative Division
America's Criminal Enterprise
Major Theft Unit

Contact Us
Your Local FBI Office
Overseas Offices
Submit a Crime Tip
Report Internet Crime
More Contacts

Learn About Us
Quick Facts
What We Investigate
Natl. Security Branch
Information Technology
Fingerprints & Training
Laboratory Services
Reports & Publications
History
More About Us

Get Our News
Press Room
E-mail Updates
News Feeds

Be Crime Smart
Wanted by the FBI
More Protections

Use Our Resources
For Law Enforcement
For Communities
For Researchers
More Services

Visit Our Kids' Page
Apply for a Job

Art Crime Team

The FBI established a rapid deployment Art Crime Team in 2004. The team is composed of twelve Special Agents, each responsible for addressing art and cultural property crime cases in an assigned geographic region. The Art Crime Team is coordinated through the FBI's Art Theft Program, located at FBI Headquarters in Washington, D.C. Art Crime Team agents receive specialized training in art and cultural property investigations and assist in art-related investigations worldwide in cooperation with foreign law enforcement officials and FBI Legal Attaché offices. The U.S. Department of Justice has assigned three Special Trial Attorneys to the Art Crime Team for prosecutive[1] support.

Since its inception, the Art Crime Team has recovered over 850 items of cultural property with a value exceeding $65 million. These include:

- Approximately 700 pre-Columbian artifacts.[2] The objects recovered in Miami were the result of a sting operation in coordination with the Ecuadorian authorities.

---

1. **prosecutive** (PRAH suh kyoo tihv): relating to legal proceedings in court against someone.
2. **pre-Columbian artifacts:** tools and objects dating from the time period before Columbus arrived in the Americas.

Courtesy of the Federal Bureau of Investigation [FBI]

IN OTHER WORDS This is the "About Us" page for the Federal Bureau of Investigation (FBI) Art Crime Team. A part of the FBI's Web site, this page gives you information about the Art Crime Team, such as when the team was created and what it does. Links to the FBI home page (Home), a "map" of everything on the site (Site Map), and frequently asked questions (FAQs) are located at the top of the page. A Search box is also at the top, so that you can search for other information on the site. Categories of other links are listed on the left side of the page. You can even learn about working at the FBI by clicking the Apply for a Job link.

A · HERE'S HOW

Vocabulary

I have never heard the word *deployment* before. I know whatever it is, this team does it fast, since *rapid* means "fast." When I look up *deployment* in the dictionary, I see that it means "act of spreading out or putting into position." I need to keep reading to know for sure, but I think this team is quickly sent out by the FBI after something happens.

B · YOUR TURN

Vocabulary

Recovered can mean "got back." It can also mean "became healthy again." Underline the meaning that makes more sense in this paragraph.

C · HERE'S HOW

Reading Focus

I want to use the *5W-How?* system to come up with good research questions as I read. At this point, I can ask and answer these questions: **When** was the Art Crime Team created? (2004) **Who** works for the team? (12 Special Agents) **What** does the team do? (They help to find stolen art objects). **Where** is the team located? (Washington, D.C.)

FBI Art Crime Team 209

A QUICK CHECK

The Art Crime Team found paintings by Heinrich Buerkel that had been stolen at the end of World War II. What did the Art Crime Team do with the paintings?

_____
_____

B YOUR TURN

Reading Focus

Ask and answer one *5W-How?* question based on the information on this page.

_____
_____
_____
_____

- Three paintings by the German painter Heinrich Buerkel (1802–1869), stolen at the conclusion of World War II and consigned[3] for sale at an auction house near Philadelphia in 2005. **A**
- Rembrandt's *Self Portrait* (1630) in a sting operation in Copenhagen carried out in cooperation with ICE[4] and law enforcement agencies in Sweden and Denmark. The FBI had previously recovered Renoir's *The Young Parisian*. Both paintings had been stolen from the Swedish National Museum in Stockholm in 2000.
- Approximately 100 paintings that had been stolen from a Florida family's art collection in a fine art storage facility. This collection included works by Picasso, Rothko, Matisse, and others that were recovered from Chicago, New York, and Tokyo.
- An extremely rare, experimental Springfield "Trapdoor" rifle to the Armory Museum in Springfield, Massachusetts. It had been stolen from the Armory Museum in the 1970s.
- Native American ceremonial material and eagle feathers belonging to the Taos Pueblo. The items included a war bonnet and a "Butterfly Bustle." With the assistance of the Bureau of Indian Affairs, the items were returned to the Taos Pueblo.
- Four rare books stolen from Transylvania University in Lexington, Kentucky. Among the items recovered were rare pencil sketches by John James Audubon and a first edition of Charles Darwin's *On the Origin of the Species*.
- Eight cylinder seals taken from archaeological sites in Iraq. **B**

3. **consigned** (kuhn SYND): sent or delivered, as goods to be sold.
4. **ICE:** acronym for U.S. Immigration and Customs Enforcement.

© Tom Gannam/AP Images

IN OTHER WORDS This is the rest of the "About Us" page. The different bullet points explain how and when the Art Crime Team has returned stolen art to its owners. The photograph on the Web page shows a man who is probably a member of the team.

COLLECTION IS FOUND TO CONTAIN STOLEN ROCKWELL ART

Based on the article from *The New York Times*

INTO THE ARTICLE
You have been reading about the F.B.I.'s Art Crime Team. This article describes one of the team's cases, which involved a famous American artist named Norman Rockwell and well-known movie director Steven Spielberg.

QUICK CHECK
What is the name of the stolen Norman Rockwell painting being discussed in this article?

LOS ANGELES, March 3

A famous painting by Norman Rockwell[1] that was stolen more than thirty years ago has been found. Movie director Steven Spielberg had the painting, the F.B.I. said Friday.

Mr. Spielberg bought *Russian Schoolroom* in 1989 from an art dealer. **C** He did not know it was stolen. Then last week someone working for Mr. Spielberg saw the painting listed on a Federal Bureau of Investigation Web site. The list was of stolen works of art. **D**

Mr. Spielberg's assistant called the F.B.I. Then experts inspected the painting. **E** They said it was the stolen work they had been looking for. The painting is thought to be worth about $700,000.

Mr. Spielberg is now helping the F.B.I. He will keep the painting until the F.B.I. can decide to where it should be returned.

The painting shows children in a classroom with a bust of Lenin.[2] Mary Ellen Shortland used to work at the Clayton Art Gallery in Clayton, Missouri. She remembers that someone paid

---
1. **Norman Rockwell** (1894–1978) was a famous American illustrator.
2. **Lenin:** Vladimir Ilich Lenin (1870–1924) is the founder of the former Soviet Union, of which Russia was part.

HERE'S HOW

Reading Focus
I think a good "How" **research question** to ask at this point would be: **How** did anyone find out that Steven Spielberg had a painting that was stolen? The answer would be: Someone working for him saw the name of the painting on a list of works of art that were stolen.

HERE'S HOW

Vocabulary
I see that the F.B.I. *inspected* the painting. From context, I think this means the F.B.I. took a close look at it.

Slightly adapted from "Spielberg Collection Is Found to Contain Stolen Rockwell Art" from *The New York Times*, March 4, 2007. Copyright © 2007 by **The Associated Press**. Retold by Holt, Rinehart and Winston. Reproduced by permission of the publisher.

A YOUR TURN

Reading Focus
How was the Rockwell painting stolen?

_____

_____

Where was it sold in 1988?

_____

When did the F.B.I. begin looking for it?

_____

"RUSSIAN SCHOOLROOM"

© AP IMAGES/TOM GANNAM

$25,000 for the painting after seeing it during a show of many Rockwell works.

The buyer agreed to leave the painting in the art show for a while, she said. A few nights later, someone smashed the gallery's glass door and escaped with the painting.

"That was all they took," Ms. Shortland said. "That's what they wanted, that painting."

There was no sign of the work for years. Then in 1988, it was sold in New Orleans.

In 2004, the F.B.I.'s Art Crime Team began searching for the painting. **A**

Russian Schoolroom first appeared in *Look* magazine, but Rockwell is best known for more than 300 covers he did for another magazine, *The Saturday Evening Post*.

Applying Your Skills

FBI Art Crime Team/Collection Is Found to Contain Stolen Rockwell Art

INFORMATIONAL TEXT FOCUS: GENERATING RESEARCH QUESTIONS

DIRECTIONS: Practice using the *5W-How?* method of **research** by completing the chart below. Think about the information you learned in the two pieces about the FBI Art Crime Team. If you were going to research the Art Crime Team, what else would you want to know? Ask 5W-How questions about the team and its work.

Who	
What	
When	
Where	
Why	
How	

VOCABULARY REVIEW

DIRECTIONS: Fill in the blanks with the correct words from the Word Box.

Word Box
- inception
- ceremonial
- recovered
- rare
- inspected

1. The painting is important because it is _____; there is no other work of art like it.
2. The agents _____ the painting closely to make sure it is really the one they had been looking for.
3. Now that the painting has been _____, it will be sent back to its original owner.

Skills Review

Collection 7

VOCABULARY REVIEW

DIRECTIONS: Each of the questions below can be answered with a word from the Word Box. Write the word that best answers each question on the lines below.

Word Box

associate
contributions
debris
evoke
generation
inspected
nuances
nuzzled
solitude
stout

1. Which word might a newspaper article use to describe the wreckage or ruins of a building that had burned down in a fire?
   _____

2. Which word would you use if you were talking about all the people in your family that were born around the same time as you?
   _____

3. If you saw a dog rubbing its nose against your sister's hand, what verb would you use to tell what the dog did?
   _____

4. When you connect thoughts together, such as seeing a leather jacket and thinking of the first day of fall, what verb describes what you are doing?
   _____

5. If you just want to be left alone, what are you looking for?
   _____

Skills Review

Language and Writing

LANGUAGE COACH: ROOT WORDS

DIRECTIONS: Many English words have Latin **roots**. The Latin word *radix* means "root." Study the list of words below. Then circle the <u>two</u> words that you think come from the Latin word *radix*.

- eradicate (IH RAD UH KAYT) *v.*: get rid of.
- phenomenon (FUH NAHM UH NAHN) *n.*: extraordinary thing.
- conceivable (KUHN SEE VUH BUHL) *adj.*: able to be understood or imagined.
- radical (RAD UH KUHL) *adj.*: extreme.
- mar (MAHR) *v.*: damage, spoil.

ORAL LANGUAGE ACTIVITY

With a partner, choose two poems that you read in this collection. Practice **reading** each poem **aloud**. Give each other tips on how to improve the reading. Once you feel comfortable with your poem, read it aloud to the rest of the class!

Collection 8

Drama

© Adam Woolfitt/Corbis

Literary and Academic Vocabulary for Collection 8

LITERARY VOCABULARY

play (PLAY) *n.:* a story meant to be acted out or performed on a stage.
I went to see a play in which the characters were two young people in love.

dialogue (DY UH LAHG) *n.:* conversation or talking.
When the young man and young woman realize they are in love, their dialogue is full of many sweet words.

monologue (MAHN UH LAHG) *n.:* a long speech by one character to one or more other characters onstage.
The young man declares his love to the young woman through a monologue full of promises to love her forever.

soliloquy (SUH LIH LUH KWEE) *n.:* a speech by a character alone onstage, who is speaking to himself or herself or to the audience.
During the character's soliloquy, I felt he was speaking directly to the audience—as if we could hear him thinking out loud.

aside (UH SYD) *n.:* dialogue that is not supposed to be heard by the other characters onstage.
The young woman whispered her thoughts in an aside, so that none of the other characters knew what she said.

ACADEMIC VOCABULARY

convention (KUHN VEHN SHUHN) *n.:* normal way of doing things.
The aside is a theatrical convention—we know the other characters are not supposed to hear it.

embody (EHM BAHD EE) *v.:* give form to.
I am writing a play that will embody my thoughts on love.

interpretation (IHN TUR PRUH TAY SHUHN) *n.:* personal idea or opinion, often about a story or play.
From the actor's interpretation, it is clear she thinks that Juliet is very innocent.

production (PRUH DUHK SHUHN) *n.:* presentation of a play; performance.
It took many months for the actors to get ready for their production of Romeo and Juliet.

Preparing to Read

from The Tragedy of Romeo and Juliet

By William Shakespeare

LITERARY FOCUS: TRAGEDY

A **tragedy** is a story about serious actions that end unhappily. As you read this play, look for these stages of its **dramatic structure**:

Exposition: the introduction of the characters, setting, and conflict.

Rising action: the conflict gets worse.

Turning point: the characters decide on actions that impact the story's end.

Climax: the moment of highest emotion in the play; in a tragedy this often involves the death of the main characters.

Resolution: the final details of the story are given.

READING FOCUS: READING A PLAY

When you **read a play**, use these tools to aid your understanding. **Read aloud** to bring dialogue to life. **Paraphrase**, or restate in your own words, to be sure you understand the meaning. **Make inferences**, or guesses based on text clues, to figure out why characters act as they do. **Predict**, or guess, what might happen next based on what you have already read. **Analyze causes and effects** to clarify what is happening.

In a play such as this one, written over four hundred years ago, some of the words used are different from the ones we use today. Here are some guidelines to understanding Shakespeare's English.

- Some verbs have different endings, like *doth* for *does* and *art* for *are*.
- *Thou* and *thee* mean *you*, and *thy* means *your*.
- *Wherefore* means *why* or *what*.

VOCABULARY

Look for these words as you read the play.

dignity (DIHG NIH TEE) *n.:* high rank or position; worth.

virtuous (VUR CHOO UHS) *adj.:* moral or good.

discourses (DIHS KOHR SUHZ) *n.:* talks or conversations.

peril (PEHR IHL) *n.:* danger, risk.

perverse (PUHR VUHRS) *adj.:* wrong or opposite.

SKILLS FOCUS

Literary Skills Understand characteristics of tragedy, including exposition, rising action, turning point, climax, and resolution; understand elements of drama, including dramatic structure, dialogue, and stage directions.

Reading Skills Read Shakespeare; read aloud and paraphrase; make inferences; analyze cause-and-effect relationships.

from THE TRAGEDY OF ROMEO AND JULIET

By William Shakespeare

INTO THE PLAY

William Shakespeare's *The Tragedy of Romeo and Juliet* was written between 1594 and 1596. In the play, a young man and a nearly-fourteen-year-old girl fall in love at first sight. Their families, the Montagues and the Capulets, are sworn enemies. Romeo and Juliet hide their love, which leads to tragedy.

© 2002 Production of Romeo and Juliet/Photo by Terry Munzo/Courtesy of the Stratford Shakespeare Festival Archives

The Prologue

[*Enter Chorus.*] **A**

CHORUS. Two households both alike in dignity
(In fair Verona where we lay our scene)
From ancient grudge break to new mutiny,[1]
Where civil blood makes civil hands unclean. **B**
From forth the fatal loins of these two foes
A pair of star-cross'd lovers take their life,
Whose misadventur'd piteous overthrows[2]
Doth with their death bury their parents' strife.
10   The fearful passage of their death-mark'd love
And the continuance of their parents' rage
(Which but their children's end naught could remove)
Is now the two hours' traffic of our stage,

---

1. Here, the word **mutiny** means "a violent outburst."
2. The phrase **misadventur'd piteous overthrows** here means "unlucky, pitiful end," and refers to the deaths of the main characters.

A HERE'S HOW

Reading Focus

I know that **reading aloud** will help me understand the play. From reading other plays, I also know the "chorus" is like the narrator. So, when I read this part aloud, I will remember that this is a different voice, not any of the characters involved in the action.

B HERE'S HOW

Vocabulary

I know the word *dignity* can mean "the quality of being honored or worthy," but here I think it means "high rank or position."

from The Tragedy of Romeo and Juliet   219

A HERE'S HOW

Literary Focus

The words here are difficult, but I see words that tell me this play will be a **tragedy**. In the opening lines, I read the words *blood*, *death*, and *rage*.

B YOUR TURN

Reading Focus

Pause at this point and consider the action so far. What do you **predict** may happen next?

_____
_____
_____
_____

C QUICK CHECK

Where does Romeo first meet and fall in love with Juliet?

_____
_____
_____
_____

D HERE'S HOW

Vocabulary

I think the word *virtuous* is related to the word *virtue*. I think *virtuous* means "moral or good."

The which if you with patient ears attend
What here shall miss our toil shall strive to mend. [*Exit.*] **A**

IN OTHER WORDS Two families of Verona, Italy, have a long-standing feud. The families must confront their hatred for each other when their children fall in love and later kill themselves because they cannot be together. Only this tragedy could bring an end to their families' rage. This is the subject of the play.

What Happens Next

As Act I opens, servants for the Montague and Capulet families meet and argue. A fight breaks out between Benvolio, a Montague, and Tybalt, a Capulet. Romeo, a Montague, tells his friend Benvolio he is in love with a woman who does not love him. To cure Romeo of his heartbreak, Benvolio suggests Romeo go with him to a masked ball at the Capulet home. **B**

Wearing masks, Romeo and Benvolio go to the home of the Capulets, their family's enemies. As he enters the party, Romeo sees Juliet for the first time and immediately falls in love. Tybalt hears Romeo's voice and, knowing that Romeo is a Montague, draws his sword. The head of the Capulet family tells Tybalt to leave the young man alone. With loving words, Romeo speaks to Juliet for the first time. She speaks to him tenderly and briefly before she is called away. **C**

Act I excerpt

Nurse. Madam, your mother craves a word with you.
Romeo. What is her mother?
Nurse. Marry[3] bachelor,
Her mother is the good lady of the house,
20 And a good lady, and a wise and virtuous. **D**
I nurs'd her daughter that you talk'd withal.

---

3. **Marry** here is taken loosely from "by the Virgin Mary."

from The Tragedy of Romeo and Juliet

I tell you, he that can lay hold of her

Shall have the chinks.[4]

Romeo. Is she a Capulet?

O dear account! my life is my foe's debt. **E**

Benvolio. Away, be gone, the sport is at the best.

Romeo. Ay, so I fear, the more is my unrest.

Capulet. Nay gentlemen, prepare not to be gone,

We have a trifling foolish banquet towards.

30 (*They whisper in his ear.*)

Is it e'en so? why then I thank you all.

I thank you, honest gentlemen. Good night.

More torches, here! Come on then, let's to bed.

Ah, sirrah, by my fay, it waxes late,

I'll to my rest.

{*Exeunt* [*Capulet and most of the others.*]}

Juliet. Come hither, Nurse. What is yond gentleman? **F**

Nurse. The son and heir of old Tiberio.

Juliet. What's he that now is going out of door?

40 *Nurse.* Marry, that I think be young Petruchio.

Juliet. What's he that follows here that would not dance?

Nurse. I know not.

Juliet. Go ask his name. If he be married

My grave is like to be my wedding bed.

Nurse. His name is Romeo, and a Montague,

The only son of your great enemy.

Juliet. My only love sprung from my only hate! **G**

Too early seen unknown, and known too late!

Prodigious[5] birth of love it is to me

50 That I must love a loathed enemy. **H**

Nurse. What's this? what's this?

Juliet. A rhyme I learn'd e'en now

---

4. When the Nurse says "he that can lay hold of her / Shall have the chinks," she means that Juliet's husband will be rich, because her family has money. She is using "chinks" to mean a chinking or clinking noise of coins.

5. The word **prodigious** (PROH DIHJ UHS) here means "huge and monstrous."

E LITERARY ANALYSIS

What emotional tone of voice do you think Romeo is using when he asks "Is she a Capulet?"

F HERE'S HOW

Language Coach

I must think about **Shakespeare's language** when he uses the word *yond*. In the dictionary, it says that *yond* is an archaic, or old, form of the word *yonder*. *Yonder* means "at a distance that I can see," or basically, "over there." So, *yond* probably means "that one over there."

G YOUR TURN

Literary Focus

Juliet has just learned that Romeo is part of the Montague family—her family's enemy. What part of the **dramatic structure** does this part of the play fall under?

H HERE'S HOW

Reading Focus

I want to try to **paraphrase** as I read, so that I make sure I understand what is happening. Using the footnote on this page, I will paraphrase lines 49–50: "Love gives me something terrible, like a monster, because the person I love is my family's hated enemy."

from *The Tragedy of Romeo and Juliet*

> **A** YOUR TURN
>
> **Literary Focus**
>
> Pause at line 71. Where do you think the play is in its **dramatic structure** at this point? Has it reached its climax yet? Explain your answer.
>
> _____
> _____
> _____
> _____

> **B** LITERARY ANALYSIS
>
> Do you agree with the Chorus that Romeo and Juliet will be able to overcome their parents' hatred of each other? Why or why not?
>
> _____
> _____
> _____
> _____
> _____
> _____

Of one I danc'd withal.
One calls within, 'Juliet!'
Nurse. Anon, anon[6]!
Come, let's away, the strangers are all gone.
[Enter Chorus.]
CHORUS. Now old Desire doth in his deathbed lie,
And young Affection gapes to be his heir.
60   That fair for which Love groan'd for and would die,
With tender Juliet match'd, is now not fair.
Now Romeo is belov'd and loves again,
Alike bewitched by the charm of looks;
But to his foe suppos'd he must complain,
And she steal love's sweet bait from fearful hooks.
Being held a foe, he may not have access
To breathe such vows as lovers use to swear;
And she, as much in love, her means much less
To meet her new beloved anywhere.
70   But passion lends them pow'r, time means, to meet,
Temp'ring extremities with extreme sweet. *[Exit.]* **A** **B**

6. The word **anon** (A NAHN), which comes up often in the play, means "soon."

222 *from* The Tragedy of Romeo and Juliet

IN OTHER WORDS When Romeo learns that the woman he has fallen in love with at first sight is a member of the Capulet family he is very upset. Juliet is also upset when she learns that Romeo is a Montague. Both of them know that their families are bitter enemies and will never allow them to marry. The Chorus suggests Romeo and Juliet can overcome their families' feud in time through their passion for each other.

What Happens Next

As Act II begins, Romeo's friends Benvolio and Mercutio have left the party and are outside the Capulet home. They look for Romeo, who has turned back to see Juliet once more. Mercutio jokes that love has made Romeo crazy. Benvolio and Mercutio stop looking for Romeo and start for home. Romeo stands beneath Juliet's balcony. **C**

Act II Excerpt

Romeo. But soft![7] What light through yonder window breaks?
It is the East and Juliet is the sun.
Arise fair Sun and kill the envious Moon,
Who is already sick and pale with grief
That thou her maid[8] art far more fair than she.
Be not her maid, since she is envious,
Her vestal livery is but sick and green,[9]
And none but fools do wear it, cast it off.

80 [*Enter Juliet at the window.*]
It is my lady! O it is my love!
O that she knew she were! **D**
She speaks yet she says nothing, what of that?
Her eye discourses, I will answer it. **E**

---

7. In this context, **soft** means "slow down" or "stay quiet."
8. **thou her maid:** Romeo is speaking of Juliet, whom he sees as a servant of the goddess of the moon.
9. **Her vestal livery is but sick and green:** Her clothing is the color of "greensickness," or anemia, a blood illness that unmarried girls were thought to have. In the next line he tells her to "cast it off," meaning she should no longer wear the color of unmarried girls.

C HERE'S HOW

Reading Focus

I want to **make inferences**, or guesses, to help me understand why the characters act the way they do. Romeo should not be at Juliet's house, because his family and her family are enemies. But it seems that he is so in love that he does not care how his family might feel.

D YOUR TURN

Reading Focus

Try **paraphrasing**, or restating, lines 82–83 on the lines below.

_____
_____
_____
_____

E HERE'S HOW

Vocabulary

According to my dictionary, *discourses* can be a noun or a verb. Here, I think it is being used as a verb, meaning "speaks."

from The Tragedy of Romeo and Juliet   223

A HERE'S HOW

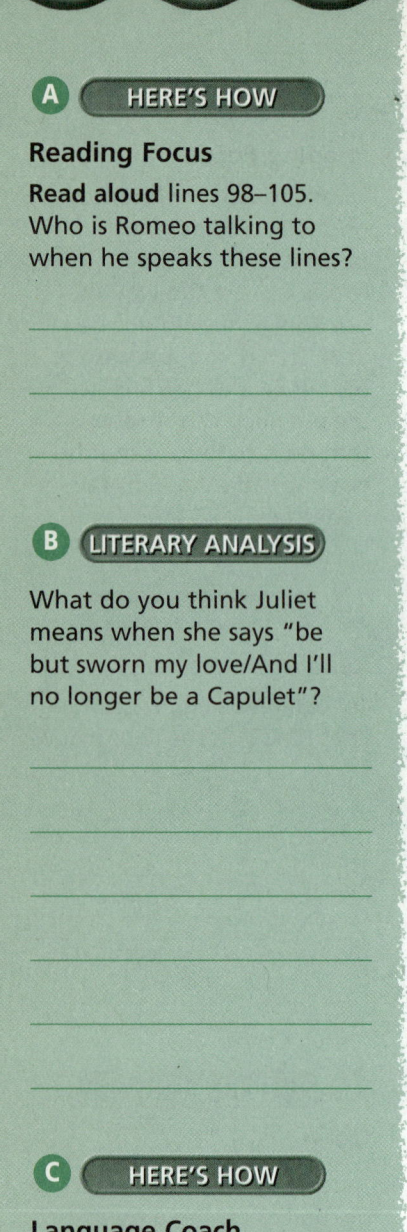

Reading Focus

Read aloud lines 98–105. Who is Romeo talking to when he speaks these lines?

_____
_____
_____

B LITERARY ANALYSIS

What do you think Juliet means when she says "be but sworn my love/And I'll no longer be a Capulet"?

_____
_____
_____
_____
_____

C HERE'S HOW

Language Coach

The phrase "Thou art thyself" uses archaic words, or words that we no longer use today. Today we would say, "You are yourself" to express what **Shakespeare** is saying here.

I am too bold, 'tis not to me she speaks.
Two of the fairest stars in all the heaven,
Having some business, do entreat her eyes
To twinkle in their spheres till they return.
What if her eyes were there, they in her head?
90 The brightness of her cheek would shame those stars
As daylight doth a lamp; her eyes in heaven
Would through the airy region stream so bright
That birds would sing and think it were not night.
See how she leans her cheek upon her hand!
O that I were a glove upon that hand
That I might touch that cheek.
Juliet. Ay me!
Romeo. She speaks.
O speak again, bright angel, for thou art
100 As glorious to this night, being o'er my head,
As is a winged messenger of Heaven.
Unto the white-upturned wond'ring eyes
Of mortals that fall back to gaze on him
When he bestrides[10] the lazy puffing clouds
And sails upon the bosom of the air. **A**

Juliet. O Romeo, Romeo, wherefore art thou Romeo?
Deny thy father and refuse thy name;
Or if thou wilt not, be but sworn my love
And I'll no longer be a Capulet. **B**
110 *Romeo.* Shall I hear more or shall I speak at this?
Juliet. 'Tis but thy name that is my enemy,
Thou art thyself, though not a Montague. **C**
What's Montague? It is nor hand nor foot
Nor arm nor face, O be some other name
Belonging to a man.
What's in a name? That which we call a rose
By any other word would smell as sweet.
So Romeo would, were he not Romeo called,
Retain that dear perfection which he owes

---

10. The word **bestrides** means "rides, as if on a horse."

120 Without that title. Romeo, doff[11] thy name,
And for thy name, which is no part of thee,
Take all myself. **D**

Romeo. I take thee at thy word.
Call me but Love and I'll be new baptiz'd,
Henceforth I never will be Romeo.

Juliet. What man art thou that thus bescreened in night
So stumblest on my counsel?

Romeo. By a name
I know not how to tell thee who I am.
130 My name, dear saint, is hateful to myself
Because it is an enemy to thee.
Had I it written, I would tear the word.

IN OTHER WORDS Romeo sees Juliet at her balcony window and admires her. He compares her beauty to the brightness of the sun. Because Romeo is a member of the Montague family and therefore an enemy of her own family, Juliet wishes he had a different name. She tells him that if she knew he loved her she would give up her own name. Juliet asks him to give up his name and be with her. Romeo tells her that his name means nothing to him compared to her love.

Juliet. My ears have yet not drunk a hundred words
Of thy tongue's utt'ring, yet I know the sound. **E**
Art thou not Romeo, and a Montague?

Romeo. Neither, fair maid, if either thee dislike.

Juliet. How camest thou hither, tell me, and wherefore?
The orchard walls are high and hard to climb,
And the place death, considering who thou art,
140 If any of my kinsmen find thee here.

Romeo. With love's light wings did I o'erperch[12] these walls.
For stony limits cannot hold love out,
And what love can do, that dares love attempt.

---

11. **Doff** is a verb meaning "to remove or put aside."
12. When Romeo says he will **o'erperch** the walls, he means "fly over them."

D HERE'S HOW

Literary Focus

Juliet asks Romeo to give up his name and family to be with her. I think we are still in the **rising action** stage, because no decision has been made yet. I see how the **tragedy** is unfolding, though, as the main characters are thinking about making decisions that will change their lives in very serious ways.

E YOUR TURN

Reading Focus

The following is a **paraphrased** version of two lines in the text: "Although your voice is not one I have heard very often, I already recognize who it belongs to." Find those two lines in the text and underline them.

A YOUR TURN

Vocabulary

Here, Juliet is talking about the dangers that Romeo faces by being beneath her garden—he may even be murdered by her family. Knowing this, what do you think *peril* means? Use your dictionary to help you.

_____

_____

B HERE'S HOW

Reading Focus

I know that it is helpful to pause sometimes and **make inferences** about a story based on text clues. Romeo says here that it would be better if he died quickly than lived without Juliet's love. I am guessing that this means before the end of the play, Romeo will actually die.

C YOUR TURN

Vocabulary

Which of the following seems like it might be the best meaning for *perverse* in line 171? Remember, Juliet is saying she is afraid Romeo might think she expressed her love for him too quickly and easily. If he thinks that, she says, she will be *perverse*—does that mean (a) stubborn and doing the opposite (b) pretty (c) overexcited?

Therefore thy kinsmen are no stop to me.

Juliet. If they do see thee they will murther[13] thee.

Romeo. Alack, there lies more peril in thine eye

Than twenty of their swords, look thou but sweet

And I am proof against their enmity. **A**

Juliet. I would not for the world they saw thee here.

150 *Romeo.* I have night's cloak to hide me from their eyes,

And but thou love me, let me find them here.

My life were better ended by their hate

Than death prorogued[14], wanting of thy love. **B**

Juliet. By whose direction found'st thou out this place?

Romeo. By Love, that first did prompt me to inquire.

He lent me counsel, and I lent him eyes.

I am no pilot, yet wert thou as far

As that vast shore washed with the farthest sea,

I should adventure for such merchandise.

160 *Juliet.* Thou know'st the mask of night is on my face.

Else would a maiden blush bepaint my cheek

For that which thou hast heard me speak tonight.

Fain[15] would I dwell on form—fain, fain deny

What I have spoke. But farewell compliment.

Dost thou love me? I know thou wilt say 'Ay,'

And I will take thy word. Yet if thou swear'st

Thou mayst prove false—at lovers' perjuries[16]

They say Jove[17] laughs. O gentle Romeo,

If thou dost love pronounce it faithfully—

170 Or if thou think'st I am too quickly won,

I'll frown and be perverse and say thee nay,

So thou wilt woo; but else, not for the world. **C**

In truth, fair Montague, I am too fond.

And therefore thou mayst think my havior[18] light,

But trust me, gentleman, I'll prove more true

---

13. **Murther** is a form of the word *murder*.
14. The word **prorogued** means "postponed."
15. **Fain** means "gladly."
16. The word **perjuries** means "broken promises."
17. **Jove** is a Roman god.
18. The word **havior** is a shortened form of *behavior*.

226 *from* The Tragedy of Romeo and Juliet

> Than those that have more cunning to be strange[19].
> I should have been more strange, I must confess,
> But that thou overheard'st, ere I was ware,
> My truelove passion. Therefore pardon me,
> 180 And not impute this yielding to light love,
> Which the dark night hath so discovered. **D**
>
> *Romeo.* Lady, by yonder blessed moon I vow,
> That tips with silver all these fruit-tree tops—
>
> *Juliet.* O swear not by the moon, the inconstant[20] moon.
> That monthly changes in her circle orb,
> Lest that thy love prove likewise variable.
>
> *Romeo.* What shall I swear by?
>
> *Juliet.* Do not swear at all,
> Or if thou wilt, swear by thy gracious self,
> 190 Which is the god of my idolatry,
> And I'll believe thee.
>
> *Romeo.* If my heart's dear love—
>
> *Juliet.* Well, do not swear. Although I joy in thee
> I have no joy of this contract tonight.
> It is too rash, too unadvised, too sudden,
> Too like the lightning, which doth cease to be
> Ere one can say it lightens. **E** Sweet, good night!

---

19. Here, Juliet means **strange** to mean "more of a stranger," or "aloof."
20. The moon is said to be **inconstant**, or changing. Juliet wants Romeo to swear by something more stable.

D LITERARY ANALYSIS

In this speech, Juliet talks about the *truth* of her love. She knows sometimes people say they are in love but are not really. She also worries that Romeo may think she seemed to fall in love too easily for the feelings to be real. Do you think that Romeo and Juliet truly believe themselves to be in love, or are they just playing a game with each other?

_____
_____
_____
_____

E HERE'S HOW

Reading Focus

I am going to try to **paraphrase** these lines in modern language. I think Juliet is saying "Don't promise you love me because it is too soon. Just like lightning which flashes and is gone, I'm afraid your love will be gone just as quickly."

from **The Tragedy of Romeo and Juliet**

> **A** HERE'S HOW
>
> **Literary Focus**
>
> Here, I see that Romeo is asking Juliet to swear she loves him as he loves her. I am not sure, but I think the **turning point** of the play may be coming soon. The turning point is when characters make important decisions that will affect how the story ends.
>
> **B** QUICK CHECK
>
> Why does Juliet suddenly have to hurry into her bedroom?
>
> _____
> _____
> _____
>
> **C** YOUR TURN
>
> **Reading Focus**
>
> Try to **predict** what will happen as the play goes on. Do you think Romeo will let Juliet know when and where he will marry her? Or do you think he will decide not to send word? On what clues do you base your prediction?
>
> _____
> _____
> _____
> _____

This bud of love by summer's ripening breath
May prove a beauteous flower when next we meet.
200 Good night, good night! As sweet repose and rest
Come to they heart as that within my breast!
Romeo. O wilt thou leave me so unsatisfied?
Juliet. What satisfaction canst thou have tonight?
Romeo. The exchange of thy love's faithful vow for mine. **A**
Juliet. I gave thee mine before thou didst request it,
And yet I would it were to give again.
Romeo. Wouldst thou withdraw it? For what purpose, love?
Juliet. But to be frank and give it thee again.
And yet I wish but for the thing I have,
210 My bounty[21] is as boundless as the sea,
My love as deep; the more I give to thee,
The more I have, for both are infinite.
I hear some noise within. Dear love, adieu—
[*Nurse calls within.*]
Anon, good Nurse! Sweet Montague, be true. **B**
Stay but a little, I will come again.
Romeo. O blessed blessed night! I am afeard,
Being in night, all this is but a dream
Too flattering-sweet to be substantial.
220 [*Enter Juliet again.*]
Juliet. Three words, dear Romeo, and good night indeed.
If that thy bent of love be honorable,
Thy purpose marriage, send me word tomorrow
By one that I'll procure[22] to come to thee
Where and what time thou wilt perform the rite,
And all my fortunes at thy foot I'll lay
And follow thee my lord throughout the world. **C**

> **IN OTHER WORDS** Juliet asks Romeo how he found her. She says her family will kill him if they find him there with her. Romeo tells Juliet that Love led him to her. Romeo says he is

---

21. Juliet's **bounty** is her ability to give.
22. **Procure** is a verb that means "to get."

from The Tragedy of Romeo and Juliet

not afraid of her family. Romeo and Juliet tell each other how much they love each other. Juliet tells Romeo that if he truly loves her and intends to marry her, he should let her know the following day where and when to meet him for the marriage ceremony.

Nurse. [*Within.*] Madam!

Juliet. I come anon. But if thou mean'st not well,

230   I do beseech[23] thee—

Nurse. [*Within.*] Madam!

Juliet. By and by, I come.

—To cease thy strife and leave me to my grief.

Tomorrow will I send. **D**

Romeo. So thrive my soul.

Juliet. A thousand times good night. [*Exit.*]

Romeo. A thousand times the worse to want thy light!

Love goes toward love as schoolboys from their books.

But love from love toward school with heavy looks.

240   *Enter Juliet again.*

Juliet. Hist Romeo, hist! O for a falc'ner's voice

To lure this tassel-gentle back again![24] **E**

Bondage is hoarse[25] and may not speak aloud,

Else would I tear the cave where Echo[26] lies

And make her airy tongue more hoarse than mine

With repetition of "My Romeo!"

Romeo. It is my soul that calls upon my name.

How silver-sweet sound lovers' tongues by night,

Like softest music to attending ears!

250   *Juliet.* Romeo!

Romeo. My sweet?

Juliet. What o'clock[27] tomorrow

---

23. **Beseech** means "to beg."
24. Juliet wishes for the voice of a falconer (someone who works with birds), to attract the **tassel-gentle**, or male falcon—meaning Romeo.
25. Juliet is in **"bondage"** to her parents and must whisper.
26. **Echo** is a character in Greek myth who could only repeat what others said.
27. Juliet is asking what time they should meet.

D HERE'S HOW

Reading Focus

I will try to understand what Juliet says in lines 229–234 by **paraphrasing** them: "If you don't truly love me, I beg you (I'm coming, Nurse!) to stop bothering me and just leave me alone. I will check with you tomorrow."

E QUICK CHECK

What is Juliet doing back on her balcony?

_____

_____

from The Tragedy of Romeo and Juliet   229

> **A LITERARY ANALYSIS**
>
> Some people who have read Shakespeare's play have said that Romeo and Juliet are more in love with love (or the idea of love) than with each other. From what you have read so far, do you agree? Why or why not?
>
> _____
>
> _____
>
> _____

> **B YOUR TURN**
>
> **Reading Focus**
>
> **Read aloud** lines 272–273, which are very famous lines in literature. Who is speaking? What kind of emotion do you think that character is feeling while saying those lines?
>
> _____
>
> _____
>
> _____

Shall I send to thee?

Romeo. By the hour of nine.

Juliet. I will not fail, 'Tis twenty years til then. **A**
I have forgot why I did call thee back.

Romeo. Let me stand here till thou remember it.

Juliet. I shall forget, to have thee still stand there,
Remem'bring how I love thy company.

260 *Romeo.* And I'll still stay, to have thee still forget,
Forgetting any other home but this.

Juliet. 'Tis almost morning, I would have thee gone,
And yet no farther than a wanton's[28] bird
That lets it hop a little from his hand,
Like a poor prisoner in his twisted gyves,[29]
And with a silken thread plucks it back again,
So loving-jealous of his liberty.

Romeo. I would I were thy bird.

Juliet. Sweet, so would I,
270 Yet I should kill thee with much cherishing,
Good night, good night! Parting is such sweet sorrow
That I shall say good night till it be morrow. **B**

Romeo. Sleep dwell upon thine eyes, peace in thy breast—
Would I were sleep and peace, so sweet to rest!
Hence will I to my ghostly friar's[30] close cell,
His help to crave and my dear hap[31] to tell. [*Exit.*]

IN OTHER WORDS With Nurse calling for her, Juliet stays on her balcony. She and Romeo talk more about their love. Juliet agrees to send someone to meet Romeo the next morning to learn where and when the marriage will take place. Romeo and Juliet pledge their love to each other before Romeo must leave.

---

28. A **wanton** is a spoiled person or child.
29. **Gyves** (JYVZ) are chains.
30. A **friar** is a monk, and the word **ghostly** here means spiritual.
31. The word **hap** means "luck."

230 *from* The Tragedy of Romeo and Juliet

Final Summary

In the remaining scenes of Act II, Romeo tells Nurse to ask Juliet to meet him that afternoon to marry him. Friar Lawrence, a monk, will perform the ceremony. Juliet arrives at Friar Lawrence's cell and embraces Romeo.

In Act III, Tybalt and Romeo argue, and Tybalt kills Mercutio. **C** Angry over Mercutio's death, Romeo kills Tybalt. When Prince Escalus, the local ruler, learns what has happened, he says that Romeo must leave Verona or die for his crime. Juliet is very upset and sends Nurse to find Romeo, give him a ring, and ask him to come and say goodbye to Juliet. Friar Lawrence tells Romeo to say goodbye to Juliet and then go to Mantua, another city in northern Italy, and stay there until the Prince forgives him. Romeo says goodbye to Juliet at her window and tells her he will see her again.

In Act IV Friar Lawrence advises Juliet to drink a potion that will cause her to look as if she's dead. **D** Then she will be taken to the family burial vault. There the Friar and Romeo will wait for her to awaken, and she will then go with Romeo to Mantua. Juliet follows Friar Lawrence's plan. When Nurse discovers her cold, motionless body, everyone believes Juliet is dead. **E**

In Act V, Romeo learns that Juliet has died and has been laid in her family's vault. Romeo buys poison, intending to kill himself

---

C HERE'S HOW

Reading Focus

I need to try to **make inferences** as I read to better understand reasons for the characters' actions. I think Romeo is less likely to argue with Tybalt now that he is married to Juliet and is worried about her family. I do not know if Tybalt means to kill Mercutio or not. Based on the text clues, I infer that everyone's temper is getting worse, and the fighting between the families is leading to more and more bloodshed.

D LITERARY ANALYSIS

Who is responsible for Juliet's decision to pretend she is dead—is it the Friar, Juliet herself, or both? Could anyone else have played a part in this decision?

_____
_____
_____
_____

E HERE'S HOW

Literary Focus

I believe I see the **turning point** of the **tragedy** now for Juliet—her decision to pretend that she is dead. Even though I'm not sure how the story will end, I think this decision will lead to a misunderstanding and more terrible events.

from The Tragedy of Romeo and Juliet

A YOUR TURN

Literary Focus

Do you see the **climax** of the tragedy yet—the point of highest emotion? What is that climax?

_____
_____
_____

B HERE'S HOW

Literary Focus

The **resolution** of the **tragedy** occurs at the end. Everyone is told exactly what happened and why, and the families finally agree to stop the fighting that started all of this.

now that his beloved Juliet is dead. Romeo does not know Juliet is really still alive. Paris, who also loved Juliet, places flowers at her burial site. Romeo is there, determined to see his beloved once last time. When Paris sees Romeo open the tomb, he believes Romeo has come to vandalize the tomb in an act of vengeance against the Capulets. Paris and Romeo struggle, and Romeo kills Paris. Romeo dies from the poison he has swallowed. When Juliet awakens in the tomb, she sees them both dead. She kisses her beloved Romeo, hoping some of the poison on his lips will kill her. Then she stabs herself and dies. **A**

At the conclusion of the play, Friar Lawrence explains to the Prince, the Capulets, and the Montagues what has happened. The families express deep sadness and remorse. Romeo's family vows to honor Juliet, and Juliet's family vows to honor Romeo. With the losses of their children, the ancient feud between the families has finally come to an end. **B**

© 2002 Production of Romeo and Juliet/Photo by Terry Manzo/Courtesy of the Stratford Shakespeare Festival Archives

from **The Tragedy of Romeo and Juliet**

Applying Your Skills

from The Tragedy of Romeo and Juliet

LITERARY FOCUS: TRAGEDY

DIRECTIONS: Below is a list of key events from Shakespeare's play. Review the different stages of **dramatic structure** on the Preparing to Read page. Decide which stage of dramatic structure is described by each event. Then write the name of that stage on the line provided.

1. Tybalt kills Mercutio. _____

2. Juliet, on the Friar's advice, decides to take a potion that makes everyone believe she is dead. _____

3. The Chorus comes on stage to tell you that this is a story about two young people in love in the city of Verona, Italy. _____

4. The Montagues and Capulets, mourning their children, agree to end their long-standing fight. _____

5. Juliet puts a dagger in her heart and ends her life, falling dead on top of Romeo, who has also killed himself. _____

READING FOCUS: READING A PLAY

DIRECTIONS: On a separate sheet of paper, **paraphrase** these lines from *Romeo and Juliet*. Refer to the footnotes from the selection to help you.

Juliet. How cam'st thou hither, tell me, and wherefore?

The orchard walls are high and hard to climb,

And the place death, considering who thou art,

If any of my kinsmen find thee here.

Romeo. With love's light wings did I o'erperch these walls.

For stony limits cannot hold love out,

And what love can do, that dares love attempt.

Therefore thy kinsmen are no stop to me.

Word Box

dignity
virtuous
discourses
peril
perverse

VOCABULARY REVIEW

DIRECTIONS: On a separate sheet of paper, write one sentence for each of the words in the Word Box.

from **The Tragedy of Romeo and Juliet** 233

Preparing to Read

"Dear Juliet": Seeking Succor from a Veteran of Love *and* from The Juliet Club

INFORMATIONAL TEXT FOCUS: PRIMARY AND SECONDARY SOURCES

When you research a topic, you mainly use two kinds of sources.

A **primary source** is written by someone who was involved in the event described. The source may take the form of a speech, an autobiography, or a letter. Since it is written from the point of view of only one person, the source may offer a limited look at the event it describes.

A **secondary source** is usually based on more than one point of view. Examples include encyclopedias, textbooks, biographies, and most newspaper articles. The writer of a secondary source was not involved in the event described. He or she may summarize or analyze the event, but will not tell you what it was like to actually *experience* it.

VOCABULARY

precipice (PREHS uh pihs) *n.:* rock face that projects out, such as a cliff; the verge of a dangerous or disastrous situation.

vital (VY tuhl) *adj.:* very important.

missives (MIHS ihvz) *n.:* written messages, such as letters.

collaborate (kuh LAB uh rayt) *v.:* work together.

melancholy (MEHL uhn kah lee) *n.:* a sad or gloomy mood.

INTO THE SELECTIONS

Verona, Italy, is a popular place for tourists to visit. Many come to visit the tomb of Juliet, the heroine (and romantic figure) of Shakespeare's *Romeo and Juliet*. As the first selection explains, Verona is also the home of the Club di Giulietta, or "Juliet Club." The club's "secretaries" respond to letters that are sent to Juliet from around the world. The second selection offers an example of one of these letters. Each year on Valentine's Day, the Juliet Club awards the *Dear Juliet Prize* for "the most beautiful letter sent to Juliet." Charlotte Schein is one of these winners.

SKILLS FOCUS

Informational Text Skills
Read primary and secondary sources; analyze primary and secondary sources.

"Dear Juliet": Seeking Succor[1] from a Veteran of Love

By Dinitia Smith
from The New York Times, March 27, 2006

"Dear Juliet," the letters all begin.

"Dear Juliet . . . You are my last hope. The woman I love more than anything in the world has left me. ... "

"Dear Juliet, I live on the third floor. My parents don't allow my boyfriend to come to my house."

"Dear Juliet, my name is Riccardo. I am 10 years old." Riccardo is in love with an older woman, 14. He saw her in Verona the summer before. Does Juliet have news of her? **A**

Every week, hundreds of letters pour into the office of the Club di Giulietta,[2] in Verona, Italy, the city that is the setting for Shakespeare's "Romeo and Juliet." Some are addressed simply "To Juliet, Verona," but the postman always knows to deliver them to the club's Via Galilei headquarters. Every letter is answered by the club's group of volunteers, no matter what the language, sometimes with the assistance of outside translators. (In the past, the owner of a local Chinese restaurant helped.) **B**

A HERE'S HOW

Reading Focus
I see that this article begins with parts of real letters. The letters are **primary sources**—firsthand accounts of experiences and feelings.

B QUICK CHECK

What is the Club di Giulietta? Why does it exist?

_____
_____
_____

IN OTHER WORDS The article begins with a few examples of how letters to Juliet, from the play *Romeo and Juliet*, sometimes begin. The writer explains that people across

1. **succor** (SUHK UHR): assistance in a difficult time; relief.
2. **Club di Giulietta** (KLUHB DEE JYOO LEE EHT UH): Italian for "Juliet Club."

From "'Dear Juliet': Seeking Succor from a Veteran of Love" by Dinita Smith from *The New York Times*, March 27, 2006. Copyright © 2006 by **The New York Times Company.** Reproduced by permission of the publisher.

A · HERE'S HOW

Vocabulary

The Preparing to Read page tells me that a *precipice* is a kind of cliff, or the edge of a bad situation. Knowing this, I am trying to understand how it would feel to be "suspended on a *precipice*." The woman must feel as if she is very close to losing control of a situation, as if she is about to fall off a cliff.

B · YOUR TURN

Vocabulary

Adjunct may be a word you do not recognize. Before looking it up in a dictionary, think about the first part of the word, the prefix *ad-*. This prefix usually means *toward* or near. Now look up *adjunct*. Does knowing the meaning of the prefix help you better understand the word itself? Explain.

_____
_____
_____

---

the world write to Juliet and send them to Verona, Italy, the same place the play was set. All of the letters are answered by members of the Club di Giulietta—the "Juliet Club." Every letter gets a reply in the same language in which it was written.

"Help me! Save me!" wrote an Italian woman whose husband had left her. "I feel suspended on a precipice. **A** I am afraid of going mad."

Her answer came from Ettore Sabina who was the custodian of Juliet's tomb for nearly 20 years, beginning in the 1930's.

"Have faith...," Mr. Solana added later in the letter. "The day of humiliation will come for the intruder, and your husband will come back to you."

Now two American sisters, Lise and Ceil Friedman, have put some of the letters and a few of the responses into a book, "Letters to Juliet," along with the story of the club and the play's historical background. It is being published in November by Stewart, Tabori & Chang. But on Wednesday, Lise Friedman, an adjunct professor at New York University, will read from it at the university's Bronfman Center for Jewish Student Life. **B**

IN OTHER WORDS In the above paragraphs, the writer gives an example of a letter the Juliet Club received and part of the Club's reply. She goes on to explain that many letters like these are about to be published as part of a book about the Juliet Club.

And what is the real history of the play? The theme of tragic love between two young people from feuding families goes back at least to Ovid. Luigi da Porto, in "Newly Discovered Story of Two Noble Lovers" (1530), set the tale in Verona with rival families, the Montecchis and Cappellettis. There is no evidence that Shakespeare ever visited Italy, and some scholars think he based "Romeo and Juliet" on a poem by Arthur Brooke, published some three decades before. But the myth of Romeo and Juliet—and it is something of a myth—has become vital to the tourism industry in Verona, where Juliet's house and tomb are supposedly located. **C** Giulio Tamassia, president of the Club di Giulietta, has said that the house on Via Cappello has been called "Juliet's" only since the 19th century. And the balcony on its front dates from the first half of the 20th century. (Shakespeare mentions no balcony in the play. For her famous Act II, Scene 2 speech, Juliet comes from "above.") **D**

IN OTHER WORDS Here the writer explains how William Shakespeare was not the first to write about two young people in love who meet a tragic end. She points out other examples of this theme before and during Shakespeare's time. She then tells the reader that the house that is supposedly Juliet's has been around for less than 200 years. That makes the house much younger than it would have to be if Juliet had actually lived there.

For years, tourists stuck notes to Juliet on the walls of the house with bubblegum. Last year the gum was removed, and white plasterboard put up for those who feel they must write. There is also a letterbox at the house, and its missives are collected and answered by the club. These days you can even send an e-mail to Juliet at info@julietclub.com. Very few letters, oddly enough, are sent to Romeo.

"There are hundreds of letters from U.S. teenagers," said Elena Marchi, the assistant to Mr. Tamassia, in a telephone interview from Verona. One reason is that "Romeo and Juliet" is part of many American high school curriculums.

"It's easier to talk to someone you don't know," said Ms. Marchi, a professional translator when she is not answering letters. "There are things you wouldn't say to your mother." **E**

Ms. Marchi goes to the club every day, she said. "Once you start," she said, "you never give up, it's so interesting."

At least since the turn of the last century, messages have been left at Juliet's tomb in a former monastery on the Via

---

C YOUR TURN

Language Coach
The **etymology** of the word *vital* is the Latin verb *vivere*, which means "to live." Two other words taken from the same Latin root are *vivid* and *vivacious*. Look both words up in the dictionary. What do the definitions of these words have in common with *vital*?

_____
_____

D YOUR TURN

Reading Focus
What source (or sources) might the author have used to find the information in this paragraph? Are the sources you list **primary** or **secondary sources**?

_____
_____
_____

E HERE'S HOW

Reading Focus
I think that a telephone interview must be a kind of **primary source**. Ms. Marchi is part of Club di Giulietta. She is giving her opinions based on her own experiences with the club. This entire article is a **secondary source**, though. It is the reporter's account of the club based on information she found, mostly through primary sources.

A QUICK CHECK

What happened in 1937 that caused the number of letters to Juliet to rise?

_____

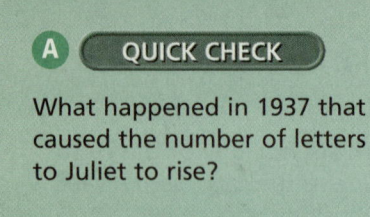

_____

B YOUR TURN

Vocabulary

You now know that to *collaborate* is to "work together." List some common situations in which you might have to *collaborate* with someone.

_____

_____

_____

---

del Pontiere, about a 15-minute walk from Juliet's house. But the letters really began flowing in 1937, the year after George Cukor's film "Romeo and Juliet" was released. That same year, Mr. Solimani was hired as the custodian of the tomb, which was probably originally an animal trough. **A** (There are no bones there. Although the two lovers are supposedly buried together, over the years Romeo seems to have vanished from the picture, and it is now usually called just Juliet's tomb.)

IN OTHER WORDS The writer now discusses the different ways people have tried to communicate with Juliet at "her house." The writer shares how many of those who write to Juliet are American teenagers. A Club member explains that people like to share their love problems with people they do not know because it seems easier. The reader is told that letters increased once a film version of the play came out in 1937. In the same year, what is supposed to be Juliet's tomb, or burial place, was made public. The writer is trying to make a connection between what people want to believe is real and what is actually real.

80   Mr. Solimani planted rose bushes and a willow tree, trained two dozen turtledoves to fly around the cloister and to land on the shoulders of female visitors, and took it upon himself to answer the letters.

In the late 1980's, the club began to answer them. It receives money from the city for stationery and postage, but is otherwise run by volunteers.

About two years ago, when the Friedman sisters who, according to Lise, "tend to finish each other's sentences" were looking for a project on which to collaborate, Ceil was given 90 some of the letters to translate. **B** She sent copies to her sister, who immediately thought they might make a book.

The club has about 50,000 letters stored in boxes. The Friedman sisters went through about 5,000, choosing representative examples from different times: A few choice

238 "Dear Juliet": Seeking Succor from a Veteran of Love

letters were remembered by the volunteers. The Friedmans have included about 75 in their book, changing the writers' names to protect their privacy.

IN OTHER WORDS The writer shares that the Juliet Club is funded by the city of Verona for stamps and paper. However, the letters are all written by volunteers. The writer also tells of how the Friedman sisters decided to write their book and how many letters they read through before choosing which ones to include.

The sisters found that during the nearly 70 years the letters have been arriving, they have become a reflection of the changing times. In 1970, a girl from Montana wrote, "Five years ago I met a Negro boy, William, at Bible camp." They had fallen in love, she explained, but added: "My parents and friends are against us getting married. William and I have separated many times, trying to get over each other."

In 1967 a Louisiana woman wrote that her husband was in Vietnam, and that she had fallen in love with his best friend. And in 1972, a soldier wrote from Vietnam itself: "I am in a bunker. Outside I hear missiles exploding, bullets being fired. I am 22 years old and I'm scared." **C**

And then there are those who have yet to find love, who write to Juliet the way children write to Santa Claus, hoping he can bring them the gift they most desire. A woman from Ukraine asks: "I have a daughter, 27, who has never been married, but is looking for a fiancé." Can Juliet help?

"It's about suspending disbelief," Lise Friedman said, trying to explain why so many people would write to Juliet, unseen, perhaps only a chimera.[3] "It's about having a life of the imagination." **D**

"It's one of those ineffable[4] things."

---

3. **chimera** (KY MIHR UH): In Greek mythology, a grotesque creature formed from a lion, a goat, and a serpent; here, a strange product of the imagination.
4. **ineffable** (IHN EHF UH BUHL): indescribable.

C LITERARY ANALYSIS

How do the letters to Juliet show how society changes during different decades? Use one of the letters described on this page as an example.

_____
_____
_____
_____

D HERE'S HOW

Vocabulary

I am trying to figure out what *suspending disbelief* means. To do this, I will use the information I have in the rest of the paragraph. I know that *disbelief* means "not believing in something." Chimeras, or imaginary creatures, are hard to believe in. But Lise Friedman says writing to the chimera Juliet is about "a life of imagination." So she thinks imagination plays a big role in why people write to Juliet. I think *suspending disbelief* must mean "stopping disbelief for a little while, in order to use your imagination."

IN OTHER WORDS As a conclusion to her article, the writer lists examples of letters the Friedman sisters found especially interesting. The different letters show how attitudes and history have changed over the years, from letters about race to letters about war to letters about a parent's wish for her daughter. One of the American authors, Lise Friedman, explains that she thinks people like writing to Juliet because it is fun to imagine that she really exists.

from THE JULIET CLUB

> **A** HERE'S HOW
>
> **Vocabulary**
> I am not sure what *fascinated* means. I get the feeling that the speaker is very interested in the love story of Romeo and Juliet. I think *fascinated* might mean something stronger than "interested," though. I checked my dictionary, and *fascinated* means "gripped the attention of, so as to take away the power to think or act." I was right that *fascinated* means something much more than simply "interested."

Dear Juliet,

My dear friend, I dream of being on your balcony, which guarded your secret love, under which Romeo declared his passion, on which you proved to him that same dangerous passion.

As I write you this letter, I'm not desperate, just a little melancholy and romantic, but still fascinated by the great power of love. **A**

Yes, Juliet, you are the hurricane and the calm, salt and sugar, tenderness and strength. But wherever did you get this strength?

I, too, listen to the song of the nightingale and the lark. I look for the dawn's light and await the tender night.

My thoughts are both timid and bold, sensible and foolish or imaginary because we are the stuff that dreams are made of.

But must we really believe that our destiny is rarely to be with our beloved?

"Letter to Juliet" by Charlotte Schein from *The Juliet Club*. Copyright © 1994 by **Club de Giulietta**. Reproduced by permission of the publisher.

A YOUR TURN

Reading Focus

Is this letter an example of a **primary** or **secondary source**? How do you know?

_____
_____
_____
_____
_____

Yes, I dream of being part of this tragedy, if only for a moment, of entering the legend of love.

Charlotte Schein

Hondschoote, France A

IN OTHER WORDS Dear Juliet, I dream of being on the same balcony where you once stood while Romeo told you he loved you. I am not hopeless, but I, too, wish to find the love of my life one day. I wish to be a part of a great and legendary love story.

Applying Your Skills

"Dear Juliet": Seeking Succor from a Veteran of Love *and* from The Juliet Club

INFORMATIONAL TEXT FOCUS: PRIMARY AND SECONDARY SOURCES

DIRECTIONS: Circle the letter of the correct answer to each question below.

1. Which of the following is a **primary source** that might tell you more about the Club di Giulietta?
   A. a history book about Italy
   B. a copy of *Romeo and Juliet*
   C. a biography of Shakespeare
   D. a journal kept by the club's founder

2. Why are **primary sources** not always dependable?
   A. They describe facts rather than opinions.
   B. They express the view of only one person.
   C. They give a broad view of the subject.
   D. They are usually difficult to understand.

VOCABULARY REVIEW

DIRECTIONS: Match each vocabulary word below with its synonym, or the word that has the same or almost the same meaning. Write the letter of the correct word in the blank.

1. _____ collaborate   a. important
2. _____ missives   b. together
3. _____ vital   c. letters
4. _____ melancholy   d. sad

Skills Review

Collection 8

VOCABULARY REVIEW

DIRECTIONS: On the blank line next to each vocabulary word, write the letter of its correct definition.

1. convention _____
2. vital _____
3. dignity _____
4. discourses _____
5. interpretation _____
6. peril _____
7. perverse _____
8. embody _____
9. production _____
10. collaborate _____
11. melancholy _____
12. virtuous _____

a. danger, risk
b. work together
c. high rank, office, or position; worthy
d. a sad or gloomy mood
e. moral or good
f. presentation of a play
g. conversations
h. normal way of doing things
i. opposite
j. very important
k. give form to
l. personal idea or opinion

Language and Writing

Collection 8

LANGUAGE COACH: SHAKESPEARE'S LANGUAGE

DIRECTIONS: Reading texts that use **Shakespeare's language** can be challenging, but can also help you better understand the roots and meanings of words we use today. Below, for each underlined word from *The Tragedy of Romeo and Juliet*, circle the letter of the modern word that you think is most similar in meaning. You can use the footnotes and sidebars in the text to help you.

1. Whose misadventur'd piteous overthrows

    a. wonderful   b. unfortunate   c. mistaken

2. I nurs'd her daughter that you talk'd withal

    a. with   b. without   c. witch

3. I am too bold, 'tis not to me she speaks.

    a. this   b. it is   c. taste

4. Or if thou wilt not, be but sworn my love

    a. you   b. we   c. thought

5. O speak again, bright angel, for thou art/As glorious to this night

    a. painting   b. artistic   c. are

ORAL LANGUAGE ACTIVITY

DIRECTIONS: As you have learned, **reading aloud** is a useful technique to practice when reading a play. Form groups of two or more students and chose a short passage from *The Tragedy of Romeo and Juliet* to practice reading aloud. Then, write a brief paragraph discussing whether you prefer reading a play yourself or hearing it read aloud. Is one way easier for you to understand?

_____

_____

_____

_____

Review 245

Collection 9

Epic and Myth

© Rijksmuseum Kroller–Muller, Otterlo, Netherlands/
The Bridgeman Art Library

Literary and Academic Vocabulary for Collection 9

LITERARY VOCABULARY

epic heroes (EH PIHK HEE ROHZ) *n.*: amazing people who go on difficult journeys to achieve something of great value to themselves or their people.
Odysseus is an example of an epic hero.

conflicts (KAHN FLIHKTS) *n.*: problems, difficulties, or obstacles.
The hero knew he would have to overcome conflicts such as the monster standing at the gate and the fire that had broken out.

external conflicts (EHKS TUHR NUHL KAHN FLIHKTS) *n.*: difficulties created by forces of nature or powers greater than nature.
The tornado tore down the bridge, causing an external conflict for Sam, the hero of the book I am reading.

internal conflicts (IHN TUHR NUHL KAHN FLIHKTS) *n.*: difficulties caused by one's own feelings or fears.
When Sam remembered falling off a bridge 20 years before, the memories and fears were internal conflicts he had to deal with.

foil (FOYL) *n.*: a character that is in opposition to another character.
Grant always lied and cheated, making him a foil to honest, reliable Sam.

myths (MIHTHS) *n.*: stories that explain natural events, teach moral lessons, and explain history.
In the myths of the ancient Greek culture, men often fought directly with gods.

ACADEMIC VOCABULARY

portrayed (PAWR TRAYD) *v.*: showed.
The author portrayed the main character, Lisa, as stubborn.

destiny (DEHS TIH NEE) *n.*: unavoidable future; fate.
Some myths describe how the destiny of its main character is fulfilled.

mutual (MYOO CHU UHL) *adj.*: done, said, or felt by each toward the other.
Sam and Lisa had a mutual attraction.

express (EHK SPREHS) *v.*: put into words; show feeling or emotion.
Sam chose to express his joy at Lisa's return by throwing a party for her.

Preparing to Read

from the Odyssey, Part One

By Homer, translated by Robert Fitzgerald

LITERARY FOCUS: EPIC HEROES AND CONFLICT

We all admire heroes in books and movies—and in real life, too. In fiction, as in real life, heroes often set out on a journey or quest to have adventures and accomplish great deeds. **Epic heroes** like Odysseus are larger than life. They often have uncommon strength and courage, and are very smart. Epic heroes face **conflicts**—struggles with other characters or with forces of nature. For example, an epic hero might have a sword fight with a villain or must guide his ship through a terrible storm. As you read about Odysseus, think about how he overcomes his conflicts. How is he heroic?

READING FOCUS: READING AN EPIC

An **epic** is a long poem that tells about the great deeds of an epic hero. When you read an epic, there are three strategies you can use to help you understand the text:

1. **Paraphrase** If a section of an epic is difficult, try to restate it in your own words.

2. **Summarize** It is important to keep track of the sequence of events in an epic. Summarize, or write a brief description, of each event in the order that it occurs.

3. **Ask questions** Ask yourself these questions to make sure you understand what you have read: *Who? What? Why? When? Where?* and *How?* For example, you might ask *Who are the main characters* or *When did this event take place?*

VOCABULARY

Look for these words and their context as you read the selection.

profusion (PRUH FYOO ZHUHN) *n.:* large supply.

adversary (AD VUHR SEHR EE) *n.:* enemy.

SKILLS FOCUS

Literary Skills
Understand heroic characters and external conflicts in epics and myths.

Reading Skills
Use paraphrasing as a strategy for comprehension; summarize as a strategy for comprehension; ask questions.

248 *from the* Odyssey, Part One

from the ODYSSEY, PART ONE

By Homer, translated by Robert Fitzgerald

THE CYCLOPS

INTO THE EPIC The *Odyssey* is an epic poem about a soldier going home from war. It is considered one of the greatest adventure stories ever told. We credit a man named Homer with writing the poem, but the story was probably told earlier and passed along by wandering poets, who sang and recited stories for a living.

In this adventure, Odysseus[1] describes his meeting with the Cyclops[2] named Polyphemus.[3] Polyphemus's father is Poseidon,[4] god of the sea. Out of curiosity, Odysseus and his men have entered the Cyclops's cave. They wait for Polyphemus to return to the cave, and they will have to be clever in order to escape.

> We lit a fire, burnt an offering,[5]
> and took some cheese to eat; then sat in silence
> around the embers, waiting. When he came
> he had a load of dry boughs on his shoulder
> 5 to stoke his fire at suppertime. **A** He dumped it
> with a great crash into that hollow cave,
> and we all scattered fast to the far wall.

A HERE'S HOW

Reading Focus

I have a **question: Who** is the *he* in line 3? I learned from the Into the Epic section that Odysseus and his men are waiting for the Cyclops Polyphemus. *He* must be Polyphemus.

---

1. **Odysseus** (OH DIHS EE UHS).
2. **Cyclops** (SY KLAHPS): a race of giants with one eye in the center of their forehead.
3. **Polyphemus** (PAHL IH FEE MUHS).
4. **Poseidon** (POH SY DUHN).
5. **burnt an offering:** in ancient cultures, people often tried to please their gods by burning offerings of meat and other things.

From "Book 9: New Coasts and Poseidon's Son" from *The Odyssey* by Homer, translated by Robert Fitzgerald. Copyright ©1961, 1963 by Robert Fitzgerald; copyright renewed © 1989 by Benedict R.C. Fitzgerald, on behalf on the Fitzgerald children. Reproduced by permission of Benedict **R.C. Fitzgerald.**

A HERE'S HOW

Vocabulary

I have seen the word *ewes* (yooz) before, but I cannot remember what they are. The poem says the Cyclops is going to milk the *ewes*. Then, the next sentence mentions rams. I am pretty sure *ewes* are female sheep.

B YOUR TURN

Reading Focus

What has happened in lines 10–12 that will make it hard for Odysseus and his men to escape from the cave?

_____

_____

_____

C HERE'S HOW

Vocabulary

I know that a *sieve* (SIHV) is a strainer that separates larger pieces out of a mixture, like tea leaves out of tea. So *sieved* must mean "strained," or "separated."

© Enrich Lessing/Art Resource, NY

Then over the broad cavern floor he ushered
the ewes he meant to milk. **A** He left his rams
10 and he-goats in the yard outside, and swung
high overhead a slab of solid rock
to close the cave. **B** Two dozen four-wheeled wagons,
with heaving wagon teams, could not have stirred
the tonnage of that rock from where he wedged it
15 over the doorsill. Next he took his seat
and milked his bleating ewes. A practiced job
he made of it, giving each ewe her suckling;[6]
thickened his milk, then, into curds and whey,[7]
sieved out the curds to drip in withy baskets,[8]
20 and poured the whey to stand in bowls
cooling until he drank it for his supper. **C**
When all these chores were done, he poked the fire,
heaping on brushwood. In the glare he saw us.

---

6. **suckling:** a young animal still feeding on its mother's milk.
7. **curds and whey:** curds are the thick lumps of soured milk used to make cheese; whey is the watery liquid that is left. Polyphemus makes cheese, which is why Odysseus and his men have cheese to eat in line 2.
8. **withy baskets:** baskets made from willow twigs.

250   *from the* Odyssey, Part One

'Strangers,' he said, 'who are you? And where from?

25 What brings you here by seaways—a fair traffic?

Or are you wandering rogues, who cast your lives

like dice, and ravage other folk by sea?' **D** **E**

We felt a pressure on our hearts, in dread

of that deep rumble and that mighty man.

30 But all the same I spoke up in reply:

'We are from Troy, Achaeans,[9] blown off course

by shifting gales on the Great South Sea;

homeward bound, but taking routes and ways

uncommon; so the will of Zeus would have it.

35 We served under Agamemnon, son of Atreus[10]—

the whole world knows what city

he laid waste, what armies he destroyed.

It was our luck to come here; here we stand,

beholden for your help, or any gifts

40 you give—as custom is to honor strangers.

We would entreat[11] you, great Sir, have a care

for the gods' courtesy; Zeus will avenge

the unoffending guest.'

IN OTHER WORDS Polyphemus enters the cave where Odysseus and his men are waiting. Polyphemus rolls a huge rock over the cave opening, then milks his sheep and starts to make his supper. Finally, Polyphemus sees the soldiers and asks them who they are. Odysseus explains that he and his men are soldiers who fought in the attack on Troy. Now they are heading home but got lost along the way. Odysseus reminds the Cyclops that Zeus, king of the gods, will punish anyone who mistreats strangers.

He answered this

from his brute chest, unmoved:

'You are a ninny,

---

9. **Achaeans** (UH KEE UHNZ): Greeks.
10. **Agamemnon** (AG UH MEM NAHN); **Atreus** (AY TREE UHS).
11. **entreat**: ask or beg.

D YOUR TURN

Vocabulary

In lines 24–27, the Cyclops is asking what kind of men these are in his cave. Underline the words that help you know what *rogues* are.

E YOUR TURN

Vocabulary

You have probably seen the word *ravage* before. Read lines 24–27 again. Then, write what you think *ravage* means on the lines below.

_____
_____
_____

from the **Odyssey**, *Part One* **251**

A HERE'S HOW

Vocabulary

I can tell that *Cyclopes* (SY KLOHPS) is the plural form of *Cyclops*.

B HERE'S HOW

Literary Focus

Usually, I do not think of lying as heroic. However, Odysseus just found out that the Cyclops does not fear the gods. Odysseus is probably smart not to trust the Cyclops. Cleverness could be a quality that an **epic hero** has. Maybe cleverness is a quality that was admired by the ancient Greeks.

C HERE'S HOW

Vocabulary

In line 67, *appalled* must mean something like "horrified." That is how the scene makes me feel, so I think that must be what *appalled* means.

---

45 or else you come from the other end of nowhere,
    telling me, mind the gods! We Cyclopes
    care not a whistle for your thundering Zeus
    or all the gods in bliss; we have more force by far. **A**
    I would not let you go for fear of Zeus—
50 you or your friends—unless I had a whim to.
    Tell me, where was it, now, you left your ship—
    around the point, or down the shore, I wonder?'

    He thought he'd find out, but I saw through this,
    and answered with a ready lie:
                                    'My ship?
55 Poseidon Lord, who sets the earth atremble,
    broke it up on the rocks at your land's end.
    A wind from seaward served him, drove us there.
    We are survivors, these good men and I.' **B**

IN OTHER WORDS The Cyclops answers that he is not afraid of any god. Then he asks where they left their ship. Odysseus lies, saying that the ship was smashed to pieces on the rocks.

    Neither reply nor pity came from him,
60 but in one stride he clutched at my companions
    and caught two in his hands like squirming puppies
    to beat their brains out, spattering the floor.
    Then he dismembered them and made his meal,
    gaping and crunching like a mountain lion—
65 everything: innards, flesh, and marrow bones.
    We cried aloud, lifting our hands to Zeus,
    powerless, looking on at this, appalled;
    but Cyclops went on filling up his belly
    with manflesh and great gulps of whey,
70 then lay down like a mast[12] among his sheep. **C**

---

12. **mast:** a tall pole that supports the sails on a ship.

IN OTHER WORDS Suddenly, the Cyclops grabs two soldiers, kills them, and eats them. Odysseus and his men watch in horror. Stomach full, the monster lies down to sleep.

My heart beat high now at the chance of action,
and drawing the sharp sword from my hip I went
along his flank[13] to stab him where the midriff
holds the liver. I had touched the spot
75 when sudden fear stayed me: if I killed him
we perished there as well, for we could never
move his ponderous[14] doorway slab aside.
So we were left to groan and wait for morning. **D** **E**

IN OTHER WORDS Odysseus pulls out his sword, ready to kill the sleeping Cyclops. Then he remembers the slab of solid rock that closes the door of the cave. Only the Cyclops is strong enough to move that rock. They are trapped in the cave. If the Cyclops dies, they all die.

When the young Dawn with fingertips of rose
80 lit up the world, the Cyclops built a fire
and milked his handsome ewes, all in due order,
putting the sucklings to the mothers. Then,
his chores being all dispatched, he caught
another brace of men to make his breakfast,
85 and whisked away his great door slab
to let his sheep go through—but he, behind,
reset the stone as one would cap a quiver.[15]
There was a din of whistling as the Cyclops
rounded his flock to higher ground, then stillness. **F**
90 And now I pondered how to hurt him worst,
if but Athena[16] granted what I prayed for.
Here are the means I thought would serve my turn:[17]

---

13. **flank:** on the side, between ribs and hip.
14. **ponderous:** heavy.
15. **quiver:** a long, narrow container for arrows.
16. **Athena** (UH THEE NUH): goddess of wisdom and the arts of war and peace.
17. **means I thought would serve my turn:** items that would help me.

D YOUR TURN

Literary Focus

In this paragraph, what two qualities of an **epic hero** does Odysseus show us that he has?

_____
_____
_____
_____

E HERE'S HOW

Literary Focus

At this point in the epic, I can see the **conflict** that Odysseus faces. He must get the Cyclops to move the large rock so he and his men can escape.

F YOUR TURN

Vocabulary

Based on the words *whistling* and *then stillness*, what do you think the word *din* means in line 88?

_____
_____

from the *Odyssey*, Part One 253

> **A** **HERE'S HOW**
>
> **Language Coach**
> A friend of mine always jokes that he is "bleeding profusely" when he gets a small cut or scrape. I know that *profusely* means "a lot." *Profusely* must be **related** to the word *profusion*. Therefore, I think *profusion* must mean "large amount."

> **B** **HERE'S HOW**
>
> **Reading Focus**
> I want to make sure I know what events have happened from lines 79–111. I will **summarize** them in order: First, the Cyclops milked his ewes. Then he ate two more men for breakfast. Next, the Cyclops left the cave to take the sheep out. While he is away, Odysseus and his men begin to make a weapon to stab into Polyphemus's eye.

a club, or staff, lay there along the fold—
an olive tree, felled green and left to season
95 for Cyclops' hand. And it was like a mast
a lugger[18] of twenty oars, broad in the beam—
a deep-seagoing craft—might carry:
so long, so big around, it seemed. Now I
chopped out a six-foot section of this pole
100 and set it down before my men, who scraped it;
and when they had it smooth, I hewed[19] again
to make a stake with pointed end. I held this
in the fire's heart and turned it, toughening it,
then hid it, well back in the cavern, under
105 one of the dung piles in profusion there. **A**
Now came the time to toss for it: who ventured
along with me? Whose hand could bear to thrust
and grind that spike in Cyclops's eye, when mild
sleep had mastered him? As luck would have it,
110 the men I would have chosen won the toss—
four strong men, and I made five as captain. **B**

IN OTHER WORDS In the morning, the Cyclops gobbles two more of the men for breakfast. Then he takes his sheep out to pasture, sealing the cave behind him. Trapped again, Odysseus looks for a weapon. He finds a giant log, which he and his men sharpen to a spike. They will jab it in the Cyclops's eye.

At evening came the shepherd with his flock,
his woolly flock. The rams as well, this time,
entered the cave: by some sheepherding whim[20]—
115 or a god's bidding—none were left outside.
He hefted his great boulder into place
and sat him down to milk the bleating ewes
in proper order, put the lambs to suck,

---
18. **lugger:** a type of sailboat.
19. **hewed:** chopped and cut.
20. **whim:** sudden desire.

and swiftly ran through all his evening chores.
120 Then he caught two more men and feasted on them.
My moment was at hand, and I went forward
holding an ivy bowl of my dark drink,
looking up, saying:

'Cyclops, try some wine.
Here's liquor to wash down your scraps of men.
125 Taste it, and see the kind of drink we carried
under our planks. I meant it for an offering
if you would help us home. But you are mad,
unbearable, a bloody monster! After this,
will any other traveler come to see you?' **C**

130 He seized and drained the bowl, and it went down
so fiery and smooth he called for more:
'Give me another, thank you kindly. Tell me,
how are you called? I'll make a gift will please you.
Even Cyclopes know the wine grapes grow
135 out of grassland and loam in heaven's rain,
but here's a bit of nectar and ambrosia!'

Three bowls I brought him, and he poured them down.
I saw the fuddle and flush come over him,
then I sang out in cordial tones: **D**

'Cyclops,
140 you ask my honorable name? Remember
the gift you promised me, and I shall tell you.
My name is Nohbdy: mother, father, and friends,
everyone calls me Nohbdy.' **E**

And he said:
'Nohbdy's my meat, then, after I eat his friends.
145 Others come first. There's a noble gift, now.'

IN OTHER WORDS Evening comes, and the Cyclops returns with his flock of sheep. He eats two more men for

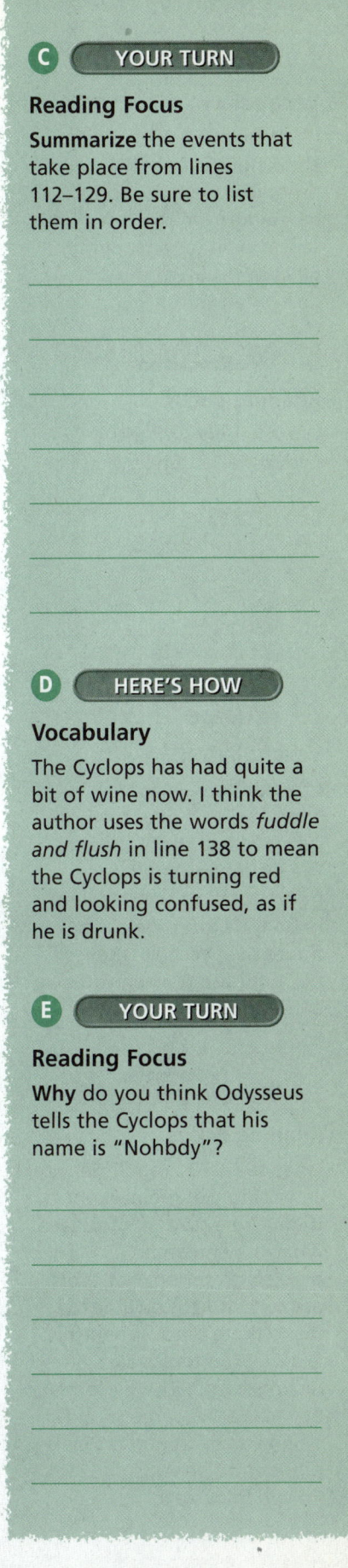

C YOUR TURN

Reading Focus
Summarize the events that take place from lines 112–129. Be sure to list them in order.

D HERE'S HOW

Vocabulary
The Cyclops has had quite a bit of wine now. I think the author uses the words *fuddle and flush* in line 138 to mean the Cyclops is turning red and looking confused, as if he is drunk.

E YOUR TURN

Reading Focus
Why do you think Odysseus tells the Cyclops that his name is "Nohbdy"?

from the Odyssey, Part One 255

A HERE'S HOW

Vocabulary

I had to look up the word *shipwright* in line 161. I should have guessed its meaning from the rest of the sentence. It is "a carpenter who works on a ship."

B YOUR TURN

Reading Focus

What happens after the Cyclops falls drunkenly asleep?

_____

_____

_____

C HERE'S HOW

Vocabulary

I thought *hale* meant "healthy," but how can iron be made healthy? I checked the dictionary, and I was right, but it also says "sound in body." I guess *hale* is a figure of speech. It is called personification when you give an object human qualities.

D HERE'S HOW

Reading Focus

Lines 167–173 are a little confusing. Let me **paraphrase** them to be sure I understand what they mean: In a blacksmith's shop, hot tools are put into cold water to make them hard. When this is done, the tool makes a hissing sound. The Cyclops's eye made this same sound when Odysseus and his men plunged their hot spike into Polyphemus's eye.

---

his dinner. Then Odysseus offers him wine. Pleased with the wine, the Cyclops asks Odysseus his name. Odysseus says he is called "Nohbdy."

Even as he spoke, he reeled and tumbled backward,
his great head lolling to one side; and sleep
took him like any creature. Drunk, hiccuping,
he dribbled streams of liquor and bits of men.

150 Now, by the gods, I drove my big hand spike
deep in the embers, charring it again,
and cheered my men along with battle talk
to keep their courage up: no quitting now.
The pike of olive, green though it had been,
155 reddened and glowed as if about to catch.
I drew it from the coals and my four fellows
gave me a hand, lugging it near the Cyclops
as more than natural force nerved them; straight
forward they sprinted, lifted it, and rammed it
160 deep in his crater eye, and I leaned on it
turning it as a shipwright turns a drill
in planking, having men below to swing
the two-handled strap that spins it in the groove. **A**
So with our brand we bored that great eye socket
165 while blood ran out around the red-hot bar. **B**
Eyelid and lash were seared; the pierced ball
hissed broiling, and the roots popped.

   In a smithy[21]
one sees a white-hot axhead or an adze[22]
plunged and wrung in a cold tub, screeching steam—
170 the way they make soft iron hale and hard—
just so that eyeball hissed around the spike. **C**
The Cyclops bellowed and the rock roared round him,
and we fell back in fear. **D** Clawing his face

---

21. **smithy:** blacksmith's shop, where iron tools are made.
22. **adze:** tool like an ax but with a longer, curved blade.

256 from the *Odyssey*, Part One

> he tugged the bloody spike out of his eye,
> 175 threw it away, and his wild hands went groping;
> then he set up a howl for Cyclopes
> who lived in caves on windy peaks nearby.
> Some heard him; and they came by divers[23] ways
> to clump around outside and call:
>
>   'What ails you,
> 180 Polyphemus? Why do you cry so sore
> in the starry night? You will not let us sleep.
> Sure no man's driving off your flock? No man
> has tricked you, ruined you?'

E HERE'S HOW

Vocabulary
I have not seen the word *ails* before. From its context, I think *ails* is a verb that means "causes pain." I checked my dictionary and I was right!

---

23. **divers:** diverse; various.

from the Odyssey, Part One **257**

A **YOUR TURN**

Vocabulary

What do you think *sage* means? Write your answer on the lines below. Check a dictionary to see if you are right.

_____

_____

IN OTHER WORDS The drunken Cyclops falls asleep. Odysseus and his men push their giant spike into the fire until it is red-hot. Then, with the help of four men, Odysseus drives the spike into the sleeping monster's eye. The Cyclops awakens, roaring in pain. Hearing his howls, other Cyclopes leave their caves and come to find out what is wrong.

          Out of the cave
the mammoth[24] Polyphemus roared in answer:

185 'Nohbdy, Nohbdy's tricked me. Nohbdy's ruined me!'
To this rough shout they made a sage reply: **A**

'Ah well, if nobody has played you foul
there in your lonely bed, we are no use in pain
given by great Zeus. Let it be your father,
Poseidon Lord, to whom you pray.'

190   So saying
they trailed away. And I was filled with laughter
to see how like a charm the name deceived them.
Now Cyclops, wheezing as the pain came on him,
fumbled to wrench away the great doorstone
195 and squatted in the breach[25] with arms thrown wide
for any silly beast or man who bolted—
hoping somehow I might be such a fool.
But I kept thinking how to win the game:
death sat there huge; how could we slip away?
200 I drew on all my wits, and ran through tactics,
reasoning as a man will for dear life,
until a trick came—and it pleased me well.
The Cyclops's rams were handsome, fat, with heavy
fleeces, a dark violet.

---

24. **mammoth:** huge.
25. **breach:** opening.

258   *from the* Odyssey, Part One

                           Three abreast
205 I tied them silently together, twining
     cords of willow from the ogre's bed;
     then slung a man under each middle one
     to ride there safely, shielded left and right.
     So three sheep could convey each man. I took
210 the woolliest ram, the choicest of the flock,
     and hung myself under his kinky belly,
     pulled up tight, with fingers twisted deep
     in sheepskin ringlets for an iron grip.
     So, breathing hard, we waited until morning. **B**

IN OTHER WORDS Polyphemus cries out that "Nohbdy" has hurt him. The other Cyclopes reply that if nobody has hurt him, there is nothing they can do to help; and so they leave. Odysseus laughs to see how well his trick has worked. But they are still trapped. Polyphemus pushes the stone away and squats in the open doorway of the cave, hoping to catch the men trying to escape. Odysseus thinks up a plan of escape. He ties the sheep together in threes, then ties a man under each middle sheep. He hides himself under the Cyclops's best ram. They wait for morning.

215 When Dawn spread out her fingertips of rose
     the rams began to stir, moving for pasture,
     and peals of bleating echoed round the pens
     where dams with udders full called for a milking. **C**
     Blinded, and sick with pain from his head wound,
220 the master stroked each ram, then let it pass,
     but my men riding on the pectoral fleece[26]
     the giant's blind hands blundering never found.
     Last of them all my ram, the leader, came,
     weighted by wool and me with my meditations.
225 The Cyclops patted him, and then he said:

---

26. pectoral fleece: wool on an animal's chest.

B YOUR TURN

Literary Focus
Although Odysseus has succeeded in injuring the Cyclops, the **conflict** between them is not over. What step is Odysseus now taking to continue to try to solve the conflict?

_____
_____
_____
_____
_____
_____
_____

C HERE'S HOW

Vocabulary
I have never seen the word *dams* used like it is in this sentence. I decided to look it up in my dictionary. The way it's used here, a *dam* is a "mother of a four-legged animal."

from the **Odyssey**, *Part One*

A YOUR TURN

Reading Focus

What is the real reason that the lead sheep is lagging behind?

_____
_____
_____

B YOUR TURN

Literary Focus

Odysseus acted like an **epic hero** by letting all his men escape from the cave before him. How does he again show his leadership in lines 251–255?

_____
_____
_____
_____
_____
_____

C YOUR TURN

Vocabulary

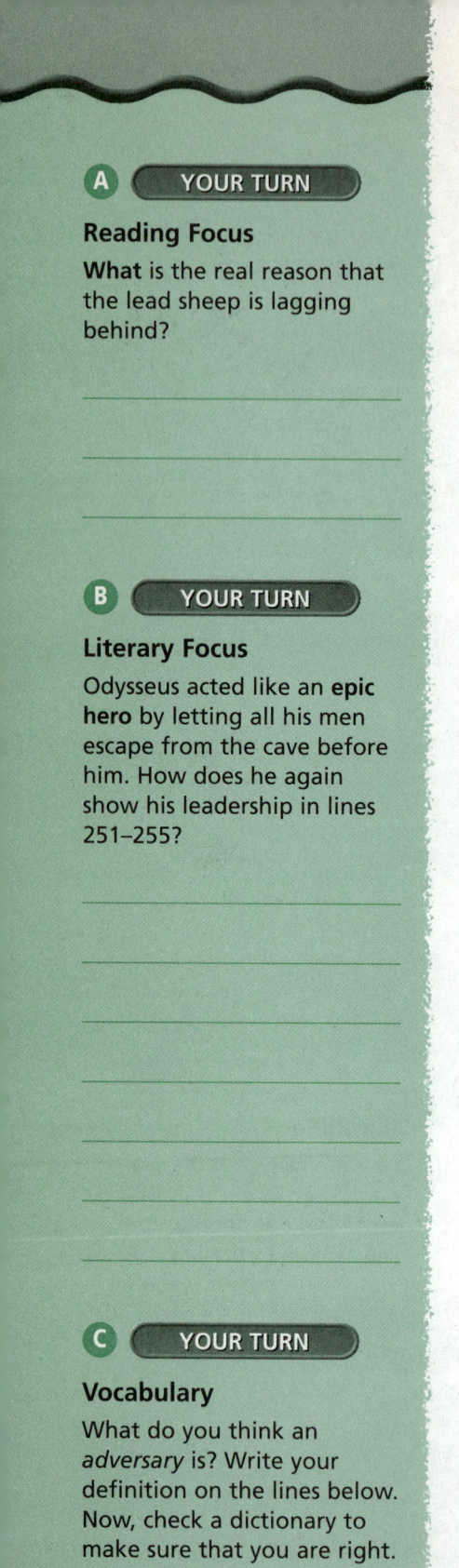

What do you think an *adversary* is? Write your definition on the lines below. Now, check a dictionary to make sure that you are right.

_____
_____
_____

'Sweet cousin ram, why lag behind the rest
in the night cave? You never linger so,
but graze before them all, and go afar
to crop sweet grass, and take your stately way
230 leading along the streams, until at evening
you run to be the first one in the fold.
Why, now, so far behind? Can you be grieving
over your Master's eye? **A** That carrion rogue[27]
and his accurst companions burnt it out
235 when he had conquered all my wits with wine.
Nohbdy will not get out alive, I swear.
Oh, had you brain and voice to tell
where he may be now, dodging all my fury!
Bashed by this hand and bashed on this rock wall
240 his brains would strew the floor, and I should have
rest from the outrage Nohbdy worked upon me.'

He sent us into the open, then. Close by,
I dropped and rolled clear of the ram's belly,
going this way and that to untie the men.
245 With many glances back, we rounded up
his fat, stiff-legged sheep to take aboard,
and drove them down to where the good ship lay.
We saw, as we came near, our fellows' faces
shining; then we saw them turn to grief
250 tallying those who had not fled from death.
I hushed them, jerking head and eyebrows up,
and in a low voice told them: 'Load this herd;
move fast, and put the ship's head toward the breakers.'
They all pitched in at loading, then embarked
255 and struck their oars into the sea. **B** Far out,
as far offshore as shouted words would carry,
I sent a few back to the adversary: **C**

IN OTHER WORDS In the morning blind Polyphemus lets his sheep out. He touches each one as it passes, but the men

---

27. **carrion rogue:** rotten scoundrel. Carrion is decaying flesh.

260 from the **Odyssey**, Part One

are safely hidden. As the last ram goes by, with Odysseus hanging beneath, Polyphemus swears to destroy "Nohbdy." Free at last, the men run for their ship, taking the sheep with them. The rest of the crew is waiting. Quickly, they load the sheep on board and begin to row away.

> 'O Cyclops! Would you feast on my companions?
> Puny, am I, in a Caveman's hands?
> How do you like the beating that we gave you,
> you damned cannibal? Eater of guests
> under your roof! Zeus and the gods have paid you!'
> The blind thing in his doubled fury broke
> a hilltop in his hands and heaved it after us.
> Ahead of our black prow it struck and sank
> whelmed in a spuming geyser, a giant wave
> that washed the ship stern foremost back to shore.
> I got the longest boathook out and stood
> fending us off, with furious nods to all
> to put their backs into a racing stroke—
> row, row or perish. So the long oars bent
> kicking the foam sternward, making head
> until we drew away, and twice as far. **D**
> Now when I cupped my hands I heard the crew
> in low voices protesting:
>
>   'Godsake, Captain!
> Why bait the beast again? Let him alone!'
>
> 'That tidal wave he made on the first throw
> all but beached us.'
>
>   'All but stove[28] us in!'
>
> 'Give him our bearing[29] with your trumpeting,
> he'll get the range and lob[30] a boulder.'

---

28. **stove:** past participle of *stave*, meaning "to smash or break up."
29. **bearing:** location.
30. **lob:** toss.

D YOUR TURN

Reading Focus
Paraphrase lines 263–273.

_____
_____
_____
_____
_____

from the Odyssey, *Part One*

A **YOUR TURN**

Reading Focus

Why do the crew members want Odysseus to stop shouting at Polyphemus? **How** does Odysseus respond?

_____
_____
_____

B **YOUR TURN**

Literary Focus

Re-read lines 282–287. What do these lines tell you about Odysseus? Does this fit your idea of an **epic hero**? Why or why not?

_____
_____
_____
_____
_____

280   'Aye
He'll smash our timbers and our heads together!'

I would not heed them in my glorying spirit,
but let my anger flare and yelled:

           'Cyclops,
if ever mortal man inquire
285 how you were put to shame and blinded, tell him
Odysseus, raider of cities, took your eye:
Laertes'[31] son, whose home's on Ithaca!' **A** **B**

IN OTHER WORDS Odysseus shouts at Polyphemus, taunting him with their escape. Enraged, the Cyclops breaks off a hilltop and throws it at the ship. The hilltop falls in the water ahead of them, making a giant wave that pushes them back to shore. The men row away again with all their might. The men beg Odysseus to leave the Cyclops alone. But Odysseus calls out to the Cyclops again, telling him his real name.

At this he gave a mighty sob and rumbled:

'Now comes the weird[32] upon me, spoken of old.
290 A wizard, grand and wondrous, lived here—Telemus,[33]
a son of Eurymus;[34] great length of days
he had in wizardry among the Cyclopes,
and these things he foretold for time to come:
my great eye lost, and at Odysseus' hands.
295 Always I had in mind some giant, armed
in giant force, would come against me here.
But this, but you—small, pitiful, and twiggy—
you put me down with wine, you blinded me.
Come back, Odysseus, and I'll treat you well,

---
31. **Laertes** (LAY UHR TEEZ).
32. **weird**: fate.
33. **Telemus** (TEHL UH MUHS).
34. **Eurymus** (YOO RUH MUHS).

262   *from the* **Odyssey**, *Part One*

> 300 praying the god of earthquake to befriend you—
> his son I am, for he by his avowal[35]
> fathered me, and, if he will, he may
> heal me of this black wound—he and no other
> of all the happy gods or mortal men.' **C**
>
> 305 Few words I shouted in reply to him:
> 'If I could take your life I would and take
> your time away, and hurl you down to hell!
> The god of earthquake could not heal you there!'
>
> At this he stretched his hands out in his darkness
> 310 toward the sky of stars, and prayed Poseidon:
>
> 'O hear me, lord, blue girdler of the islands,[36]
> if I am thine indeed, and thou art father:
> grant that Odysseus, raider of cities, never
> see his home: Laertes' son, I mean,
> 315 who kept his hall on Ithaca. Should destiny
> intend that he shall see his roof again
> among his family in his fatherland,
> far be that day, and dark the years between.

---

35. **avowal:** a public announcement or acknowledgment; a proclamation.
36. **blue girdler of the islands:** a reference to the sea, which girdles, or surrounds, the islands. Poseidon is god of the sea.

C YOUR TURN

Reading Focus
Paraphrase what Polyphemus says to Odysseus in lines 295–304.

A **YOUR TURN**

Reading Focus

What is the result of Odysseus's taunting of the Cyclops? **How** do you predict the rest of Odysseus's journey will go?

_____
_____
_____
_____
_____

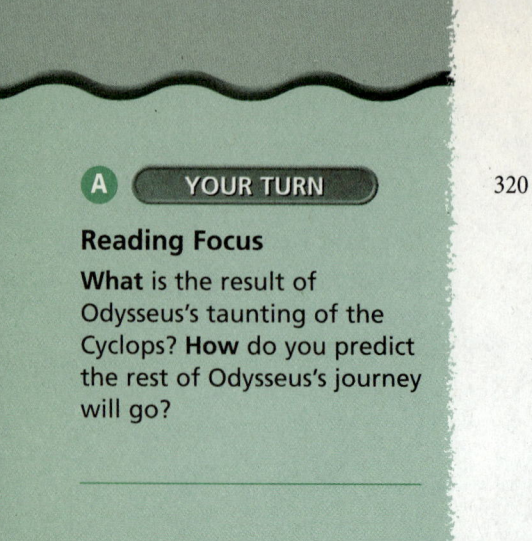

Let him lose all companions, and return
320 under strange sail to bitter days at home.' ..." **A**
(*from* Book 9)

IN OTHER WORDS Long ago, a wizard said that Polyphemus would be blinded by Odysseus. Hearing this name, the Cyclops realizes that his fate has come to pass. He asks Odysseus to come back, saying that he is the son of the god Poseidon, and that he will ask his father to treat Odysseus well. Odysseus responds with threats and insults. Polyphemus calls out to Poseidon, begging him to make sure that Odysseus never reaches home. Or, if that is impossible, to make his journey long and hard, and his final return full of grief.

264 *from the* **Odyssey**, Part One

Applying Your Skills

from the Odyssey, Part One

LITERARY FOCUS: EPIC HEROES AND CONFLICT

DIRECTIONS: Odysseus is an **epic hero**. He has all of the qualities of an epic hero listed in the first column of the table below. In the second column, explain how each quality helped Odysseus solve the conflict between himself and the Cyclops. Use examples from the epic to support your answers.

Quality	How it helped Odysseus
Strength	
Courage	
Intelligence	

READING FOCUS: READING AN EPIC

DIRECTIONS: Answer the following questions to check your understanding of the selection. Write your answers on a separate sheet of paper.

1. **Who** are the main characters of this epic?
2. **Where** are Odysseus and his men trapped?
3. **When** does Odysseus begin building a weapon to strike the Cyclops with?
4. **Why** does Odysseus tell the Cyclops that his name is "Nohbdy"?
5. **How** does Odysseus use sheep to get his men out of the cave?
6. **What** does Polyphemus say to try to lure Odysseus back to the cave after he has escaped?

VOCABULARY REVIEW

DIRECTIONS: Write two sentences, each using one word from the Word Box correctly.

Word Box
- profusion
- adversary

1. _____
2. _____

Preparing to Read

from Shipwreck at the Bottom of the World *and* Tending Sir Ernest's Legacy

INFORMATIONAL TEXT FOCUS: SYNTHESIZING SOURCES: MAKING CONNECTIONS

One way to increase your understanding as you read is to **synthesize**—or bring together—what you have learned from different sources on one topic. You can also connect what you are reading to your own experiences.

Whenever you read, you look for connections between what you are reading and the world you know. You think about how the subject—a childhood memory, for example—**connects** with your own experience. You ask yourself whether the work seems true to you based on what you already know or have experienced.

You can also connect and compare your reading with other works you have read. For example, you might **compare** a brave character from one story to the hero of another. You could then consider how those two characters are alike and different, and what each tells you about bravery. Each work you read on a subject adds to your overall understanding of the topic.

As you read the following biography and interview, paraphrase the ideas in each source. Then ask yourself the following questions:

- How are these sources similar?
- How are they different?
- What other works on this topic do these pieces remind me of?
- How have these sources added to my understanding of life?

SKILLS FOCUS

Informational Text Skills Synthesize information from several sources on a single topic; make connections to or from a text.

VOCABULARY

provisions (PRUH VIHZH UHNZ) *n.:* supplies, usually of food.

plummeted (PLUHM IH TIHD) *v.:* dropped; plunged.

ambitious (AM BISH UHS) *adj.:* wanting to achieve a goal.

optimism (OP TUH MIZ UHM) *n.:* positive outlook.

from SHIPWRECK AT THE BOTTOM OF THE WORLD

By Jennifer Armstrong

> ### INTO THE BIOGRAPHY
> In 1915, Ernest Shackleton and his crew of 28 men were stranded in the Antarctic, the most dangerous environment on earth. Their ship, the *Endurance*, was caught in ice and frozen in place for the winter. When spring came, ice pushed the ship over and crushed it. The crew crowded onto three lifeboats and made it to a small island on April 16, 1916, after six days on the water. There was nothing on the island, and Shackleton knew that somebody had to get help or they would all die. Shackleton picked five men to go with him. They rebuilt the lifeboat, called the *James Caird*, and went to try to find help.

On the morning of Monday, April 24, all hands were roused at six o'clock to help lash up and stow the *Caird*. As Wild[1] oversaw the preparation of the boat, Shackleton and Worsley climbed up a small hill they used as a lookout and surveyed the ocean. The ice was within five or six miles of the shore, drifting northeast. Large, grounded icebergs made wide gaps in the ice as they streamed past them. The rescue party would escape through one of those leads. **A**

Below, the *Caird* was dragged down to the surf and loaded with the bags of ballast,[2] boxes of stores, a hand pump, a cook pot, six reindeer-skin sleeping bags, and the rest of the provisions. At noon the men heaved the laden boat out on the backwash of a breaking wave, and the remainder of the stores was ferried out on the *Stancomb Wills*. Shackleton and Worsley rejoined the

---
1. **Wild:** Frank Wild, second-in-command of the *Endurance*.
2. **ballast** (BAL uhst): something heavy carried in a ship's hold to steady it.

A HERE'S HOW

Reading Focus
The way this text begins gives me a chance to practice **connecting** the text to my own experiences. I can imagine being nervous about starting a trip. I know I was terrified the first time I went on an airplane. I will try to think about this feeling of anxiety and nervousness that the crew may have as I keep reading.

From *Shipwreck at the Bottom of the World: The Extraordinary True Story of Shackleton and the* Endurance by Jennifer Armstrong. Copyright © 1998 by Jennifer M. Armstrong. Reproduced by permission of **Crown Publishers**, a division of Random House, Inc., www.randomhouse.com.

A QUICK CHECK

What nickname did the men have for Shackleton?

B HERE'S HOW

Vocabulary

I know that *porpoise* is a noun that refers to a kind of animal that lives in the ocean. My teacher says that *porpoised* in line 20 is a verb that means "moved forward with a rising and falling motion in the manner of a porpoise." I think this sentence is just saying that the penguins were moving in the water along with the boat.

---

group. There were handshakes all around. The six members of the relief party boarded the boat, and they shoved off.

Behind on the beach, the remaining twenty-two men cheered and waved. "Good luck, Boss!" they shouted. **A** Shackleton looked back once and raised his hand in farewell.

20 Gentoo penguins porpoised along beside the boat as they raised the sail and plunged forward into the rolling waves. **B** The Boss stood with one arm around the mast looking forward, directing Worsley at the helm around the ice.

IN OTHER WORDS While shipwrecked and stranded on an island in the Antarctic Ocean, Ernest Shackleton picked five members of his 28-man crew to join him on a rescue mission. The men loaded supplies onto a lifeboat called the *James Caird*, and with one man named Worsley steering the ship, set out to find help.

They made good speed for two hours and then reached the loose belt of ice they had seen from the lookout. They turned east along it, searching for the leads that would let them through. Huge, lopsided remnant bergs bobbed and heaved in the waves, and small chunks of broken floe[3] knocked and scraped along the sides of the *Caird*. The whole jumble of loose pack hissed and
30 rustled as it rose to the swell. After an hour's run, they found an opening and turned north to sail through it. Just before dark they

---

3. **floe** (FLOH): sheet of floating ice.

© Bettmann/Corbis

268 *from* Shipwreck at the Bottom of the World

were on the other side, and when they looked over their shoulders they saw Elephant Island as a small shadow far astern.

Shackleton and Worsley had agreed that the safest plan was to get as far north as possible before heading east. For one thing, they would be glad to get away from the most frigid weather as soon as they could. Furthermore, they would be sailing day and night, and they needed to get beyond the limit of floating ice: if they rammed a chunk in the dark, their journey would be a short one. By 10:00 P.M. the water seemed relatively clear of ice, and their spirits rose: so far, so good. In the darkness, they steered by keeping an eye on the small blue pennant that streamed from the mast in the wind.

IN OTHER WORDS After a few hours at sea, the crew of the *Caird* navigated around some dangerous ice. Shackleton planned to first head north to escape the cold, then east for dry land. The crew sailed both day and night, using a flag tied to the mast as a guide in the darkness.

The living arrangements on board were uncomfortable and cramped. The men were divided into two watches: Shackleton, Crean, and McNeish steered, bailed, and pumped for four hours, while Worsley, Vincent, and McCarthy slept—or tried to. Then the watches traded places—watch and watch, every four hours. The sleeping bags were forward, under the improvised decking on the bow. To reach them, the men had to crawl on hands and knees over the stone ballast, then wriggle forward on their stomachs over the crates of stores. Then, with barely enough room to turn around, they wormed themselves into the sleeping bags and attempted to sleep as the boat bucked up and down through the heavy swell. At the end of each four-hour watch, the men would change places, wriggling past each other in the cramped space. **C**

C QUICK CHECK

What conditions do these explorers face? Why must they have four-hour watches for the boat?

_____
_____
_____
_____

from Shipwreck at the Bottom of the World 269

A **HERE'S HOW**

Vocabulary

I have not seen the word *oilskins* before. My teacher says that *oilskin* is a type of waterproof fabric used by fisherman.

B **HERE'S HOW**

Reading Focus

I can **connect** this passage to an experience of my own. One time, I went camping and it rained for the entire week—I thought I would never feel dry again. Shackleton's crew must have felt the same.

© Royal Geographical Society

It was a tossup which was worse—being pounded up and down in the bow of the boat in a sorry excuse for sleep, or huddling in the cockpit as icy seas swept across the thwarts[4] and gunwales.[5] There were no oilskins, and the men were dressed in wool, which got wet and stayed wet for the duration of the voyage. **A** With temperatures below freezing, and no room to move around to get their blood stirred up, they were always cold. Miserably cold. Waves broke over the bows, where bucketfuls of water streamed through the flimsy decking. The bottom of the boat was constantly awash, and the two men on watch who weren't steering were always bailing or pumping. The reindeer-skin sleeping bags were soaking wet all the time, and beginning to rot. Loose reindeer hair found its way into the men's nostrils and mouths as they breathed, into their water and their food as they ate. **B**

IN OTHER WORDS The men worked in four-hour shifts: three of them sailed the ship, while three tried to sleep below deck. Conditions were crowded, though. The men were always wet from water splashing over the ship's sides. Even their sleeping bags were wet.

---

4. **thwarts:** rowers' seats extending across a boat.
5. **gunwales** (GUN EHLZ): upper edges of the sides of a boat.

from **Shipwreck at the Bottom of the World**

Crean had taken over as cook for the journey. In the pitching and rolling of the boat, preparing meals was a tricky business. Crean and Worsley would sit on opposite sides of the boat with their feet out, bracing the Primus camp stove. **C** Crean would light the stove and begin stirring up chunks of sledging ration[6] in water as Worsley held the pot. With each dip and plunge of the boat, Worsley swooped the pot up in the air lest their precious hoosh[7] go slopping into the bilges.[8] When the hoosh was cooked, Crean doled it out into six bowls, and the men ate it scalding hot, hunched under the decking. Whoever finished first went out to relieve the man at the tiller[9] so that he could eat his hoosh before it cooled. In addition, Shackleton allowed hot milk and sugar at regular intervals: the only way to keep going was by fueling themselves constantly.

By the third day of sailing, the weather turned rotten. A gale blew up with snow squalls and heavy seas, and waves broke incessantly over the boat. The *James Caird* clawed its way up the face of one hissing wave and then plunged down the other side as spray lashed into the men's faces. The gale continued into the fourth day, finally blowing them north of the sixtieth parallel. Floating past them went two pieces of wreckage from a lost ship. The men watched it disappear, and hunched their shoulders and struggled to keep their little boat on course. As Shackleton put it, "So small was our boat and so great were the seas that often our sail flapped idly in the calm between the crests of two waves. Then we would climb the next slope, and catch the full fury of the gale where the wool-like whiteness of the breaking water surged around us." **D**

C QUICK CHECK

Why did Crean and Worsley have to brace the camp stove while they cooked every meal?

D YOUR TURN

Reading Focus

Try to **connect and compare** this part of the text with other reading you have done. Have you ever read about someone else who had to complete a dangerous and difficult task? Who was this character, what situation was he or she in, and why?

IN OTHER WORDS Preparing meals was tricky while waves tossed the small ship around. Two men had to hold

---

6. **sledging ration:** crew member's daily food allotment while on an Antarctic expedition.
7. **hoosh:** thick stew made from pemmican (mixture of dried meat, fat, and cereal), a thickener such as ground biscuits, and water.
8. **bilges** (BIHLJ IHZ): bottom of a ship's hull.
9. **tiller:** the bar or handle at the stern of the boat used for steering.

The Open Boat Journey: The First Ten Days 271

A HERE'S HOW

Language Coach

I think the word *calculations* must be a **derivation**, or another form, of the word *calculate*. *Calculations* looks like a noun, and I think it means "the results of calculating." I checked my dictionary, and I was right.

B YOUR TURN

Vocabulary

Plummeted means "plunged" or "dropped." Why does Shackleton's journey become more difficult and dangerous when the temperature *plummeted*?

_____
_____
_____

---

the camp stove steady while they cooked thick stew for every meal. Shackleton believed it was important for the crew to be well fed, though. On the third day of sailing, the *Caird* entered a windstorm. The crew faced huge waves for about a day before passing through the storm.

100   For Worsley, navigating had ceased to be a science and had turned into a kind of sorcery. To get a sight of the sun meant Worsley had to kneel on the thwart, where Vincent and McCarthy would hug him around the waist to keep him from pitching out of the boat as it bucked and leaped over the waves. Then, while Shackleton stood by with the chronometer,[10] Worsley would wait until the boat reached the top of the wave and the horizon came into sight, then shout "Now!" as he shot the sun. His books were fast turning into useless pulp. His sun sights were the crudest of guesses, and to look up positions in
110   the tables he had to peel apart the wet pages one by one. Making his calculations with a pencil became laughably impossible. **A** The boat pitched and rolled so badly that he could barely read his own scribbles. The weather was so foul that in the whole journey he managed to take a sight of the sun only four times.

Since leaving Elephant Island, the six men had been accompanied by an albatross, who soared and dipped through the air. The bird could have reached South Georgia in a matter of hours, if it chose, while the men in the *James Caird* were crawling like a beetle over the surface of the ocean. Each time Worsley
120   calculated the number of miles they had put behind them, the bird seemed to mock their slow progress.

On their seventh day at sea, the wind again turned into a gale roaring up from the Pole; the temperature plummeted. **B** The men began to fear that the sails would freeze up and cake with ice, becoming heavier and heavier until the boat toppled upside down. With the gale howling around their ears, they took down the sails and rolled them up, stuffing them into the cramped space below.

---

10. **chronometer** (KRUH NOM UH TUHR): clock or watch that keeps exact time and is used to determine longitude at sea.

Then they rigged a sea anchor, a canvas cone dragged through the water to keep the boat turned into the storm.

IN OTHER WORDS Considering the many obstacles he faced, Worsley did an impressive job navigating the ship. While the men of the *Caird* moved slowly north, they were followed by an albatross, a large seabird, seemingly mocking their progress. On the seventh day, winds picked up again and the temperature fell. The crew dropped an anchor to wait out the storm.

130   Throughout the night, waves crashed over the *James Caird* and quickly turned to ice. At first the crew was relieved, since it meant the flimsy decking was sealed against further leaks. But when they awoke on the eighth day, they felt the clumsy, heavy motion of the boat beneath them and knew they were in trouble: fifteen inches of ice encased the boat above the waterline, and she was rolling badly. "We saw and felt that the *James Caird* had lost her resiliency," Shackleton said later. "She was not rising to the oncoming seas. The weight of the ice was having its effect, and she was becoming more like a log than a boat." **C**

140   The ice had to come off. Taking turns, the men crawled on hands and knees over the iced deck, hacking away with an ax. "First you chopped a handhold, then a kneehold, and then chopped off ice hastily but carefully, with an occasional sea washing over you," Worsley explained. Each man could stand only five minutes or so of this cold and perilous job at a time. Then it was the next man's turn. **D**

And the gale continued through the next day, too. As Shackleton crawled out to relieve Worsley at the tiller, a large wave slammed the skipper right in the face. Shackleton took the
150   tiller ropes and commented, "Pretty juicy," and both men managed a weak laugh.

IN OTHER WORDS On the eighth day, the crew realized that the ship was frozen in the ice. They took turns chipping

---

C   YOUR TURN

Reading Focus
How does this quote by Shackleton **connect** to the rest of the story?

_____
_____
_____
_____
_____

D   QUICK CHECK

Why could the men only chop away the ice for about five minutes at a time?

_____
_____
_____
_____

from **Shipwreck at the Bottom of the World**   273

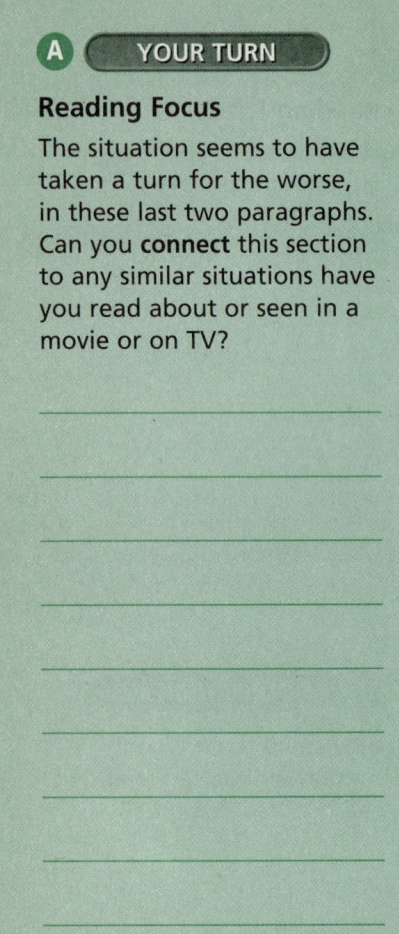

> **A** **YOUR TURN**
>
> **Reading Focus**
> The situation seems to have taken a turn for the worse, in these last two paragraphs. Can you **connect** this section to any similar situations have you read about or seen in a movie or on TV?
>
> _____
> _____
> _____
> _____
> _____
> _____
> _____

away the ice with an axe while the storm continued raging around them. Because of the cold, each man could only stand to work on the ice for about five minutes at a time.

As the storm continued, a large buildup of ice on the sea anchor's rope had kept the line swinging and sawing against the stern. Before noon on the ninth day, the sea anchor broke away, and the boat lurched heavily as seas hit her broadside. Before the gale ended that afternoon, the men had had to crawl onto the deck three times to get rid of the boat's shell of ice. The men all agreed that it was the worst job any of them had ever been forced to do.

By the time the gale ended, everything below was thoroughly soaked. The sleeping bags were so slimy and revolting that Shackleton had the two worst of them thrown overboard. Even before the storm, however, the men had been suffering from the constant wet. "After the third day our feet and legs had swelled," Worsley wrote later, "and began to be superficially frostbitten from the constant soaking in seawater, with the temperature at times nearly down to zero; and the lack of exercise. During the last gale they assumed a dead-white color and lost surface feeling." **A**

IN OTHER WORDS On the ninth day, the rope on the ship's anchor broke. Three times that day, the men had to remove ice that was building up on the ship's deck—which they all agreed was the worst job ever. The freezing temperatures and water were beginning to take their toll on the crew.

Exposure was beginning to wear the men down. In spite of two hot meals a day, they were hungry for fresh meat. Cape pigeons often darted and flitted around the boat, but the men couldn't bring themselves to kill the friendly birds, and ancient superstition forbade them from killing the albatross that still followed majestically above. But the men were in pain. They were cold, frostbitten, and covered with salt-water blisters. Their legs were rubbed raw from the chafing of their wet pants. Conditions below were almost unbearable: the stinking, rotting sleeping bags made the air putrid, and the molting hairs choked the men as they tried to gasp for breath. Their bodies were bruised and aching from their pounding up and down in the bows, and they were exhausted from lack of sleep. McNeish, who was more than fifty, was beginning to break down. Vincent, who should have stood the conditions well, was also close to collapsing. Shackleton, Worsley, Crean, and McCarthy took up the slack. When someone looked particularly bad, the Boss ordered a round of hot milk for all hands. The one man he really wanted to get the hot drink into never realized that the break was for his benefit and so wasn't embarrassed, and all of the men were better off for having the warmth and nourishment. **B**

The night after the gale ended, Shackleton was at the tiller, crouched in a half-standing, half-sitting position against the thwart with his back hunched against the cold. He glanced back toward the south and saw a line of white along the horizon. "It's clearing, boys!" he shouted. But when he looked back again, he yelled, "For God's sake, hold on! It's got us!" Instead of a clearing sky, the white line to the south was the foaming crest of an enormous storm wave bearing down on them. Worsley was just crawling out of his sleeping bag when the wave struck, and for a few moments the entire boat seemed to be submerged.

IN OTHER WORDS The men were hungry for meat, but they could not bring themselves to kill the albatross or other passing birds. Shackleton insisted that everyone drink hot milk to stay warm and keep spirits high. The night after the storm ended, a huge wave crashed down on the *Caird*, seemingly covering the entire ship.

Worsley, Crean, Vincent, McCarthy, and McNeish frantically pumped and bailed with anything they could find—the cook pot, dippers, their hands—anything that would get the water out of the boat. For an hour they labored to keep the water from capsizing the *Caird*. They could hardly believe they had not foundered,[11] and they prayed they would not see another wave like that one again. **C**

---

11. **foundered:** sank.

B LITERARY ANALYSIS

In what way do Shackleton's actions here show his leadership abilities?

_____
_____
_____
_____
_____

C YOUR TURN

Language Coach

Circle the word in this paragraph that is a **derivation** of the word *frantic*, meaning "desperate" or "wild with fear."

The Open Boat Journey: The First Ten Days   275

A LITERARY ANALYSIS

Judging by what Shackleton wrote, how would you describe his character? How would you guess this rescue mission ended?

_____
_____
_____
_____
_____
_____
_____
_____

On the tenth day, the sun showed its face long enough for Worsley to get a fix. He calculated that they had made 444 miles from Elephant Island, more than half the distance. The men rejoiced as the weather cleared and they had the first good weather of the passage. They brought wet sleeping bags and clothes up on deck and hung them from the masts, halyards, and rigging.[12] The sleeping bags and clothing didn't dry, but they were reduced from soaking wet to merely damp. All their spirits were lifted. They were more than halfway to South Georgia Island.

"We were a tiny speck in the vast vista of the sea," Shackleton wrote later. "For a moment the consciousness of the forces arrayed against us would be overwhelming. Then hope and confidence would rise again as our boat rose to a wave and tossed aside the crest in a sparkling shower like the play of prismatic colors at the foot of a waterfall." **A**

They had less than half the distance left to go.

IN OTHER WORDS The crew quickly began bailing the water out of the ship. They worked for an hour to keep the ship from tipping over; they could hardly believe it did not sink. On the tenth day, the storm calmed and the sun came out. Worsley guessed that they were over halfway to their destination. Shackleton later recalled that although things seemed grim, hope always returned as the ship passed successfully over the waves.

---

12. **halyards** (HAL yuhrdz), **and rigging:** ropes used on a ship to raise or lower something, such as a flag or sail, or to support the masts, yards, and sails.

276 The Open Boat Journey: The First Ten Days

TENDING SIR ERNEST'S LEGACY

Based on the interview with Alexandra Shackleton from *NOVA Online*

Sir Ernest Shackleton would be proud of his only granddaughter, Alexandra Shackleton. She is the president of the James Caird Society. This organization honors Shackleton and shares information about his life. Here, Ms. Shackleton talks about the great man. **B**

NOVA: Why did your grandfather want to cross Antarctica?

Shackleton: I think he considered it the last great Antarctic adventure—to cross the Antarctic from the Weddell Sea to the Ross Sea, a distance of about 1,800 miles.

10 **NOVA:** It was a pretty ambitious plan. **C** Was the challenge what made him want to do it?

Shackleton: It was ambitious, but I think he thought it was possible. He would never have tried anything that he thought could not be done. He always had the lives of his men to think about. **D**

From "Tending Sir Ernest's Legacy: An Interview with Alexandra Shackleton" by Kelly Tyler from *NOVA Online*, 2002. Copyright © 2002 by **WGBH Educational Foundation**. Reproduced by permission of the publisher.

B **HERE'S HOW**

Reading Focus

I want to **compare** and **synthesize** sources as I read. I already recognize that this text will be about Ernest Shackleton—the same person I read about in the previous article. I remember that he led an expedition and rescued his stranded men.

C **HERE'S HOW**

Vocabulary

I am not sure what *ambitious* means. Even after reading the surrounding sentences, I am still not sure. I checked my dictionary, and *ambitious* means "wanting to achieve a goal."

D **YOUR TURN**

Reading Focus

Compare Alexandra Shackleton's comments about her grandfather here to what you read about him in the last article. Do you agree or disagree with what she says? Explain your answer.

_____
_____
_____

A QUICK CHECK

How did Shackleton act seeing his ship sink?

_____
_____

B YOUR TURN

Language Coach

Reassure is a **derivation** of the word *assure,* which means "to secure" or "to confirm." What do you think the word *reassured* means?

_____
_____

C HERE'S HOW

Reading Focus

I can **connect** this part of the text to what I already know. I remember that the previous article also described how Shackleton gave hot milk to his crew to keep them warm and make them feel better.

NOVA: How do you think your grandfather felt when the *Endurance* was stuck in the ice, and he realized he would never cross Antarctica?

Shackleton: Well, it wasn't sudden. The crew gradually understood that the ship was not going to get out. My grandfather said to the captain, "the ship can't live in this." Then he started making plans for what could be done. He was a great planner.

For several weeks the ship had been making creaking and groaning noises. Then they saw the ship disappear. He found it extremely upsetting. It was the end of his dream.

Yet he said to his men, quite calmly, "ship gone . . . now we will go home." His new goal was bringing every one of his 27 men home alive, from a part of the world where nobody knew they were. **A**

NOVA: He must have been so disappointed. And yet he held himself together.

Shackleton: Yes, and the men felt reassured. **B** After losing the ship, they felt lost, and yet he helped them. He gave them something to do.

NOVA: On the journey to South Georgia on the lifeboat, how did your grandfather help the men deal with the terrible conditions?

Shackleton: Every man was fed every four hours. And if he noticed anyone weakening, he would order hot milk right away, not just for him, but for everybody. That way this man would not be embarrassed. When he noticed one man was particularly cold, he would find him a pair of gloves. **C**

NOVA: How do you think your grandfather felt when he finally saw South Georgia?

278 Tending Sir Ernest's Legacy

Shackleton: When they saw South Georgia for the first time, he felt huge relief. But there was a storm, and it took two days before they could land.

NOVA: Even today that journey is seen as a miracle.

Shackleton: Yes. Many believe that was the greatest small boat journey in the world. They went 800 miles across the stormiest seas in the world in a boat not even 23 feet long, They had to deal with terrible storms, thirst, hunger, everything. It was a huge achievement. **D**

NOVA: Was the *Endurance* expedition the greatest achievement of his life?

Shackleton: I think so, because in the worst situation he brought his 27 men home safely. Climbing across the mountains of South Georgia with no equipment was remarkable. To this day, no one has ever beaten his record of 30 miles in 36 hours.

NOVA: What did your grandfather think were the most important qualities for an explorer in the South Pole to have?

Shackleton: He said first optimism, second patience, third imagination, and fourth, courage. **E** He thought every man had courage. **F**

NOVA: What qualities do you think made him such a strong leader?

Shackleton: His men were so important to him. Leadership was a two-way thing. It wasn't men following him just because he was the leader; he really cared for them. It was a very close relationship. It took four tries to rescue his men from Elephant Island. But when he got to Elephant Island and found all well, he was alright again.

NOVA: Do you think he was happiest when he was in the Antarctic?

D HERE'S HOW

Vocabulary

I am not sure what the word *achievement* means. By looking at it's context. I think *achievement* means "something accomplished."

E HERE'S HOW

Vocabulary

I think I have heard the word *optimism* before and that it is a view that puts everything in a positive light. That makes sense in this sentence, where Alexandra Shackleton is talking about important qualities for this kind of explorer.

F QUICK CHECK

According to Shackleton, what were the four most important qualities for an explorer in the South Pole to have?

_____
_____
_____
_____

A YOUR TURN

Reading Focus
Shackleton was happiest doing what he loved. How does this knowledge **connect** to something from your own experiences?

_____
_____
_____
_____
_____
_____
_____

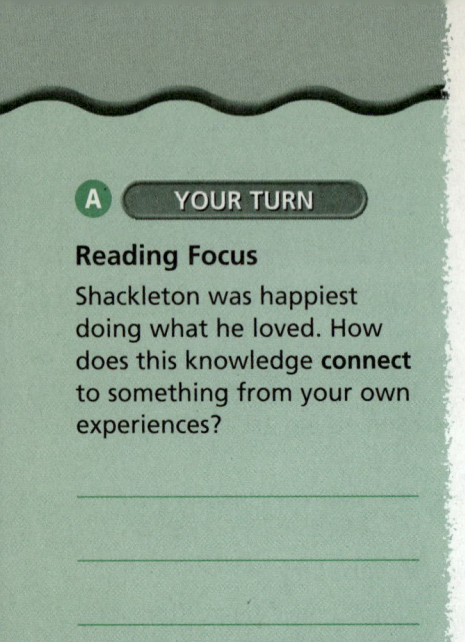

Shackleton: Yes. He wrote to my grandmother, "I'm not much good at anything else but being an explorer." He loved her and his home, but he needed to explore. For a man who loved open spaces, Antarctica was amazing. It's like nowhere else. He wrote to a little sister, "you cannot imagine what it is like" to walk where no man has trod walked before. **A**

Interview conducted by Kelly Tyler, NOVA producer, "Shackleton's Voyage of Endurance"

Applying Your Skills

from Shipwreck at the Bottom of the World *and* Tending Sir Ernest's Legacy

INFORMATIONAL TEXT FOCUS: SYNTHESIZING SOURCES: MAKING CONNECTIONS

DIRECTIONS: Now that you have read two sources about Ernest Shackleton and his voyage, use your knowledge from **synthesizing** the sources to answer the questions that follow. Circle the letter of the best answer in each case.

1. Which of the following points do *both* Jennifer Armstrong and Alexandra Shackleton make?

   A. Shackleton was angry because he failed to reach the Antarctic.

   B. Shackleton was mysterious and kept his ideas to himself.

   C. The entire crew survived the expedition because of Shackleton's leadership.

2. Which of the following statements highlights a key *difference* in the selections?

   A. The interview gives more details about the expedition.

   B. Jennifer's Armstrong's biography lacks quotations.

   C. Jennifer Armstrong's biography focuses more on the hardships of the journey to Antarctica.

3. Which statement synthesizes themes from the two selections?

   A. Good leaders put the well-being of their crews first.

   B. Being a leader means being a hero.

VOCABULARY REVIEW

DIRECTIONS: Fill in the blanks with the correct words from the Word Box.

Word Box
- provisions
- plummeted
- ambitious
- optimism

1. When the temperature _____, the crew had to worry about staying warm.

2. The crew stocked the *Caird* with plenty of _____, or food and supplies, for their long journey.

Skills Review

Collection 9

VOCABULARY REVIEW

DIRECTIONS: Read each sentence below. Then choose the letter of the word that best fits in the blank.

1. The temperature _____ quickly, and it was soon bitterly cold.
   A. plummeted   B. increased   C. portrayed

2. The character was _____ as a kind and generous woman.
   A. portrait   B. portrayed   C. portion

3. Odysseus stood up to his _____, the evil Cyclops.
   A. ally   B. adversary   C. friend

4. Every time I go to the store, I buy bottles of water and keep them in my garage. After several trips to the store, I had a _____ of water bottles in my garage.
   A. profusion   B. provision   C. protrusion

5. It is important for an explorer to have _____, or a positive attitude.
   A. options   B. optimism   C. opinions

6. The waves splashed into the boat, soaking the crew's _____, or supplies.
   A. provisions   B. protein   C. programs

7. According to legend, the hero's _____ was to kill the dragon.
   A. desperately   B. dizzy   C. destiny

Language and Writing

Collection 9

LANGUAGE COACH: WORD DERIVATIONS

DIRECTIONS: You can understand new words more quickly and completely if you recognize their word roots. Below, match each word from the selections you have read with the word from which it was **derived**, or originated from. Write the letters on the correct blanks.

_____ 1. aching   A. warm
_____ 2. frostbitten   B. stick
_____ 3. warmth   C. ache
_____ 4. proud   D. frost
_____ 5. stuck   E. pride

ORAL LANGUAGE ACTIVITY

DIRECTIONS: Now that you have learned to **connect** and **compare** as you read, work with a small group to discuss the connections between Ernest Shackleton and Odysseus. Here are some of the questions you might talk about together:

- How were the two men's journeys similar?
- How were they different?
- Did the two men have any of the same character qualities?
- Was either man a hero?
- Why or why not?

During your discussion, take notes about what your group thinks. Then compare the results of your discussion with those of the other groups in your class.

Collection 10

Reading for Life

© Masterfile Royalty Free

Literary and Academic Vocabulary for Collection 10

LITERARY VOCABULARY

consumer (KUHN SOO MUHR) *n.:* someone who buys or uses something.
You are a consumer every time you buy something.

consumer documents (KUHN SOO MUHR DAHK YOO MUHNTS) *n.:* pieces of written information that come with something you buy.
My bicycle came with several consumer documents.

product information (PRAH DUHKT IHN FUHR MAY SHUHN) *n.:* a document that tells you about what you are buying and is often found on the box or label.
The product information for my bicycle said it had 10 speeds and excellent hand brakes.

instruction manuals (IHN STRUHK SHUHN MAN YOO UHLS) *n.:* documents that tell you how to set up and use a product.
The instruction manual for my bicycle explained how to put it together.

warranties (WAWR UHN TEEZ) *n.:* documents that explain what happens if a product does not work as it should and what you have to do to get it repaired or replaced.
My bicycle's warranty said that if it broke within two years, I could bring it back to the store where I bought it for a replacement.

ACADEMIC VOCABULARY

consequences (KAHN SE KWEHNS EHZ) *n.:* results; outcomes.
The consequences of poorly written directions could be confusion and frustration.

function (FUHNGK SHUHN) *n.:* typical role or action of something.
The function of consumer documents is to tell consumers about products or services.

coherent (KOH HIHR EHNT) *adj.:* clear; logical; connected; understandable.
It is easy to understand a coherent document.

specify (SPEHS UH FY) *n.:* state in detail.
Product information on clothing labels may specify the size and the materials used.

Preparing to Read

Following Technical Directions

INFORMATIONAL TEXT FOCUS: FOLLOWING TECHNICAL DIRECTIONS

Instructions for using computers as well as other scientific, mechanical, and electronic products and activities are called **technical directions**. You follow technical directions when you read instructions on how to fix a flat tire on your bicycle, program the remote control for your TV, or install software on your computer. Technical directions may seem hard to understand at first, but if you pay attention and follow each step carefully, you can reach your goal.

READING FOCUS: SKIMMING AND SCANNING

You can use tools such as skimming and scanning to help you read and understand an informational document.

- **Skimming** helps you get an idea of what the whole document is like. You look quickly at the title, heads, and subheads, and read the first line or two of each paragraph.

- **Scanning** helps you find information in the document. You search for **boldface** or *italic* words, pictures, and other details that act like a "map" to help you find the information you are looking for. This is different from the way "scanning" is talked about in the document. Make sure you know the difference between when we are talking about reading the text, and when we are talking about copying a picture onto a computer.

VOCABULARY

Look for these words as you read this selection.

scan (SKAN) *v.:* copy words or pictures from paper onto a computer.

image (IHM IHJ) *n.:* a picture or graphic.

options (OP SHUHNZ) *n.:* choices.

SKILLS FOCUS

Informational Text Skills
Follow technical directions.

Reading Skills
Skim and scan.

286 Following Technical Directions

MANUAL

Adding Graphics to Your Web Site **A**

The following technical directions show how to *scan*, edit, and save an *image* for your Web site using a made-up photo-editing program called PhotoEdit. The directions assume you have a scanner and it is set up properly to work with your computer. Reading through these instructions will make you familiar with the process of following **technical directions** so that when you choose your own picture-editing program, you'll have no trouble getting the results you want. **B** **C**

Setting Up

1. Make sure the scanner is turned on.
2. Place your image in the scanner. The image should lie face down on the glass, aligned according to the page-size indicators on the scanner.
3. Open up the PhotoEdit program.

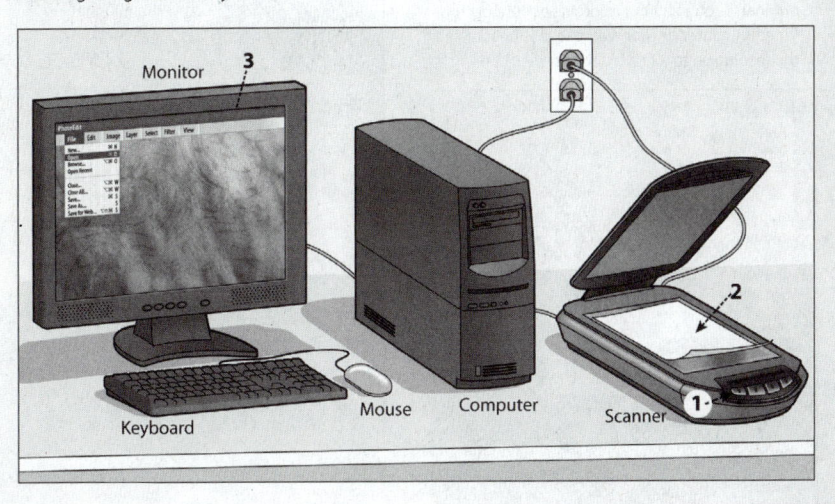

[Illustration showing a computer setup with labels: Monitor (3), Keyboard, Mouse, Computer, Scanner (1), and image placement (2)]

1194 Unit 6 • Collection 10

IN OTHER WORDS These directions tell you how to take an image, or picture, from a piece of paper and put it onto your computer so you can put it on a Web site. Place your picture in a machine called a *scanner*, which you will use to copy your picture onto the computer.

A **YOUR TURN**

Reading Focus

Before you begin reading, practice the technique of **skimming**. Underline the title. Circle any heads or subheads you find. Draw an arrow next to any graphics. Then go back and read just the first sentence of each paragraph. What do you think this document will teach you how to do?

_____
_____
_____
_____
_____

B **HERE'S HOW**

Language Coach

The word *scan* has **multiple meanings,** or several possible definitions. *Scan* can mean: (1) read quickly; (2) mark the rhythm of a line of poetry; or (3) copy words or pictures from paper onto a computer. In this document, I think *scan* means "copy words or pictures from paper onto a computer."

C **HERE'S HOW**

Vocabulary

I have heard the word *edit* used in my English class before. When I *edit* my essay, I change things in it. I think that in this sentence, *edit* is a verb meaning "change."

Following Technical Directions   **287**

A HERE'S HOW

Vocabulary

I am not sure what a *dialogue box* is, but I think I can figure it out. A *dialogue* is a conversation. Maybe this term means "a screen that allows you to tell the computer something or choose an option."

B HERE'S HOW

Reading Focus

I know that **scanning** will help me find specific information quickly. I see a sentence in boldface, which means it is probably very important. I guess the image has to be in the scanner for everything to work!

Scanning

4. In PhotoEdit, under the File menu, choose Import; then select your scanner's name under the list of options. This will open up a scanning dialogue box within PhotoEdit. A preview of your picture will also appear. **Do not remove original image from the scanner.** **B**   **A**

5. With the cursor, select the area of the image you want scanned.

6. Set the size and resolution of the image. In general, scan your image at a larger size than the original (such as 200%) to provide more options for editing later on. For Web use, it is best to set the resolution to 72 dpi (dots per inch).

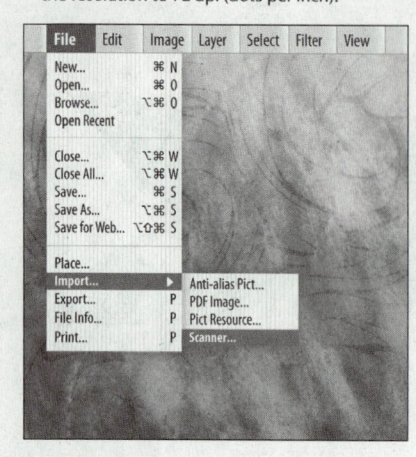

7. Click on SCAN. Your image will now open as an untitled document in PhotoEdit, ready to be edited.

Technical Directions **1195**

IN OTHER WORDS You can use a computer program called PhotoEdit to find the picture that is in the scanner. Choose the part of the picture you want to use, decide how big and clear it should be, and click SCAN to put your picture on the computer.

288 Following Technical Directions

Editing

8. You may now perform any number of edits to ready your image for Web use. You can crop, adjust the color, retouch, and sharpen the image in PhotoEdit. **C**

9. In order to resize the image, you must decide how big you want it to appear on the Web page. First, make sure you are viewing the image at 100% (actual size). Next, go to the Image menu and choose the Image Size option. A dialogue box will open. If you want your image to be large, you may set the pixel size to 800 width x 600 height. If you would like your image to be a thumbnail size, set the width to a size of around 180 pixels. If the "Constrain proportions" option is enabled in this box, the image height will be set automatically. **D**

10. Once you have entered the desired values, hit OK. You will now see the resized image.

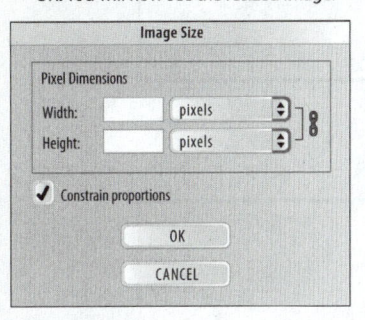

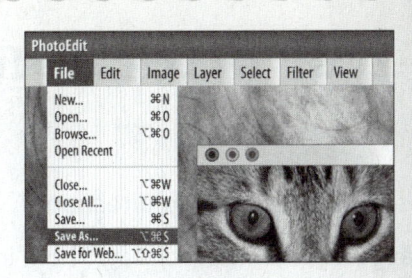

Saving

11. When you are satisfied with the way your image looks, go to the File menu and select Save As.

12. When you name your file, be sure not to exceed 31 characters, including the file extension.

13. Choose JPEG under file format (a JPEG is a compressed version of the file, suitable for Web use). When saving an image as a JPEG, you will have the option of setting the image quality and file size. For the Internet, it is best to choose a "medium" setting for these options.

14. Click OK. Your image is now ready to be uploaded onto your Web site. **E**

1196 Unit 6 • Collection 10

IN OTHER WORDS Now that your picture is on the computer, you can make a lot of changes to it. You can change the size of the picture to be as big or as small as you want it on your Web site. When you are done working with your picture, give it a short name. Save it on the computer as a JPEG, a kind of picture that does not take up a lot of space. Medium-quality pictures look good and show up quickly on a Web site.

C YOUR TURN

Vocabulary

The word *crop* can be a noun meaning "plants that grow on a farm," or a verb meaning "to trim or cut the edges off." Which definition makes more sense here?

_____
_____

D YOUR TURN

Reading Focus

Use **scanning** to find out how to resize an image. Under what heading and number is this information?

_____
_____

E QUICK CHECK

What should you do when you are happy with how your image looks?

_____
_____
_____
_____

Following Technical Directions 289

Skills Practice

Following Technical Directions

USE A CHAIN OF EVENTS CHART

A chain of events chart can help you organize step-by-step directions.

DIRECTIONS: Think of a simple task that you perform every day. Then, in the chart below, list the steps involved in completing your task.

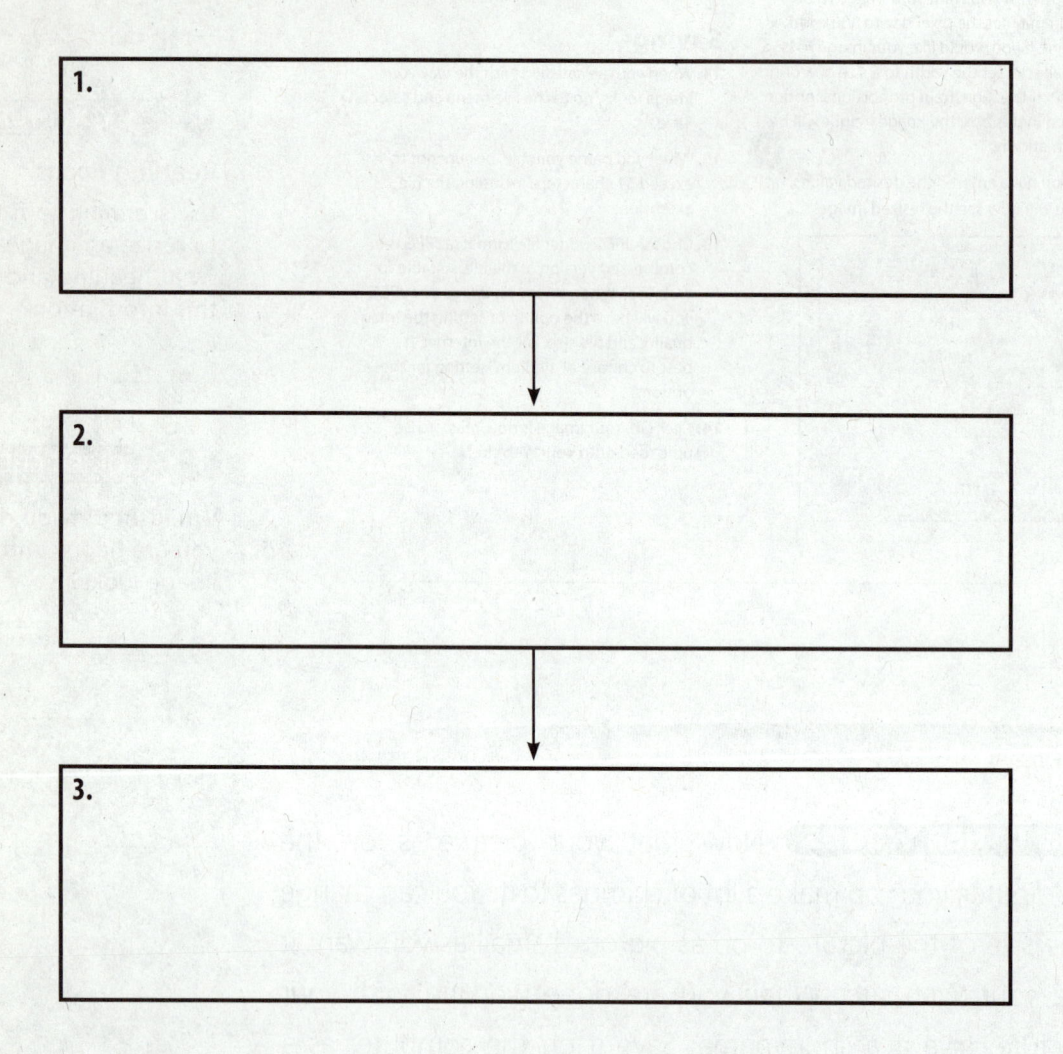

1.

2.

3.

Applying Your Skills

Following Technical Directions

INFORMATIONAL TEXT FOCUS: FOLLOWING TECHNICAL DIRECTIONS

DIRECTIONS: Use the techniques of **skimming** and **scanning** to answer the questions about the selection you have just finished.

1. What is the name of the computer program you will be using?
   _____

2. What is the very first thing you should do when you decide to scan an image?
   _____

3. Should you scan your image at a larger or smaller size than the original?
   _____

4. Which of these can you NOT do with your image using this program: crop, adjust the color, retouch, resize, animate, sharpen?
   _____

5. What file format should you choose when saving your image?
   _____

Word Box
- scan
- image
- options

VOCABULARY REVIEW

DIRECTIONS: Write two sentences telling about what you can do with PhotoEdit. Use at least one word from the Word Box in each sentence.

1. _____
   _____

2. _____
   _____

Preparing to Read

Functional Workplace Documents

INFORMATIONAL TEXT FOCUS: ANALYZING FUNCTIONAL WORKPLACE DOCUMENTS

When you read a workplace document, it is important to notice the **structure**, or the order and the way the document is put together. Also pay attention to the **format**, or how the document looks on the page. Here are some examples:

- A business letter begins with the sender's address on the right and then the address of the person the letter is written to on the left.
- Contracts usually have short numbered sections with boldface headers.
- User guides and technical directions often include **graphics** such as **charts**, **diagrams**, and **illustrations**.
- Web sites have many different structures and formats and often include attention-grabbing graphics such as colorful type.

READING FOCUS: ADJUSTING READING RATE

When you read workplace documents you might find yourself **adjusting**, or changing, **your reading rate**—how fast or slow you read. You may quickly skim the address on a business letter and slow down to pay attention to the main part of the letter. You might look quickly through a user guide until you find the information you want. You should always read contracts and other legal documents very slowly and carefully.

VOCABULARY

Look for these words and their context as you read.

diligent (DIHL uh juhnt) *adj.*: hard-working.

differentiate (DIHF uh REHN shee ayt) *v.*: create a difference between.

en route (AHN ROOT) *adv.*: along the way.

SKILLS FOCUS

Informational Text Skills
Analyze workplace documents.

Reading Skills
Adjust your reading rate.

292 Functional Workplace Documents

BUSINESS LETTER

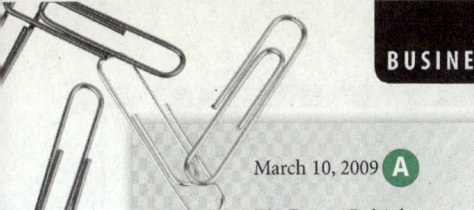

March 10, 2009 **A**

Ms. Donna Pulsipher
Senior Editor
GearTroll Magazine
5100 South Nixom Lane
Grand Rapids, MI 49503

Dear Ms. Pulsipher:

For the past several months, I have been designing a computer game, and I have recently created a new Web site to promote it. Because you know so much about this industry, I wonder if you would be willing to offer your opinion. I want the site to be clear, interesting, and easy to use, and I would love to hear your ideas and suggestions. **B** **C**

I am a diligent student, and I like to spend my spare time developing my design and programming skills. I want to create new video games that will appeal to young adults like me. Now I have developed a game that I think can be very successful, and I want to make it available to users all over the world. **D**

If you have any time available, I would also enjoy the opportunity to meet with you in person to discuss the Web site and my project. Please feel free to contact me at any time. You can reach me at the above address or at gdesigner@wysiwygames.com.

Again, thank you so much for your help. I am very much looking forward to your insight.

Sincerely,

G. Designer

G. Designer

WYSIWYGAME ARTS

A HERE'S HOW

Reading Focus

I want to pay attention to the **structure** and **format** of the documents I am reading. I believe this first document is a business letter, since I can see it starts with addresses and the line "Dear Ms. Pulsipher."

B HERE'S HOW

Vocabulary

I think that Ms. Pulsipher is in the business of computer games—so the word *industry* must mean "business."

C YOUR TURN

Reading Focus

Does your **reading rate** get faster or slower when you get to this first paragraph? Why?

_____
_____
_____
_____

D YOUR TURN

Vocabulary

Use your dictionary to find the meaning of the word *diligent*, and write the definition below.

_____
_____

IN OTHER WORDS This is a business letter from G. Designer to Ms. Pulsipher, the Senior Editor of a magazine that writes about computers. In the letter, G. Designer tells Ms. Pulsipher that he has spent the last few months creating a computer game and has made a Web site to show his game to others. He asks Ms. Pulsipher if she would mind taking a look at the Web site and give her opinions on how the site is set up.

Functional Workplace Documents

A QUICK CHECK

Does Ms. Pulsipher like or dislike the Web site sent to her by G. Designer?

_____

B YOUR TURN

Language Coach

Differentiate begins with a short *i* sound. How would you pronounce this word **fluently**, or smoothly? Practice saying *differentiate* out loud.

C YOUR TURN

Vocabulary

What do you think *differentiate* means? (Hint: What root word do you see?)

_____
_____

D QUICK CHECK

What is the purpose of the Shareware Agreement?

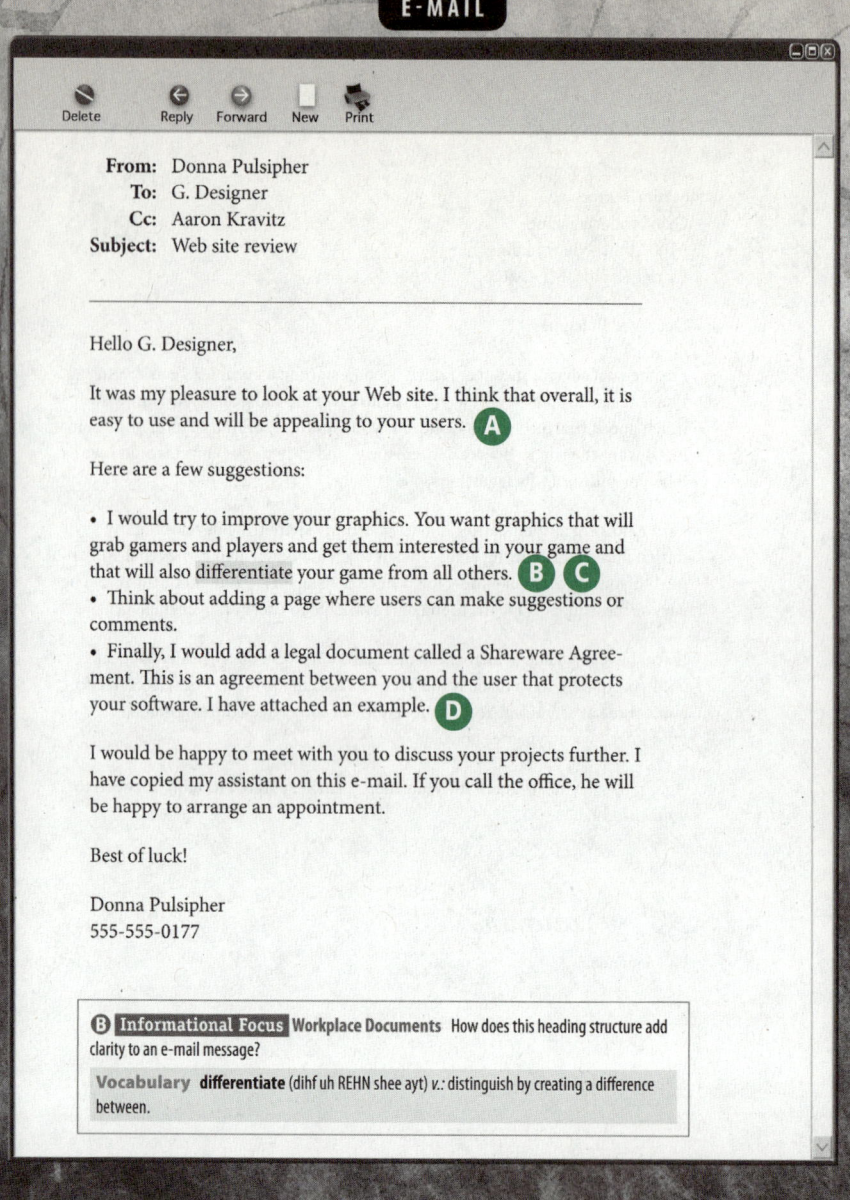

_____
_____

E-MAIL

From: Donna Pulsipher
To: G. Designer
Cc: Aaron Kravitz
Subject: Web site review

Hello G. Designer,

It was my pleasure to look at your Web site. I think that overall, it is easy to use and will be appealing to your users. **A**

Here are a few suggestions:

- I would try to improve your graphics. You want graphics that will grab gamers and players and get them interested in your game and that will also differentiate your game from all others. **B** **C**
- Think about adding a page where users can make suggestions or comments.
- Finally, I would add a legal document called a Shareware Agreement. This is an agreement between you and the user that protects your software. I have attached an example. **D**

I would be happy to meet with you to discuss your projects further. I have copied my assistant on this e-mail. If you call the office, he will be happy to arrange an appointment.

Best of luck!

Donna Pulsipher
555-555-0177

B Informational Focus Workplace Documents How does this heading structure add clarity to an e-mail message?

Vocabulary **differentiate** (dihf uh REHN shee ayt) *v.*: distinguish by creating a difference between.

IN OTHER WORDS This is an email from Donna Pulsipher. Ms. Pulsipher is answering G. Designer's letter about his computer game and Web site. Ms. Pulsipher says that she likes the Web site, but has some suggestions about how to fix it up. She "copies" her assistant on the email, meaning that she has also sent this email to her assistant.

294 Functional Workplace Documents

WEB SITE

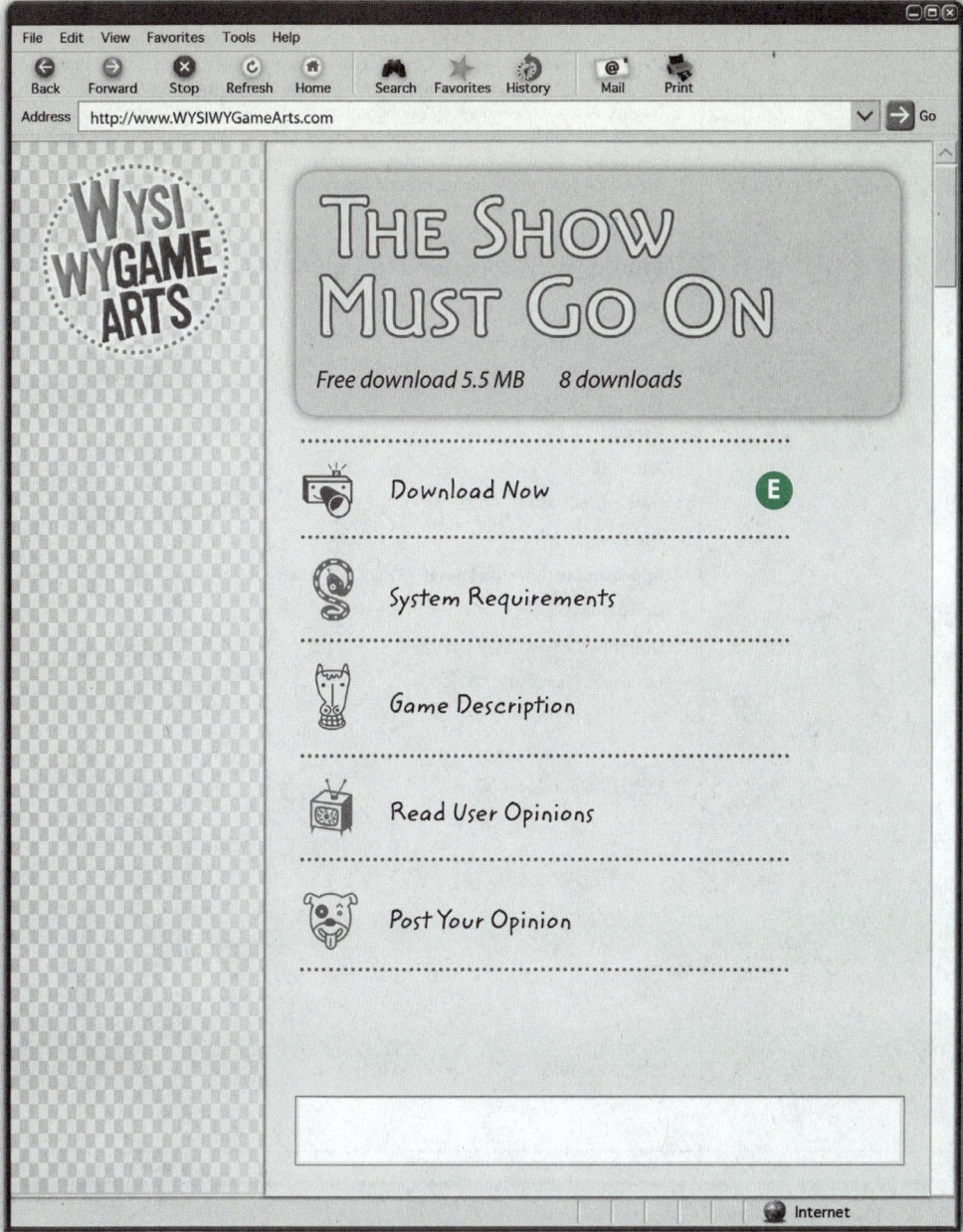

WYSIWYGAME ARTS

The Show Must Go On

Free download 5.5 MB   8 downloads

- Download Now **E**
- System Requirements
- Game Description
- Read User Opinions
- Post Your Opinion

E YOUR TURN

Reading Focus

Circle all of the **graphics** that appear on this page. Do these graphics add to this Web site? Explain your answer?

_____

_____

_____

_____

IN OTHER WORDS Here is G. Designer's Web site. The Web site gives information about the computer game that Designer created. On this page, there is a list of different places to go on the site. You can click on "Game Description" to take you to a page that explains the game.

Functional Workplace Documents   **295**

A YOUR TURN

Reading Focus

Is your **reading rate** fast or slow here?

_____

_____

B HERE'S HOW

Reading Focus

I think the Game Facts has the **format** of a list. I think this is so you can easily and quickly see all the pieces of information.

Game Description

You, Candy Rapper, are trying to get to the stadium to sing at the big benefit concert to aid the farmworkers. En route, though, you are stopped by different characters—Terry Techno and Coyote Cowboy, for example—who demand that you play them _their_ songs before they let you pass. With a quick check of the playlist, you dial up a song on your boombox. If you play the right song, you gain points and move on toward the stadium. If not, you lose points and have to stay until you find the right song. Can you make it to the stadium in time? If you do, you perform to a standing ovation accompanied by a fireworks display. **A**

Would you recommend this game?

YES   NO   Post My Opinion

Game Facts

Version 1.0

Ages: 10–16

Date added: April 6, 2009

File size: 5.5 MB

Approximate download time: 13 min. at 56 kbps

Downloads: 8

Opinions (5): 80% YES; 20% NO

Licensee: Shareware **B**

Download Now

IN OTHER WORDS This is the "Game Description" page. The page lets the viewer answer whether or not he or she would recommend, or suggest, this game to other people. There are also the basic computer game facts, like how much room the game will take up on your computer. The "Download Now" button, when clicked, lets the viewer download the game right onto his or her computer.

Functional Workplace Documents

CONTRACT

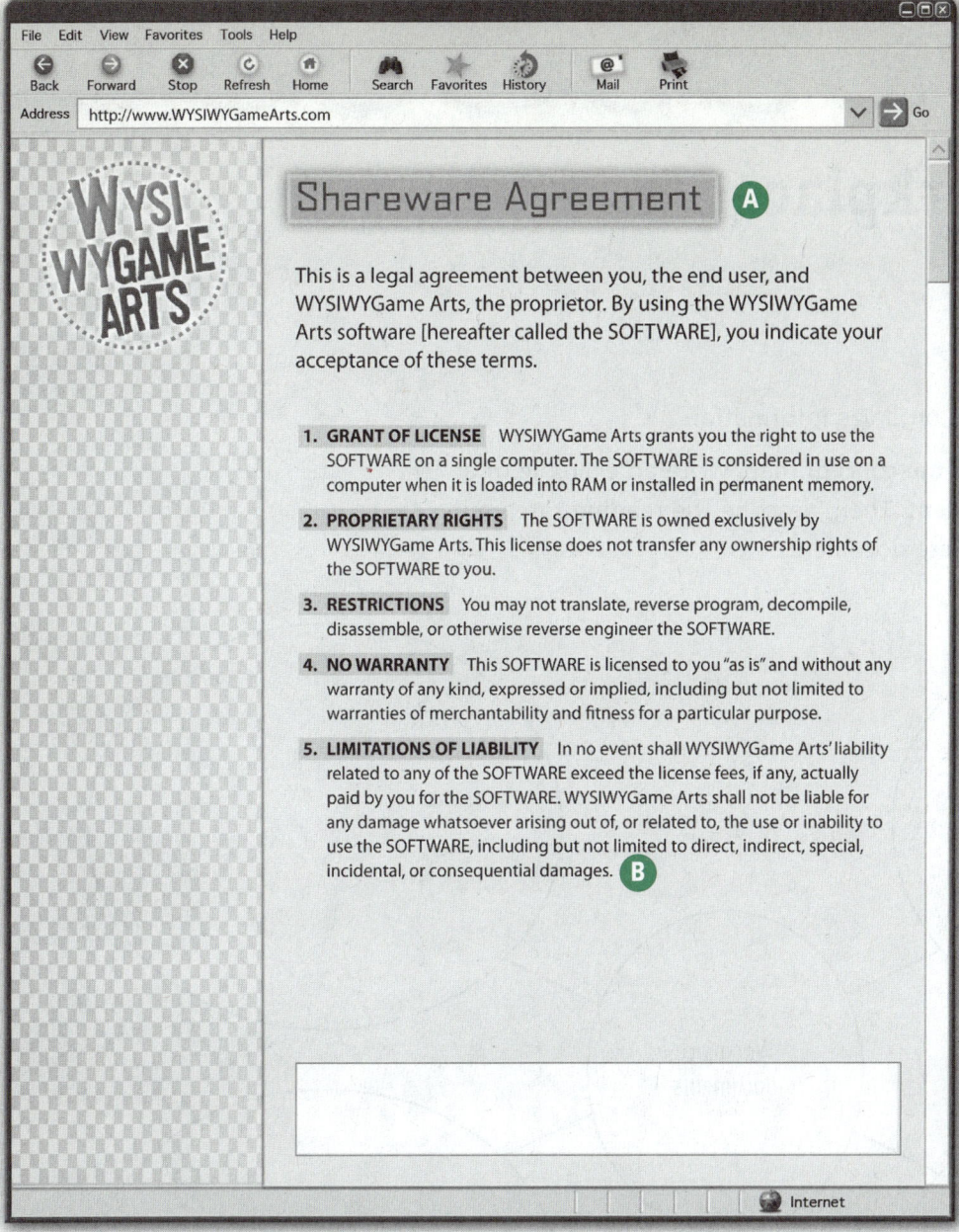

Shareware Agreement

This is a legal agreement between you, the end user, and WYSIWYGame Arts, the proprietor. By using the WYSIWYGame Arts software [hereafter called the SOFTWARE], you indicate your acceptance of these terms.

1. **GRANT OF LICENSE** WYSIWYGame Arts grants you the right to use the SOFTWARE on a single computer. The SOFTWARE is considered in use on a computer when it is loaded into RAM or installed in permanent memory.

2. **PROPRIETARY RIGHTS** The SOFTWARE is owned exclusively by WYSIWYGame Arts. This license does not transfer any ownership rights of the SOFTWARE to you.

3. **RESTRICTIONS** You may not translate, reverse program, decompile, disassemble, or otherwise reverse engineer the SOFTWARE.

4. **NO WARRANTY** This SOFTWARE is licensed to you "as is" and without any warranty of any kind, expressed or implied, including but not limited to warranties of merchantability and fitness for a particular purpose.

5. **LIMITATIONS OF LIABILITY** In no event shall WYSIWYGame Arts' liability related to any of the SOFTWARE exceed the license fees, if any, actually paid by you for the SOFTWARE. WYSIWYGame Arts shall not be liable for any damage whatsoever arising out of, or related to, the use or inability to use the SOFTWARE, including but not limited to direct, indirect, special, incidental, or consequential damages.

IN OTHER WORDS A Shareware Agreement is between the creator of software and the computer user who is going to download that software. Here, the agreement is between G. Designer and whoever wants to download his computer game.

A HERE'S HOW

Reading Focus

When I read this contract, I am **adjusting my reading rate** to read more slowly. This is because there are many words I am not familiar with. I want to make sure I understand what I am reading.

B YOUR TURN

Reading Focus

Of all the documents in this selection for which one was your **reading rate** the quickest? Why do you think that was the case?

_____

_____

_____

_____

Functional Workplace Documents

Skills Practice

Functional Workplace Documents

USE A CONCEPT MAP

You can use a concept map to help organize information.

DIRECTIONS: In the outer circles of the concept map, write an example of a different type of **workplace document**. Then, describe the **reading rate** you would expect to use for each of these documents.

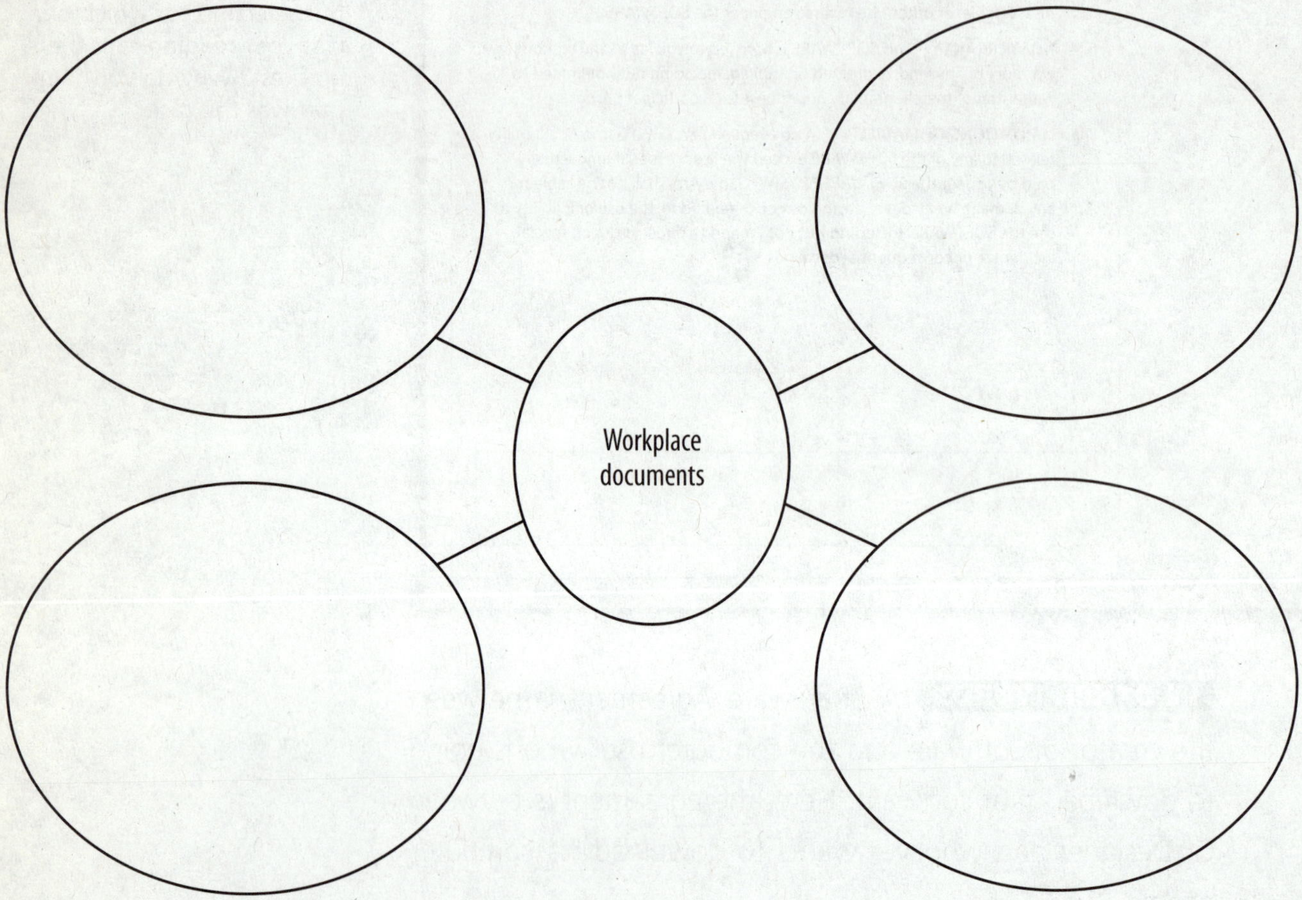

Applying Your Skills

Functional Workplace Documents

INFORMATIONAL TEXT FOCUS: ANALYZING FUNCTIONAL WORKPLACE DOCUMENTS

DIRECTIONS: Below, match the **format** or **structure** details to the kind of document where you are most likely to see such details. Write the correct letter on each blank line.

_____ 1. Web site   A. Sender's address
_____ 2. Contract   B. Colorful type
_____ 3. Business letter   C. Charts and diagrams
_____ 4. User guide   D. List with boldface headers and numbers

DIRECTIONS: Circle the letter of the best answer for each question below based on the documents you have just read.

1. What percentage of people would recommend the described computer game?
   A. 20 %
   B. 40 %
   C. 80 %

2. Which is a suggestion Ms. Pulsipher makes about the Web site?
   A. Change the story on which the computer game is based.
   B. Add a page for comments.
   C. Make sure everyone can copy the game whenever they want to.

3. What is Ms. Pulsipher's job title?
   A. Senior Manager, GameNET
   B. Senior Editor, GearTroll Magazine
   C. Senior Leader, Web Systems Inc.

READING FOCUS: ADJUSTING READING RATE

DIRECTIONS: On a separate piece of paper, write a brief paragraph explaining when and why you adjusted your **reading rate** while reading the previous workplace documents.

VOCABULARY REVIEW

DIRECTIONS: Write a brief note to G. Designer, making suggestions about his Web site. In your note, include at least one of these vocabulary words: _diligent_ and _differentiate_.

_____
_____

Functional Workplace Documents 299

Skills Review

Collection 10

VOCABULARY REVIEW

DIRECTIONS: Write "yes" on the line if the underlined vocabulary word is used correctly. Write "no" if the underlined word is not used correctly.

1. I hope these directions are clear and <u>coherent</u> so I can follow them easily.
   _____

2. Having the correct tools <u>function</u> me to complete the job quickly.
   _____

3. I want to add this <u>image</u> to my Web site to illustrate my idea.
   _____

4. There are many dinner <u>options</u> available to me on the restaurant's menu.
   _____

5. The <u>diligent</u> of my Web site is to allow people to see my ideas.
   _____

6. I will stop at the grocery store, since it is <u>en route</u> to my apartment.
   _____

7. When I work, I am <u>differentiate</u> about finishing everything carefully.
   _____

300   Reading for Life

Language and Writing

Collection 10

LANGUAGE COACH: MULTIPLE MEANING WORDS

DIRECTIONS: Many words have **multiple meanings**, or several possible definitions. For the words below, choose the letter of the definition that does NOT belong to the word above it. Use your dictionary to help you.

1. function
   A. typical role or action.
   B. purpose.
   C. result.

2. crop
   A. windstorm.
   B. plant or animal grown to use or sell.
   C. cut or trim.

3. scan
   A. technical.
   B. search for words in a document.
   C. copy words or pictures from paper onto a computer.

WRITING ACTIVITY

DIRECTIONS: Choose a product that you have in your home. On a separate sheet of paper, write a product information document for that item. Remember to describe how it is used. Share this consumer document with a partner. Does he or she get a good idea of the product from what you have written? If he or she has any questions or comments, use those to add to, change, or edit your product information document to create a final version.

_____

_____

_____

Index of Authors and Titles

4 Little Girls 203
About StoryCorps 159
Alvarez, Julia 35
American History 65
Armstrong, Jennifer 267

Ballad of Birmingham 200
Blessing, A 183
Branch, Taylor 199

Cask of Amontillado, The 93
Cinderella's Stepsisters 167
Cofer, Judith Ortiz 65
Collection Is Found to Contain Stolen
    Rockwell Art 211
Connell, Richard 3
Cub Pilot on the Mississippi 149

"Dear Juliet": Seeking Succor From a
    Veteran of Love 235

Ebert, Roger 203
Einstein, Albert 139, 140, 141

FBI Art Crime Team 209
Foer, Joshua 174
Following Technical Directions 287
Functional Workplace Documents 293

Gift of the Magi, The 133
Grandfather, The 155
Great Escape, The 43

Henry, O. 133
History Behind the Ballad, The 199
Homer 249
Hughes, Langston 55
Hurst, James 113

I Wandered Lonely as a Cloud 191
If Poe Had Only Succeeded When He
    Said Nevermore to Drink 105
Interlopers, The 87
Interview with Dave Eggers, An 73

Juliet Club, *from* The 241

Kaavya Syndrome 174

Kaavya Viswanathan: Unconscious
    Copycat or Plagiarist? 171
Legal Alien/Extranjera Legal 195
Letter to President Roosevelt 140
Liberty 35

Mora, Pat 195
Morrison, Toni 167
Most Dangerous Game, The 3

Nankani, Sandhya 171

Odyssey, *from the* 249
On the Abolition of the Threat
    of War 141

Poe, Edgar Allan 90
Poe's Death Is Rewritten as Case of
    Rabies, Not Telltale Alcohol 104
Poe's Final Days 99

Randall, Dudley 200
Romeo and Juliet, The Tragedy of 219

Saki 87
Scarlet Ibis, The 113
Shakespeare, William 219
Shipwreck at the Bottom of the World 267
Silverman, Kenneth 99
Smith, Dinitia 235
Soto, Gary 155

Tending Sir Ernest's Legacy 277
Thank You M'am 55
Twain, Mark 149

Walker, Alice 187
Weapons of the Spirit 139
Women 187
Wordsworth, William 191
Wright, James 183

302 Index of Authors and Titles